Trinity: Mother of Churches

TRINITY: MOTHER OF CHURCHES

An informal history of Trinity Parish in the City of New York

CLIFFORD P. MOREHOUSE

THE SEABURY PRESS · NEW YORK

ACKNOWLEDGMENTS

Grateful acknowledgment is made to the following authors and publishers for permission to use copyrighted material from the sources listed:

Coward-McCann, Inc.—Edward Robb Ellis, *The Epic of New York City.* Copyright © 1966 by Edward Robb Ellis.

Dodd, Mead & Company, Inc.—Allan Nevins, ed., *The Diary of Philip Hone.*

Macmillan Co.—Allan Nevins and Milton Halsey Thomas, eds., *The Diary of George Templeton Strong.*

Oxford University Press—Powel Mills Dawley, *The Story of the General Theological Seminary.*

Random House—Lloyd Morris, *Incredible New York.* Copyright © 1951 by Random House.

Charles Scribner's Sons—W. A. Swanberg, *The Rector and the Rogue.*

Gwenith Heuss Severance—"A Loyalist Church During the American Revolution." An unpublished thesis; Wesleyan University.

University of North Carolina Press—Carl Bridenbaugh, ed., *Gentleman's Progress.*

Library of Congress Catalog Card Number: 72-94206
ISBN: 0-8164-0246-9
Design by Carol Basen
Printed in the United States of America

Foreword

On May 6, 1697, William III, King of England, granted a Royal Charter to the Parish of Trinity Church in the City of New York. The Charter, under which the Parish continues to operate, did not establish a neighborhood parish, but rather founded "The Church in New York."

From the earliest days Trinity has been faithful to this larger responsibility for mission and ministry. The original patrimony granted by William III, and later augmented by Queen Anne and others, has been shared to an astonishing degree with the City and Diocese of New York, the Episcopal Church, and the Anglican Communion.

The year from May, 1972 to May, 1973 is being celebrated as the 275th Anniversary of Trinity Parish. *Mother of Churches* is a historical survey of all the years that lead to this milestone. It is a fascinating account of the life and work of a parish once described by the Bishop of London as "unique in the whole of Christendom."

Perhaps the most exciting part of the story is the ending, for the ending is the account of a new beginning. In 1969, Dr. John V. Butler, XIV Rector of the Parish, appointed an *ad hoc* committee of the Vestry to review the whole question of the nature of the Parish, the use of its human and financial resources, and the broad policies to be followed in the 1970s.

The resulting report, called "One Peppercorne," was adopted by the Vestry on September 24, 1970. It calls upon Trinity "to make a transition over several years to being a parish that again provides the City and the whole Church with powerful leadership by demonstrating how any church can faithfully use all of its resources to maximum effect."

Since the adoption of the report, many significant steps toward its implementation have been taken. It appears that the future is taking shape as a worthy continuation of a noble past. In this Anniversary Year, it is the prayer of those who have the guardianship of Trinity's trust and responsibility for her mission that this be so.

No introduction to *Mother of Churches* would be complete without a sincere expression of gratitude to its author, Dr. Clifford P. Morehouse. Dr. Morehouse, one of the distinguished lay leaders of the Episcopal Church in modern times, long-time Vestryman and Warden of Trinity Parish, is presently Historiographer of the Parish. Through his skill as a writer he has brought together in this volume a long, loving, and intimate knowledge of the parish and an unsurpassed understanding of the contemporary church in an historical context. The result is fascinating reading.

ROBERT RAY PARKS
xv Rector
of the Parish of Trinity Church
in the City of New York

Preface

I am greatly indebted to Miss Helen Rose Cline, recorder and archivist of Trinity Parish, for her invaluable help in research, her reading and correction of the manuscript at all stages, and her meticulous attention to names, dates, and circumstances, as well as for duplicating and circulating draft copies for criticism and evaluation. Without her help, this book would have been impossible.

I also wish to express my appreciation to the readers who have criticized the manuscript at various stages and made many helpful suggestions. Among these are the Rev. Dr. John V. Butler, Dr. Joseph W. Barker, Mrs. John Heuss, the Rev. Dr. Powel M. Dawley, Mr. and Mrs. Theodore Baumeister, and the Rev. Fr. Robert C. Hunsicker.

The present rector, the Rev. Dr. Robert R. Parks, has given generous encouragement to the project, as did his predecessor, Dr. Butler.

All of those named above, and many others, are entitled to share in whatever is good about this book; the author alone is responsible for any errors or inadequacies of the work.

CLIFFORD P. MOREHOUSE

Sarasota, Florida
June 12, 1972

Contents

Illustrations

Trinity: Mother of Churches

William Vesey, the First Rector

1

The First Trinity Church

1691-1698

New York in the 1690s was a great place to live—that is, if you were a member of the establishment or on good terms with the royal governor and his associates. And that wasn't always easy, as each governor allied himself with a different faction in the city, and seemed chiefly concerned to undo the work of his predecessor.

SEVENTEENTH-CENTURY NEW YORK

The city itself was a beautiful one. Captured from the Dutch in 1664, retaken by them in 1673, and finally recaptured by the English in 1674, it still retained much of the flavor of the days when it had been known as New Amsterdam. Neat gabled Dutch houses lined its few streets; prosperous farms with peach and apple orchards lay north of the protecting wall, and vast wheatlands in the Hudson Valley, each with its picturesque Dutch windmill, supplied the city with the flour that soon became one of its leading products, and made New York the granary of the northern colonies. With the establishment of manufacturing and packaging, known as "bolting," made a monopoly of a few leading citizens, the flour industry became a mainstay of the city's first business boom, with nearly two-thirds of the citizens dependent in one way or another upon its processing and shipping.

Although smaller than Boston and Philadelphia, New York's 4,000 inhabitants were already a cross-section of Europe's polyglot population. For besides the English and Dutch, who retained much of their power under English rulers, there were Irish, Swedes, Germans, and Scots; also some French Huguenots who had come via England or the West Indies. There were an unknown number of Negroes, most of them slaves of the aristocratic families; and slavery, both of Blacks and of Indians, was to continue and increase for the next century, though never so prevalent as in the southern colonies. There were also indentured servants, brought from the Old World under labor contracts, who might gain their freedom after the agreed period of manual service.

The English Revolution of 1688, whereby James II was deposed and William of Orange and Mary II came to the English throne, had its repercussions in New York. Two years before that, the colony of New York had been annexed to New England. New York's Roman Catholic governor, Thomas Dongan, was forced to resign, and Sir Edmund Andros had been appointed the royal governor of the combined dominion. He established his headquarters in Boston, and the new lieutenant governor, Francis Nicholson, exercised the royal authority in New York. When news reached America about the English Revolution, Governor Andros was jailed by the people of Boston, who chose a Council of Safety to carry on the government until further directions should be received from England. In New York, Nicholson refused to proclaim the accession of William and Mary until he received official word from them. He repaired Fort James, facing what later became known as Bowling Green, and ordered the militia to supplement the few English regular troops stationed there.

The senior captain of the militia, Jacob Leisler, a rich Calvinist married to the widow of a Dutch citizen, and himself a deacon in the Dutch Reformed Church, seized power and demanded that Nicholson surrender the keys to the fort. The lieutenant governor at first refused, but when faced with a show of force by the militia, he handed over the keys and Leisler took command of the fort, and the effective control of the city. For two years Leisler ruled New York, claiming that he held it until the English monarchs should recognize his authority or appoint a new royal governor. Meanwhile the erstwhile militia captain governed with an iron hand. He expelled the Roman Catholics (who had enjoyed Governor Dongan's favor and had been tolerated by Nicholson), and Dongan and Nicholson fled for their lives. Meanwhile Leisler raged because William and Mary failed to recognize him, and became so tyrannical that petitions against him were sent to England.

The new king and queen actually appointed Col. Henry Sloughter as the new royal governor of New York on September 2, 1689, with Richard Ingoldsby as lieutenant governor. The new officials sailed from England in a fleet of ships, but these were scattered in a storm and the governor's ship grounded in Bermuda and was laid up for repairs.

Ingoldsby's ship, with two others and a force of regular troops, was the first to arrive in New York; but the official papers proclaiming the new authority were with Sloughter in faraway Bermuda. Ingoldsby demanded that Leisler surrender the fort, but Leisler refused to do so without a written order from the king or the new governor. After waiting four days, Ingoldsby disembarked his troops, quartered them in the city hall, and demanded release of council members whom Leisler had imprisoned in the fort.

For six weeks there was an impasse, with no word from Governor Sloughter. Then Ingoldsby began to collect militiamen to reinforce his regulars and seize the fort. Leisler demanded that Ingoldsby disband his forces; when he refused, Leisler ordered his men to fire on the royal troops. Few were killed or injured; but Leisler had gone too far, and some of his own militiamen deserted him and returned to their homes.

Two days later, Governor Sloughter's ship finally arrived. The governor landed, joined Ingoldsby at the city hall, read aloud his royal commission, and ordered the instant surrender of the fort. Leisler sent his son-in-law, Jacob Milborne, to parley with the governor, but Sloughter threw him into jail. After some further parleying, in which Leisler demanded conditions, the governor commanded Ingoldsby to order the men in the fort to lay down their arms, promising freedom from prosecution to all but Leisler, Milborne, and their closest associates. When the troops obeyed this order, the royal troops entered the fort. Leisler and his staff were accused of treason; after a week's trial, Leisler and Milborne were summarily executed.

Although there was relatively little bloodshed in what became known as Leisler's Rebellion, the effects of it were to be felt for many years. New Yorkers continued to be divided in their loyalties, some feeling that Leisler was the defender of the people and others that he was a rebel and traitor. Thus the electorate was split into two parties—a division that was to affect the city for years to come, with subsequent governors supporting one or the other of the two groups, as expediency and conviction might demand. It was thus a very divided city, with hatred and bitterness upon both sides, that entered into the last decade of the seventeenth century.

If New York was divided politically, the religious situation was even more complicated. Under the Dutch regime, the Dutch Reformed Church had been the established one, and Governor Peter Stuyvesant had given scant toleration to other religious bodies. When the Lutherans became strong enough, in 1654, they appealed to the governor and later to the Dutch West India Company for a clergyman of their own; both appeals were denied, on the ground that if the Lutherans were permitted a minister, the Anglicans and others would demand the same right. The first English governors, Nicolls and Lovelace, granted a measure of toleration, especially to Lutherans and Quakers, and aided the Dutch to get a new minister from Holland, providing him with a rent-free house and a generous salary—thus virtually continuing the establishment of the Dutch Reformed Church. Independents (Congregationalists) were also tolerated. Anglicans were ministered to by a series of chaplains at the fort; and apparently these services were continued (along with Dutch ones) during the brief time that the Dutch reoccupied New York.

Upon restoration of the English rule in 1674, Col. Edmund Andros was sent out as governor, with instructions "to permit all persons of what Religion soever, quietly to inhabit within the precincts of your jurisdiction, without giving them any disturbance or disquiet whatsoever for or by reason of their differing opinions in matter of Religion: Provided they give no disturbance to the public peace, nor do molest or disquiet others in the exercise of their religion." In particular, it was agreed that the Dutch inhabitants should retain their customary church privileges and church discipline, as well as their laws and customs in the division of their inheritances.

Governor Andros himself, in one of his early reports to London, describes the state of religion in New York in 1678:

> The Duke maintains a Chaplain, wh^ch^ is all the certaine allowance of Chirch of England but peoples free gifts to ye ministry, And all places oblidged to build churches & provide for a minister, in wh^ch^ most very wanting, but presbiterians & Independents desierous to haue and maintaine them if to be had, there are ab^t^ 20 churches or Meeting places of wh^ch^ above halfe vacant their allowance like to be from 40 li (pounds) to 70 li a yeare and a house and garden. Noe beggars but all poore cared ffor, If good Ministers could be had to goe thither might doe well and gaine much upon these people.

Shortly thereafter, Governor Andros made a voyage to England to report in person. On his return, he brought with him an Anglican priest, the Rev. Charles Wolley, with commission to serve as chaplain to the forces. He was the first such chaplain to be known by name, though others had preceded him. He remained two years; and his manner of conducting services from the Book of Common Prayer, with short sermons in place of the interminable ones to which Dissenting ministers were prone, caused some astonishment. Some Dutch Protestants thus described one of his services:

> We went at noon today to hear the English Minister, whose services took place after the Dutch Church was out. There were not above twenty-five or thirty people in the Church. The first thing that occurred was the reading of all their prayers and ceremonies out of the prayer book, as is done in all Episcopal churches. A young man then went into the pulpit and commenced preaching, who thought he was performing wonders; but he had a little book in his hand, out of which he read his sermon, which was about a quarter of an hour or half an hour long. With this the services were concluded, at which we could not be sufficiently astonished.

Chaplain Wolley enjoyed his tour of duty in New York, which he described in a book published after his return to London as "a place of as sweet and agreeable air as I ever breathed in, and the inhabitants both English and Dutch very civil and courteous." However, if the Dutch had found his conduct astonishing, Wolley's estimate of their clergy was far from flattering:

> In the same City of New York where I was Minister to the English, there were two other Ministers or Domines as they were called there, the one a Lutheran a German or High Dutch, the other a Calvinist an Hollander or Low-Dutchman, who behav'd themselves one towards another so shily and uncharitably as if Luther and Calvin had bequeathed and entailed their virulent and bigotted Spirits upon them and their heirs forever.

In 1682 Governor Andros was succeeded in office by Thomas Dongan, a devout Roman Catholic, who brought with him, as the government chaplain, an Anglican priest, the Rev. Dr. John Gordon, and also, as his private chaplain, a Jesuit, the Rev. Thomas Hardy. Later, Chaplain

Gordon was replaced by another Anglican chaplain, the Rev. Josias Clarke. During the interim between the two, Anglican services in the fort were conducted by lay readers. Dongan was a conscientious governor and continued the policy of religious toleration.

Governor Dongan in one of his reports gave his own estimate of the state of religion in New York:

> New York has first a chaplain, belonging to the Fort, of the Church of England; secondly a Dutch Calvinist, thirdly a French Calvinist, fourthly a Dutch Lutheran. Here bee not many of the Church of England; few Roman Catholicks; abundance of Quakers; Sabbatarians; Anti-sabbatarians; Some Anabaptists, some Independents; some Jews; in short of all sorts of opinions there are some, and the most part of none at all. The Great Church which serves both the English and the Dutch is within the Fort which is found to bee very inconvenient; therefore I desire that there may bee an order for their building another, ground already being layd out for that purpose and they wanting not money in Store where with all to build it. The most prevailing opinion is that of the Dutch Calvinists.

It is noteworthy that it was this Roman Catholic governor who urged the building of a new church, presumably Anglican, shortly before the English Revolution of 1688, and mentioned that the ground was already laid out for it. Old maps of the walled city show that this ground was just within the north wall, at about what would today be Wall and Broad streets. But it was to be nearly a decade later, and under quite a different political situation, when steps were taken to erect the first Trinity Church, not quite on that location, but on Broadway, at the head of Wall Street, which retained its name after the fortified wall had been torn down.

BUILDING THE FIRST TRINITY CHURCH

Governor Sloughter's administration, following the disastrous Leisler regime, lasted less than two years. He died suddenly in July 1691 under circumstances that at first caused suspicion of poisoning. However, in the first autopsy conducted in New York, a panel of six doctors concluded that he had died of acute alcoholism following a drunken debauch.

During his short term, however, Sloughter initiated two important moves that were to have far-reaching effects. One was the calling of a representative assembly, elected on a broader basis than those of Governors Andros and Dongan, many of whose members had been imprisoned by Leisler. The other was an instruction to the Assembly to provide for the settlement of the ministry in every town. It remained for his successor, however, to secure the legislation to accomplish this object.

The new royal governor, Benjamin Fletcher, did not arrive until August of 1692, with Major Ingoldsby exercising authority during the interim. Governor Fletcher was greeted with a great parade, thus inaugurating New York's policy of honoring notables in that fashion. Fletcher was a staunch Anglican, and immediately renewed Sloughter's recommendations that the Assembly provide for a settled ministry. When the Assembly delayed, he reminded them:

> Lett us not forgett that there is a God that made us who will protect us if we serve him. That has been alwayes the first thing I have recommended, yet the last in your consideration.

Eventually the Assembly passed a law providing for

the establishment in each place of a "good sufficient Protestant Minister"—one in New York City, one in Richmond (Staten Island), two in Westchester, and two in Queens County—to be paid by a tax to be levied by wardens and vestrymen who would be elected by the inhabitants of the respective areas.

The Act was not entirely satisfactory to the governor, as it did not specify that these ministers were to be Anglicans; and indeed the assembly had no intention that they should be. The first "town vestry," as it came to be known, for New York City consisted of two wardens (both Dissenters) and ten vestrymen, only three of whom were Anglicans. This vestry levied the tax provided for in the Act, and expressed "ye opinion of the board that a dissenting Minister be called to officiate and have the Care of Souls for this Citty." However, they were unable to agree on a minister to be called, and went out of office without making any appointment.

A second town vestry, consisting mostly of Dutch worthies, again with a small Anglican minority, did in fact nominate an Anglican, William Vesey, as rector; but when the governor opposed their choice (preferring the fort chaplain, the Rev. John Miller) they let the matter drop, and apparently did not even notify Mr. Vesey of his call. A third town vestry had as little success in coming to an agreement with the governor.

Meanwhile the Anglicans, anxious to have a church of their own, took matters into their own hands and petitioned Governor Fletcher for leave to purchase land, gather funds independently of the tax moneys (which in fact had not been collected), and erect a church. For this purpose they organized themselves as a board known as "Managers of the Church of England." This petition met with the favor of the governor, and was granted by him on March 19, 1696.

Anticipating the approval of the governor, the managers actually held their first meeting on January 27, 1696, and laid plans for the purchase of land and erection of a church. There were eleven men at that first meeting, the minutes of which have been carefully preserved, and they appointed a twelfth, thus rounding out the traditional number for an apostolic band. It is well to record their names here, as they were the actual founders of Trinity Church.

First named, and presumably chairman of the managers, was Col. Caleb Heathcote, who was later to become Lord of the Manor of Scarsdale and mayor of New York. Next was the incumbent mayor, William Merrett. Others were John Tuder, James Emott, Richard Ashfield, James Evetts, Direck Vanderburgh, and Capts. William Morris, Thomas Clarke, Ebenezer Willson, and Jeremiah Tothill—the last-named having been one of the Anglican members of the original town vestry. They appointed Robert Lurting to be the twelfth member of the group.

They agreed "that the Ground lying on the South West Side of the burial place of this Citty is the most Convenient place for the building of the Said Church, and Whereas the Lutheran Congregation doe Claime a Right to the said ground, Itt is Agreede at the Request of Mr. Direck Vanderburgh (one of the Elders of the said Congregation) that Capt. John Tuder, Mr. James Emott, Capt. Thomas Clarke & Capt. Ebenezer Willson doe meet Such Persons as shall be Appointed by the Said Lutheran Congregation" as to their rights in the property and willingness "to agree and Bargaine for the Same if they shall See Convenient."

Colonel Heathcote and Captain Clarke reported that they were already at work securing subscriptions, and had "gott to the Value of four hundred and Seaventy pounds or thereabouts, and that there is a Prospect of farther Incouragement." Accordingly, the tasks immediately before them were divided up on a "do-it-yourself" basis. Colonel Heathcote and James Evetts were to purchase and procure all the timber boards, shingles, and scaffolding for the building; Captains Clarke and Tothill to "gett Stones for the Aforesaid building"; and Direck Vanderburgh (a master mason) and Captain Ebenezer Willson to purchase and procure the necessary lime. All were to report on the following Monday "how farr they have proceeded & what Prospect they have for Procuring the said Materials."

By the following Monday, the committee to deal with the Lutherans reported that their congregation held the desired land by patent from former Governor Nicolls, and that they would sell it to the Anglicans for "the Sum of twenty pounds Current Money of New Yorke," and further would voluntarily give the managers "a Certaine piece of Ground Lying in the rear of the Ground Aforementioned Near the Locust Trees, which was Given to the Said Lutheran Congregation by one Lawrence Anderson Late of New Jersey Deceased, they onely Desireing Liberty of burying their Dead in the Church yard, paying for the Same as is or shall be Customary by any of the Congregation of the Said English Church." Thus by the generosity of the Lutherans, the future Trinity Church gained the commanding property at the head of Wall Street, and the nucleus of a burying ground as well. Apparently the dual membership of Mr. Vanderburgh in both congregations was helpful in this early ecumenical gesture.

The managers continued to meet every Monday "att four of ye Clock afternoon," and their minutes make fascinating reading. As the gathering of materials and building of the church progressed, new tasks were assigned to the members, many of whom brought their own servants to do the manual labor. They also paid the contractors and laborers each week—the first known instance of a weekly pay day in New York's history. At the same time they continued to raise funds, including a contribution of a hundred pounds sterling from the governor, and loans secured by the credit of the managers, all of whom were citizens of substance, at the rate of 6 percent interest. Others volunteered various services; it is interesting to note that Capt. William Kidd (later to gain fame as a privateer or notoriety as an alleged pirate) "has lent a Runner & Tackle for the hoiseing up Stones as long as he stays here." The only one of the managers to be paid for his labors was Direck Vanderburgh, who as the practical master mason must have devoted most of his time to the project. His laborers were allowed sixpence per day, "for to provide themselves drinke for one month."

Meanwhile Colonel Heathcote, Mayor Merrett, and Mr. Emott, a leading lawyer of the colony, were appointed a committee to see the king's attorney general about a charter, and to draft the articles to be contained in it, and also to request a grant of land "for the building of a Free School house &c."—a notable instance of concern for education in a colony that as yet had no schools except small private ones, mostly on manor properties outside the city.

The progress in building the new church, and the approval of the governor, appear to have stimulated the town vestry to take action with regard to "a good sufficient Protestant minister." Governor Fletcher having relinquished his objection to the election of William Vesey (largely at the instigation of Colonel Heathcote), and upon the recommendation of the Rev. Samuel Myles and the wardens of King's Chapel, Boston, the vestry again elected Mr. Vesey, and on his acceptance of the election, voted funds to defray his expenses on a voyage to England to receive Anglican ordination.

Meanwhile the building of the church continued, with the managers taking turns in supervising the work. Negotiations with the royal attorney general for a charter also continued; and at last, on May 6, 1697, this important document was promulgated by Governor Fletcher in the name of King William III, "by the grace of God King of England, Scotland, France and Ireland, Defender of the Faith, etc." It was a long and detailed document, granting all that the managers had wished, and was enthusiastically received by them. When the attorney general read it to them at their next meeting, they appointed a committee to wait upon the governor at 8 o'clock the following morning, to express their appreciation and to secure "his Excell further direction therein."

The Charter set forth the Act of 1693 providing for the settlement of a minister in the city of New York, and declared the rector of Trinity Church to be the "good sufficient Protestant Minister" designated in the said Act. The church was to be recognized as the parish church of the city, and was to be designated and consecrated in accordance with the rites and ceremonies of the Church of England and to continue in communion with the Mother Church, with the usual rights and privileges of English church law. The Bishop of London was designated as the first rector, and was to have an assistant in priest's orders, together with a clerk. The Charter also named Thomas Wenham and Robert Lurting as the first wardens, and twenty men (all Anglicans, and mostly members of the Board of Managers) as the first vestrymen, providing for election of their successors annually on the Tuesday in Easter week.

As consideration for the granting of the Charter, it was provided that "the quitrent . . . be one pepper corne as desired." This quaint provision, equivalent to the modern "one dollar and other sufficient considerations," was to be remembered more than two and a half centuries later as a slogan for reorganization of the parish, still operating under the Royal Charter as amended and reaffirmed by the New York legislature after the Revolution.

Thus the first Anglican parish in New York became a reality, even while its walls were beginning to rise upon the fair site overlooking the North River. The work proceeded with new vigor, in the hope that it might be completed by the time William Vesey returned from England to serve as its rector; for it was never contemplated that the Rt. Rev. Henry Compton, Bishop of London, would actually serve in that capacity, except for the purpose of organization of the parish.

With the granting of the Charter, Governor Fletcher gave further aid to the new parish by granting it a lease of the King's Farm, a substantial piece of property north of the city which was a perquisite of the royal governor, and which was later to become the most important financial asset of Trinity Parish, and the source of many of its troubles as well.

Still other perquisites of the parish were the release of certain sums contributed for the ransom of victims of the Barbary pirates and no longer needed for that purpose, and a patent to the wardens of rights to all drift whales "and whatsoever else Drives from the high sea and is lost below high water mark and not having a lawful Owner within bounds and limits of his Majesties Province of New York." This interesting provision, never repealed, accounts for the fact that to this day, when the beaching of a whale is reported in the New York papers, the wardens of Trinity remain incommunicado until the Department of Sanitation has dealt with the matter, since drift whales are far more of a liability than an asset in the twentieth century.

While these developments in the building and endowing of Trinity Church were under way, Mr. Vesey was in England seeking Holy Orders. On July 8, 1697 he received the degree of Master of Arts from Merton College, Oxford; and on July 25 and August 2 he was ordained deacon and priest respectively by the Bishop of London. Armed with letters from the bishop (who, it will be remembered, was designated in the Charter as the first rector of Trinity), commending his choice and promising aid toward the completion of the church, he returned to New York in December, ready to enter upon his duties as soon as he might be lawfully inducted into the parish.

Although the new church was not yet completed, Governor Fletcher was anxious to induct the new rector. Accordingly, on Christmas Day 1697 the ceremony of induction was performed in the new stone church of the Dutch Reformed congregation in Garden Street, with the governor presenting the keys symbolizing the rector's office, and two of the Dutch ministers serving as official witnesses. For about three months thereafter, Mr. Vesey and the pastor, Domine Henricus Selyns, preached alternately in that church, the former officiating in English and the latter in the Dutch language.

The new rector also had an important personal matter to attend to, for about the first of March 1698 he was

married to one Mary Reede. She was possibly a daughter of Vestryman Lawrence Reade (the name appears both ways), but more likely a widow with whom Vesey had been acquainted before his departure for England, since the license describes her as "Mrs. Mary Reede." There is a tradition that she appeared at Trinity Church as a bride the first time it was opened for public worship, but there is no firm evidence of that fact. What is of record is that she was the gracious first lady of the parish throughout her husband's rectorship, and that after his death she was married to a Trinity vestryman, Judge Daniel Horsmanden.

On March 7, 1698, the church being substantially completed, the managers directed that three of their number "do take care that the Church be cleared and put in the best posture they can in order that Divine Service and the Communion be there administered the next Sabbath Day." Accordingly, on Sunday, March 13, the Rev. Mr. Vesey conducted the first services in Trinity Church, taking the occasion to declare "his unfeigned assent and consent to all and every thing contained in and by the book Entituled the book of Common prayer" and "did read a certificate from the Rt. Reverend father in God Henry Lord Bishop of London that he had subscribed the acknowledgement or Declaration according to the act of uniformity."

Trinity Church was now fully organized, and ready to begin its long and fruitful ministry as the parish church of the City of New York.

2

Troubles Within and Without

1698-1743

The first Trinity Church was a modest rectangular building, with a high mansard roof and a small entrance porch. Writing to the Archbishop of Canterbury, in an appeal for additional furnishings, the vestry said: "The situation of our church is very pleasant, between two rivers on eminent ground. We have a large burying place, adjoining it a good fence and adorned with rows of Lime trees, which will make a pleasant shade in a little time."

In the custom of the day, pews were rented and set aside for families of the congregation, many of whom were members of the local aristocracy, landowners, and prosperous merchants. The choice pew was assigned to Governor Fletcher; on his return to England he presented it to the corporation (vestry), and gave a Bible and other books. A later governor, Lord Cornbury, gave the church a black pall for funerals, "on condition that no person dying and belonging to Fort Anne should be deny'd the use thereof"; he also presented to the church two Books of Common Prayer, "and to the Library Lord Clarendon's first part of the history of the Civil Wars of the Kingdome of England."

WHY CAPTAIN KIDD WAS NOT IN CHURCH

One of the initial pewholders, however, was probably never able to worship in the new church, though his wife and daughter doubtless did so. He was Captain Kidd, who had lent his tackle "for the hoiseing up Stones as long as he stays here." He did not stay in New York long enough to see the opening of the new church, for he had already been commissioned a privateer, with the assignment of capturing pirate ships and those sailing under letters of marque from the French and Spanish governments, with whom the mother country was intermittently at war. Among his sponsors in that venture were Robert Livingston of New York, the Earl of Bellomont (who was to succeed Fletcher as governor of New York, and of New England as well), other members of the English aristocracy, and—it was rumored—King William himself.

Captain Kidd sailed from New York in September 1696 in the *Adventure Galley*, with a crew of 155 men, on a mission that had the full approval of the government. Not until a year later did he reach the Red Sea, where he captured two small prizes. Then at last Kidd "hit the jackpot" by capturing a 500-ton merchant vessel, the *Quedagh Merchant*, which he sailed to the West Indies. There Kidd learned of rumors that he had turned pirate, and that orders had been issued from England for his arrest and return for trial. This piece of news caused "great consternation" to Kidd and his crew. The captain thereupon determined to leave his prize ship in Hispaniola, and sailed for New York in a smaller vessel, the *Antonio*, taking with him only a small part of the plunder. He was apparently confident that Bellomont, one of his backers, and now the governor, would set the record straight and get the charges withdrawn, or have a King's Pardon issued.

Finding that Governor Bellomont had removed to Boston, Captain Kidd put in at Gardiners Island in Long Island Sound, and sent messages to influential friends in New York.

To Gardiners Island, in due course, came James Emott, a leading New York lawyer and vestryman of Trinity, who had been to Boston to see Bellomont on Kidd's behalf. In the course of his interview with the governor, Emott may have delivered to him the letters of marque captured from the *Quedagh Merchant* and other ships, which would have served as a powerful defense of Kidd against the charge of piracy. At any rate, the way seemed clear for Kidd to proceed to Boston, and he did so. First, however, he took the precaution of sending certain of his treasures ashore, where they were buried on Gardiners Island. Some brocades and silks were presented to John Gardiner, the proprietor and lord of the island, in return for provisions for the ship.

Arriving in Boston, Kidd soon learned that he had been lured into a trap. Bellomont had no desire to clear him, but did demand his share of the prizes. Kidd replied that most of the plunder was in Hispaniola, and asked the governor to furnish a ship to retrieve it. But the governor threw Kidd into jail, summoned John Gardiner for an accounting of the merchandise left with him, and eventually shipped Kidd in irons to England, to stand trial for piracy.

Arriving in England, Kidd was thrown into Newgate Prison, where he was kept for nearly a year. Meanwhile a debate was held in the House of Commons, where Kidd's backers were under fire for financing the alleged piratical expedition; in trying to hush up the scandal, they turned against Kidd and made him the scapegoat. To avoid bringing prominent names into court, Kidd was tried and convicted of murder by striking a mutinous gunner with an iron-bound bucket—an act that might have been considered a normal exercise of discipline under other circumstances. He was then tried on five charges of piracy. Broken in health, denied counsel, and without the documents that might have been adduced in his defense, he was unable to defend himself adequately; and on May 23, 1701 he was hanged at Execution Dock along with seven other men.

Two hundred years later the French letters of marque that he had taken from the captured vessels were found in the Public Records Office in London. Had they been available for his defense, they might have cleared him of the piracy charges, and could perhaps have saved his reputation, if not his life.

Neither Bellomont nor any of Kidd's other backers received any of the missing treasure. The *Quedagh Merchant* and its rich cargo disappeared from history; and if any substantial part of the plunder was buried, it has never been found, despite many and conflicting legends.

Governor Bellomont was determined to do all that he could to support the Leislerian party, and to counteract many of the constructive measures of his predecessor,

Governor Fletcher. His first act was to dissolve the Assembly and call a new one. Before that legislature he denounced Fletcher, accusing him of dishonesty, oppression, and collusion with pirates. And since Fletcher had been the patron of Trinity Church, he also attacked the parish and its rector, whom he stigmatized as "a Jacobite." Indeed he wrote the Lords of Trade in London to urge them to take steps to deprive Mr. Vesey of his rectorship, "for it cannot be thought that I will ever go to Church while that fellow continues as Minister here."

Bellomont's hostility took the form of an attack on the Charter of Trinity Church, which he claimed to be invalid and which he sought to have revoked. But the vestry also wrote to England, and presented its case directly to the king. In reply, Governor Bellomont was directed:

> . . . that in case any Suit be already commenced, or shall hereafter be commenced against their said Charter, to ye prejudice of their said Church, or any of ye Rights or Revenues thereunto belonging, that you do not proceed definitively thereupon, until their said Charter, or an Authentic Copy thereof, together with ye whole state of ye matter be first transmitted hither, and laid before us in our Councill, and Our further Pleasure be thereupon signified unto You.

Frustrated in his attack on the Charter, the governor turned to an attempt to cancel Trinity's lease to the King's Farm, contending that he needed it for a pasturage for his own horse and cow. On this pretext he persuaded the Assembly to pass an act vacating the lease; but only over strong opposition and by his own casting vote. Before he could do more damage to the infant church, the governor died suddenly of "gout in the stomach"; his successor, Lord Cornbury, renewed the lease for the duration of his tenure as governor.

A PERIOD OF TROUBLES (1702-1743)

Trinity's political troubles were not over with the death of Governor Bellomont. During the interval before the arrival of Lord Cornbury in 1702, there was another interregnum, during which the Leislerian party was again in power. Lord Nanfan, brother-in-law of Bellomont, was the nominal head of the government of the province as lieutenant governor. One of his first acts was to imprison Nicholas Bayard, one of the most conspicuous of the anti-Leislerians and a prominent member of Trinity Church. He was put on trial for his life before Chief Justice Atwood on a charge of high treason, found guilty, and sentenced to death. The trial was hastened when the Rev. Mr. Vesey came to the defense of Bayard in a sermon from the pulpit of Trinity; Atwood replied, "We will not give Mr. Vesey an opportunity for another sermon against us." But before Bayard could be executed, Governor Cornbury arrived, superseded Nanfan, and freed Bayard—who was later elected a vestryman of Trinity. Atwood, fearing that he would be held to account for his violations of law and justice, fled from the colony.

Cornbury brought with him a new commission from Queen Anne, who had succeeded William III in 1702. This called upon him to strengthen and establish the church, and to see that "the Book of Common prayer as by law established, (be) read each Sunday and Holyday, and the blessed Sacrament administered according to the rites of the Church of England."

Another boost for the Anglican Church in the colonies was the sending of the Rev. George Keith to New England and New York. A former Quaker, Keith was employed by the infant Society for the Propagation of the Gospel (S.P.G.), founded in England in 1701. His mission was to travel through the colonies and report upon the religious needs of the Church. Landing in Boston, he preached at King's Chapel, the only Anglican church in New England (though a missionary had recently been sent to Newport, R. I.), and then traveled slowly through the colonies as far south as North Carolina, visiting small congregations of Anglicans wherever he could find them, and thrusting himself into Quaker meetings to engage in debate whenever possible.

In Connecticut, a Puritan colony, there were no Anglican churches. However, a few churchmen in Stratford sent a message to the rector of Trinity Church, New York, asking him to hold services for them. As the distance was too great, and Mr. Vesey too occupied with the affairs of his own parish, he referred the petition to the Rev. George Muirson, the Society's missionary at Rye, N. Y. Colonel Heathcote, Trinity's intrepid vestryman and a correspondent of the S.P.G., agreed to accompany Muirson into Connecticut, and in 1706 the two set out for Stratford and Fairfield, where Muirson held the first services of the church. It was well that Heathcote, well armed and ready to protect the priest, accompanied him on this and subsequent journeys, for the Puritan ministers sent circular letters to their churches warning against the intruders, and threatening their arrest. On a second visit to Stratford, when Mr. Muirson administered Holy Communion to the small group of Anglicans, two justices stationed themselves and other persons along the roads to intercept the two Anglicans and to warn the people against attending their services.

The Puritans also sent one of their ablest ministers, the Rev. Timothy Cutler, to Stratford to combat the attempt to establish an Anglican church there. This proved to be a strategic error, for Cutler was secretly inclined toward episcopacy. Stratford did not get a permanent Anglican minister until 1722. By that time, Cutler had become president of Yale; and at commencement that year he and six other ministers announced that they had decided to become Anglicans. Four of the "Yale converts," as they were called, went to England to obtain Holy Orders. One died there of smallpox, but Timothy Cutler, Samuel Johnson, and James Wetmore were ordained and returned to America. Wetmore and Johnson later became members of the Trinity staff, and Johnson became the first president of King's College in New York.

Trinity Church further aided the young congregation at Stratford by responding to a request from Colonel Heathcote in 1708 for "the Lone of one hundred pounds for two years towards building a church at Stratford in the Colony of Conecticut & he & the Rev. Mr. Muirson would be security for the same." This is the first record of a gift from Trinity Church to a church outside of New York, and the beginning of its recognition as "Mother of Churches."

The queen's strictures about regularity of Prayer Book services was scarcely necessary for Trinity Church. In a report to the Bishop of London in 1722 the rector set forth the schedule of services which had apparently been in force almost from the beginning. Services were held "every Sunday, holiday, Wednesday, and Friday in the year . . . and on Sundays there is a great congregation. The Sacrament of the Lord's Supper," he noted, is administered "once in six weeks, and the usual number of Communicants is One hundred and upwards, but on the three great festivals Christmas, Easter & Whitsuntide more than two hundred." This was more than twice as many celebrations of Holy Communion as was customary in the eighteenth century, when many churches were content with a quarterly celebration, including Christmas and Easter.

The Society for the Propagation of the Gospel assisted with supplies, and also furnished a catechist and later an ordained assistant, especially for the training of children. In addition, there was a Charity School, with about forty poor children, under a lay headmaster, William Huddleston, and with a small but growing library.

Nor were the slaves neglected. There were in the early 1700s about 1,500 Negro and Indian slaves in the city, the system of slavery having been introduced by the Dutch. These were ministered to by a devoted catechist, Elias Neau, a former elder of the French Church who became an Anglican in 1705, and was commissioned by the Venerable Society (as the S.P.G. was called) to minister to "the humble classes."

At first Mr. Neau visited the slaves from house to house, but later obtained permission for many of them to gather at his house after the close of the workday, and after the afternoon service on Sundays. By 1708 he had more than 200 catechumens under instruction, and these were presented to Mr. Vesey for baptism as rapidly as he felt them to be sufficiently instructed. Some were later admitted to Holy Communion. All this was particularly notable in a time when, according to an early historian,

> the Negroes were much discouraged from embracing the Christian religion, upon account of the very little regard

showed them in any religious respect. . . . Their marriages were performed by mutual consent only, without the blessing of the Church; they were buried by those of their own country or complexion in the common field, without any Christian office, perhaps some ridiculous heathen rites were performed at the grave by some of their own people. No notice was given of their being sick that they might be visited; on the contrary frequent discourses were made in conversation that they had no souls and perished as beasts.

It is to the honor of the rector and his assistants, and the glory of the congregation that, in the light of the prevailing view, they did all they could to help these unhappy and often miserable people. Indeed there was a time, during the so-called insurrection of the Negroes in 1712 (when many false rumors about them caused much unnecessary bloodshed), when Elias Neau was in danger of his life for sheltering some of his catechumens from the violence of mob action.

By 1711 the number of Negro slaves had increased, and most wealthy whites "owned" several of them. A slave market was opened at the eastern end of Wall Street, within sight of Trinity Church, and these miserable people were bought and sold as chattels. Slave ships entered New York harbor, but they generally unloaded their cargoes on the New Jersey side, to avoid the head tax on their victims.

Shortly after midnight on April 7, 1712 some twenty-three Negroes, armed with guns, hatchets, and knives, met in an orchard at Maiden Lane. Two of them set fire to the home of a Dutch burgher, and raced back to the orchard. All then headed for the burning house, and attacked those who came to put out the fire. Nine white men were killed, and several wounded.

Reprisals were swift and drastic. Governor Hunter,

aroused from sleep, sent soldiers to the troubled area. When the Negroes scattered, he posted sentries at the river crossings to prevent them from leaving the island of Manhattan. Shortly after daybreak, the Negro mobsters were flushed from cover. Six of them killed themselves, rather than endure the fate awaiting them. Then, says Edward Robb Ellis in *The Epic of New York City*:

> The town churned with rage and fear. White people told one another that this never would have happened if Elias Neau hadn't opened a school for Negroes and stuffed their minds with inflammatory ideas. What need had Negroes for education? All they had to know was to do as they were told, work hard, and keep their places. The kind-hearted Neau was abused so shrilly that for a while he hardly dared appear in public.

Then the populace turned to the punishment of the guilty Negroes—and any others who were suspected of complicity in the plot. After a brief semblance of trial, the slaves were tortured unmercifully. One was suspended alive in chains without food or water until he died after days of agony. Two were roasted alive over a slow fire. Another was tied to a cart and dragged through the town, with ten bloody lashes inflicted at each street corner. A woman was hanged. Another man was broken on the wheel. In all, twenty-one Negroes were executed; others, who turned state's evidence and testified against their comrades, were banished from the province.

It was a dark day in the history of New York City —one that was conveniently forgotten in later years, when New Yorkers were to rail at Southerners for alleged inhumanity to their slaves—many of whom would have been sold to them by enterprising New York and New England traders.

When the frenzy died down, and the situation was more soberly estimated, "there were not any found," according to an unsigned memorandum probably written by the Rev. Mr. Vesey, "either Actors or Accomplices in the Conspiracy who had attended the Catechetical instruction, but two were accused, one of which had been formerly baptised and dyed protesting his innocence, and was, but too late for him, pitied & declared guiltless even by the Prosecutors. The other had made some proficience but was not admitted to Baptism thro' the reluctance of his Master whom he had often Solicited for it."

In due time, Neau was able to resume his ministry to the slaves, with the hearty support of the rector, and at least the tacit support of the pewholders, many of whom were themselves slave owners.

Queen Anne showed her generosity to Trinity by bestowing on the parish, in perpetuity, the Queen's Farm, and also a smaller tract of land, now the south section of the churchyard of Trinity, known as the Queen's Garden. Little is known of the former use of the garden, which was described as "fronting on Broadway on the east and extending to low water mark on the west." The Queen's Farm, however, was to play an important part in the history of Trinity Church, becoming in the nineteenth century both the source of great wealth and the cause of innumerable lawsuits and litigation. Eventually, however, the right of Trinity Church to the ownership of this valuable property in lower Manhattan was firmly established, beyond any shadow of legal doubt.

The description of the property granted by Queen Anne as the Queen's Farm was somewhat indefinite, as few streets, other than Broadway, had yet been laid out. The description in the grant describes the property as "bounded on the east partly by the Broadway, partly by the Common and partly by the Swamp and on the west by Hudson's River." In more modern terms it is described, in a survey by a title guarantee company, as extending along Fulton Street from Broadway to the Hudson River, north to Christopher Street to a point just east of Hudson Street, and then south and east back to Broadway near Duane Street.

This large parcel of land, in what was to become the heart of downtown Manhattan, has had an interesting history, going back well before the founding of Trinity Church. In the days when the Dutch ruled Manhattan (which they were reputed to have bought from the Indians for $24.00 worth of wampum and trinkets), the farm belonged to one Anneke Jans, wife of the manager for the first Patroon of the Van Rensselaer Manor near Albany. Her husband died, leaving three daughters and one son. In 1638 Anneke Jans married the Rev. Everardus Bogardus, the Dutch pastor, by whom she had four more children.

Pastor and Mrs. Bogardus apparently lived on the farm, while he served the Reformed congregation, until 1647 when Bogardus was lost at sea on a voyage to his homeland. His widow retained the title to the farm, but removed to Albany, where she died in 1663. In her will she directed that the farm on Manhattan Island should be sold, the proceeds to be divided principally among the four children by her first husband.

The farm was bought by the English governor of the province, Francis Lovelace. It was Lovelace who surrendered New York the second time to the Dutch; he was disgraced and heavily in debt to the proprietor, the Duke of York. Consequently, when New York reverted to English rule after the peace between England and Holland in 1674, all of Lovelace's property, including the farm, passed into the possession of the duke, who was to become King James II. Thereafter, it became known as the Duke's Farm and later as the King's Farm.

With the duke's approval, the rental of the farm became a perquisite of the English governor, though the title vested in the Crown. Consequently, in 1697 Governor Fletcher leased the farm to "the Managers of the Church of England" for a period of seven years. His successor, Lord Bellomont, tried to void the lease and recover the farm for his own use. But the next governor, Lord Cornbury, again leased the property to Trinity Church, for the duration of his governorship, the rental value at that time being £36 per annum.

At first, Trinity let the land to a tenant farmer; but as early as 1703 Colonel Morris and Colonel Heathcote recommended that a part of the land be set aside for the establishment by the Society for Propagation of the Gospel as the site of a college. It was perhaps with this possibility in mind that in 1705 Queen Anne made the generous grant of the farm, now known as the Queen's Farm, to Trinity Church. It is noteworthy that in due course a college, known as King's College, and later as Columbia, was founded in 1754 under the auspices of Trinity Church and on its property.

Queen Anne further showed her favor to Trinity Church by the gift of a handsome silver set of Communion plate, still used in the church on special occasions.

It was not until more than a century later, in 1833, that certain so-called Bogardus heirs sued Trinity over the grant of the Queen's Farm, alleging that the transfer of title to Governor Lovelace was invalid, because one of the heirs, Cornelius Bogardus, did not sign the deed. After a trial of thirteen days, the court held that the alleged defect was insufficient to cloud the title to the land, and that in any case "at the expiration of sixty years from that time (1705) the right of the complainants' ancestors if it previously had any was completely barred" by the statute of limitations. Similar claims, arising from time to time after that date, were rejected by the courts; and indeed some lawyers attempting to organize the alleged heirs of Anneke Jans to claim their "inheritance" were fined or disbarred on grounds of fraud. Attempts to upset Trinity's title by appeal to the New York legislature and to Congress have also been unsuccessful; and it is safe to say that probably no property in Manhattan has been so thoroughly examined and so completely established as that granted in 1705 to Trinity Church under the name of the Queen's Farm.

Despite the favor of Queen Anne, Trinity Church continued to have troubles with the successive royal governors, and with the city vestry, upon which Mr. Vesey was dependent for his salary. One difficulty was that the Anglican Church in the colonies, despite its episcopal organization, had no resident bishop to exercise authority over the parishes and to protect them from intrusion by the secular authorities. As early as 1705, the rector and vestry of Trinity Church wrote to the queen and to the Bishop of London asking that this situation be remedied. Regarding the episcopate, they wrote:

> We conceive it to be highly necessary for securing the Establishment of the Church in these Provinces and Enlarging her Borders that the Ecclesiasticall Government according to the Apostolic fform and order should be establisht among us in like manner as in England & Ireland. We therefore become humble suppliants to your Majesty that you will be graciously pleased to Establish Bishops who may reside among us to govern the Church to Ordain some, Confirm others and bless all in our Redeemer's Name which we doubt not (by the blessing

of God) will be the most sure and effectual means to propagate Religion and Sound Doctrine and preserve the Church in Unity and Peace.

However, this plea, echoed by churches in New Jersey, Virginia, and other provinces, fell upon deaf ears. It was simply inconceivable to eighteenth-century Englishmen to contemplate bishops who were not also secular lords and judges in ecclesiastical courts; and the Nonconformists in America were violently opposed to episcopacy as they had known it in England, and as they feared it might be developed in the colonies. Thus for 177 years (from the founding of Jamestown, Va. in 1607 to the consecration of the first American bishop in 1784) the only episcopal supervision of Anglican churches in the American colonies was the very remote and nebulous authority of the Bishop of London and the Archbishop of Canterbury. In the absence of resident bishops, no one could be confirmed and no priests or deacons ordained in the colonies. For ordination, it was necessary for candidates to make the long and hazardous voyage to England; and one out of five of those who undertook that journey did not return from it. Some authority was exercised by commissaries in priest's orders, commissioned by the Bishop of London and sent out by the Society for the Propagation of the Gospel; but they had little power except that of moral suasion, and could not confirm or ordain. (In his later years, Mr. Vesey was appointed commissary for the province of New York, and helped as best he could to unite the various Anglican churches in that area.)

By 1714 the situation in New York City had become so acute, with the feeling against the church fomented by radical agitators who did not hesitate on occasion to invade the church building itself and commit sacrilegious outrages, that the vestry determined to send the rector to England to make efforts to protect the church against her enemies, and to secure more adequate direction from the Mother Church. Despite the opposition of Governor Hunter, the Bishop of London approved the voyage, and the parish vestry arranged for a supply of preachers during the rector's absence. However, the city vestry refused to pay Mr. Vesey's salary for the time he was absent, and it was necessary for the S.P.G. to vote a sum of money for his relief while in London, where for a time he became ill and was temporarily incapacitated. Nevertheless, on his return to New York in 1715 with his appointment as commissary, he was able to report that he had met with a large measure of success in acquainting the English church authorities with the problems of the churches in the colonies, though unable to convince them of the need for a resident bishop.

Meanwhile, both New York and Trinity Church were growing and developing into more of an urban community and parish. William Bradford, the pioneer printer of the colony (and a vestryman of Trinity) began a weekly newspaper and published the first map of the city. He also, on commission from Trinity Parish, published the first Colonial edition of the Book of Common Prayer, identical with that in use in England but locally printed and distributed.

Bradford's map showed only three streets between Trinity Church and the fort, with four other streets to the north of Trinity, extending to the Queen's Farm. Thereafter a road continued Broadway to the north and west, in the direction of Harlem.

Trinity Church was embellished and enlarged from time to time, as was the Charity School operated by it.

A new belfry was added, to which the Jews of the city made a substantial contribution (since they could enjoy the bells even though they did not worship in the church); and the first accident recorded in parish annals occurred when one of the workmen fell from the belfry to the ground, "by which," according to Bradford's *Gazette*, "most of his bones were broken, but is yet alive." However, in the next issue it was reported that the man had died.

By 1737 Trinity Church had been considerably enlarged and beautified, and in 1741 the first organ was installed. Writing a few years later, a local historian, William Smith, described the church:

> It stands very pleasantly upon the banks of Hudson's River, and has a large Cemetery on each side, inclosed in the front by a painted pale fence. Before it a long walk is railed off from the Broad-way, the pleasantest street of any in the whole Town. The building is about 148 feet long, including the Tower and Chancel, and 72 feet in Breadth. The Steeple is 175 Feet in Height. . . . The church is, within, ornamented beyond any Place of publick Worship amongst us. The Head of the Chancel is adorned with an Altar-piece, and opposite to it, at the other End of the Building, is the Organ. The Tops of the Pillars which support the Galleries, are decked with the gilt Busts of Angels winged. From the Ceiling are suspended two Glass Branches, and on the Walls hang the Arms of some of its principal Benefactors. The Allies are paved with flat Stones.

The steeple and belfry were the highest points in colonial New York; for a fee of sixpence visitors could gain a breathtaking panorama of the city, the fort, and the boats in the harbor.

In 1742 a further addition was made to the church, when it was ordered "that a new gallery be built on the

North side the Church, and that the Pulpit be Removed near the Chancell." Apparently, too, the congregation had wearied of the innumerable "gilt Busts of Angels winged," for it was further ordered that "upon the pillars under the galleries there be a Crown and Cherub alternately instead of all Cherubs."

All in all, Trinity was no doubt considered a magnificent specimen of the church architecture of the day, and one to give great satisfaction to the pewholders who gathered week by week to worship God and to be edified by the sermons of Mr. Vesey or an assistant or occasional visiting preacher.

3

The Years Prior to the Revolution

1744-1775

In June of 1744 New York was visited by one of the most indefatigable and articulate of colonial travelers, Dr. Alexander Hamilton of Annapolis, Md. This well-educated, Scottish-born physician and bachelor prescribed for himself a long journey on horseback, "intended only for health and recreation," while recovering from a bout of illness that left him with "an Incessant cough, which no medicine whatsoever can abate or diminish; this makes me apprehensive that the consequences will be a confirmed Consumption." Despite this, accompanied only by his Negro slave Dromo, he traveled some 1,624 miles, to York, Maine, and return; with a side trip by boat from New York to Albany. His candid diary gives an excellent account of the journey, with keen observations of the manners and customs of the many places visited.

DR. ALEXANDER HAMILTON'S REPORT

Of New York, on his first visit, he observes: "This city makes a very fine appearance for above a mile all along the river, and here lyes a great deal of shipping. I put my horses up att one Waghorn's att the Sign of the Cart and Horse." This establishment was a popular tavern on what is now William Street, between John and Fulton streets. Later he took up lodgings at the residence of one Mrs. Robert Hogg, at the corner of Broad and William streets. The next afternoon he "took a turn thro' severall of the principall streets in town, guarding against staring about me as much as possible for fear of being remarked for a stranger, gaping and staring being the true criterion or proof of rustick strangers in all places."

Nevertheless, Dr. Hamilton kept his eyes open, and continued:

> I found this city less in extent but, by the stirr and frequency upon the streets, more populous than Philadelphia; I saw more shipping in the harbour; the houses are more compact and regular and, in generall, higher built, most of them after the Dutch modell with their gavell ends fronting the street. There are a few built of stone, more of wood, but the greatest number of brick, and a great many covered with pan tile and glazed tile with the year of God when built figured out with plates of iron upon the fronts of severall of them. The streets, in generall, are but narrow and not regularly disposed. The best of them run paralell to the river, for the city is built with logs of wood piled upon a stone foundation. . . . The women of fashion here appear more in publick than in Philadelphia and dress much gayer. They come abroad generally in the cool of the evening and go to the Promenade.

Trinity Church he described as "a spacious church belonging to the English congregation with a pritty high but heavy, clumsy steeple built of freestone fronting the street called Broadway." On the following Sunday he met at breakfast Thomas Jeffrys, a customs officer who had once been in Maryland, and with him the doctor went to Trinity for the morning service, of which he wrote:

> The minister who preached to us was a stranger. He gave us a good discourse upon the Christian virtues. There was a large congregation of above a thousand [doubtless an exaggeration, as the church would hardly hold that many] among which was a number of dressed ladies. This church is above 100 foot long and 80 wide. Att the east end of it is a large semicircular area in which stands the altar, pritty well ornamented with painting and guilding. The gallerys are supported with wooden pillars of the Ionick order with carved work of foilage and cherubs' heads guilt betwixt the capitals. There is a pritty organ att the west end of the church consisting of a great number of pipes handsomly guilt and adorned, but I had not the satisfaction of hearing it play, they having att this time no organist, but the vocall musick of the congregation was very good.

Dr. Hamilton went with his new friend, Mr. Jeffrys, to the home of Stephen Bayard (soon to be New York's mayor) to dine, then to the coffeehouse, and later to tea at "a gentlewoman's house, whose name I know not, being introduced there by Mr. Jeffrys." At six o'clock the two set out again, to visit the fort and the Battery. Hamilton continued:

> The castle, or fort is now in ruins, having been burnt down three or four years ago by the conspirators, but they talk of repairing it again. The Leutenant Governour had here a house and a chapell, and there are fine gardens and terrass walks

from which one has a very pritty view of the city. In the fort are severall guns, some of them brass and cast in a handsome mould. The new battery is raised with ramparts of turf, and the guns upon it are in size from 12 to 18 pounders. The main battery is a great half moon or semicircular rampart bluff upon the water, being turf upon a stone foundation about 100 paces in length, the platform of which is laid in some places with plank. Upon it there are 56 great iron guns, well mounted, most of them being 32 pounders. Mr. Jeffrys told me that to walk out after dusk upon this platform was a good way for a stranger to fit himself with a courtezan, for the place was the generall rendezvous of the fair sex of that profession after sun set. He told me there was a good choice of pritty lasses among them, both Dutch and English. However, I was not so abandoned as to go among them but went and supped with the Club att Todd's.

The "pritty organ," to which Dr. Hamilton referred, was built by John Clemm, of Philadelphia; and his son, John Clemm, Jr., had served for three years as organist. However, in 1743 the vestry had sent to England "to procure for the Church a Good Sober Organist; but not to exceed forty pounds Sterling per annum, nor to agree for a longer term than three years." Accordingly John Rice of London arrived in November, 1744, his transportation from England being paid by the vestry. Canon Edward N. West, writing of the music of Old Trinity, notes that "Mr. Rice was so sober that he attracted no attention during the seventeen years in which he held this post." The choir consisted of boys trained by the organist, and the music consisted mostly of metrical psalms. Not until 1753 did Trinity acquire a truly great musician, in William Tuckey, trained in the cathedral at Bristol, England. Tuckey raised the number of boys in the choir to fifty-six, trained them to sing hymns, and composed music not only for the organ but for accompaniment by an instrumental band as well.

TRINITY'S FIRST CHAPEL

By 1745 the Anglican Church in New York colony had grown to some twenty-two congregations, over which Mr. Vesey had a measure of authority as commissary for the Bishop of London. Many of these, as well as some in Connecticut, had been started or aided by Trinity, which was already becoming known as the "Mother of Churches." But the venerable rector was growing old and somewhat infirm; his last attendance at a vestry meeting was on April 3, 1746, and on July 11th of that year he died at his residence at the age of seventy-two, having served faithfully as rector of Trinity for forty-nine years.

As second rector (the nominal rectorship of Bishop Compton not being counted), the vestry chose a noted missionary to the Indians, the Rev. Henry Barclay. On October 23, 1746 Mr. Barclay was inducted by the royal governor, George Clinton, in the presence of the wardens, vestrymen, and congregation, and "did openly and publickly before the congregation assembled declare his unfeigned assent and consent to all and Everything and things contained and prescribed in and by the book Intituled the Book of Common Prayer." At the time of his election and induction, Barclay was thirty-four years old, and had served as pastor of the Mohawk Indians for eight years. Native-born, he was a graduate of Yale College. As rector of Trinity, he continued his interest in the Indians, and in 1762 he supervised a new edition of the Prayer Book in the Mohawk tongue.

Two years after the beginning of his rectorship, Mr.

Barclay appointed the Rev. Samuel Auchmuty as assistant minister, and the two cooperated closely together in the work of the parish during Barclay's brief rectorship. In December, 1749, on successive days, the rector and his assistant were married in Trinity Church, the former to a daughter of the late Capt. Anthony Rutgers and the latter to the widow of the late Captain Tucker—"both Ladies," according to a contemporary account, "of great Merit and valuable Accomplishments."

In 1749 the congregation of Trinity Parish had grown to the extent that need was felt for a second church to accommodate those living to the north at some distance from the mother church. Accordingly, ground was purchased in an area east of the present William Street, and a "chapel of ease," 92 feet in length and 72 feet in breadth, was constructed. The architect was Robert Crommelin, a vestryman, and the new building was consecrated as St. George's Chapel.

Despite its growth, New York was still a green and pleasant city, rivaling Boston and Philadelphia in size. A Swedish traveler in 1748 noted an abundance of trees along the chief streets, "which in summer give them a fine appearance, and during the excessive heat of that time, afford a cooling shade. I found it extremely pleasant to walk in the town, for it seemed quite like a garden." He also wrote of an abundance of birds nesting in the trees, but noted that there were also numerous frogs, who "are very clamorous in the evening and in the nights (especially when the days had been hot, and a rain was expected) and in a manner drown the singing of the birds." Indeed, he added, "they frequently make such a noise that it is difficult for a person to make himself heard."

The houses, this traveler observed, were of brick, many

having gables turned to the street, with balconies on the roof where the people spent their evenings. The walls within were whitewashed, and often the walls were covered with all sorts of drawings and pictures in small frames. The churches were mostly of stone, and he noted nine of them: Trinity, distinguished by a steeple with a bell, the old and new Dutch churches, a Presbyterian church which "was built but lately," two German churches, one Lutheran and one Reformed, a French church, "for Protestant refugees," and also a Quaker meeting house and a Jewish synagogue.

For the most part, Trinity continued on an even keel during Mr. Barclay's rectorship, though there was some trouble with the Bogardus heirs, who had to be evicted from church property when they attempted to build a shack on it. The Charity School, with some fifty scholars, also flourished until 1750, when it was unfortunately destroyed by fire of unknown origin. The same fire set Trinity's steeple ablaze, and destroyed the parish registers, containing the records of baptisms, marriages, and burials. A year later the schoolhouse was rebuilt, but the loss of the parish records was irreparable.

Political affairs in the colony were increasingly vexing. The French and their Iroquois allies were on the warpath, and the northern parts of the colony were frequently ravaged by them. There was fear that New York City itself might be invaded; and the Indians of the Six Nations, who had traditionally been allied with the British, declared that they would fight against the French no more. Governor Clinton, unpopular with the colonists, "wracked by rheumatism and richer by 80,000 pounds," returned to England in 1753; his successor, Sir Danvers Osborn, committed suicide shortly after his arrival. Mr. Barclay buried him, after a ruling that the governor had killed himself while insane. He was succeeded by the lieutenant governor, James DeLancey, who had his hands full trying to cope with political and ecclesiastical dissent until the arrival of the new royal appointee, Sir Charles Hardy, two years later.

However, Mr. Barclay and the Trinity vestry had the great satisfaction of participating in the founding of King's College, later to become Columbia University. Funds had been raised, in the custom of the time, by two state-sponsored lotteries, and vested in a board of ten trustees, seven of whom were Trinity vestrymen.

A clergyman of the Church of England, Dr. Samuel Johnson, was elected the first president of the new college; and, since his salary as president was inadequate, he was also named an assistant minister of Trinity. The parish also made a generous grant of land to the college, "lying & being on the West side of the Broadway . . . fronting easterly to Church street between Barclay street and Murray street, . . . thence running westerly between and along the said Barclay street and Murray street, to the North River." The consideration for this transfer of land was the nominal sum of ten shillings; a hundred years later the land was valued at $400,000.

King's College received its charter on October 31, 1754. It provided that the president of the college "forever and for the time being" must belong to the Church of England, and Trinity's land grant contained a similar proviso. This requirement was deleted from the charter in 1810, when the college was incorporated by the State of New York as Columbia College; but it remained in the Trinity grant deed for nearly two centuries. In 1950 a twentieth-century vestry waived the rule at the request of the Columbia trustees, who had elected Dwight D. Eisenhower as the first non-Anglican president of the university.

The cornerstone of the first King's College building was laid on August 23, 1756. Until this building was ready for use, the college classes met in Trinity's schoolhouse. Thus the sixth college in the American colonies began its life as a virtual ward of Trinity Parish.

ST. PAUL'S CHAPEL

In July of 1762, while workmen were repairing Trinity's steeple, a heavy thunderstorm arose and the steeple was struck by lightning. The workmen, it was reported, "received no Hurt, otherwise than remaining feeble for a short space," and the resulting fire was "happily extinguished." But the vestry, apparently aware of Benjamin Franklin's experiments with lightning, determined to protect the church against future catastrophes of that nature. Accordingly they ordered "that the Spire of the Steeple of Trinity Church be wholly New shingled and scuttles be made with hooks that may be thought proper to go up to the top of the spire and that a proper Iron conductor or conductors be affixed up from the Spindle of the Cock to come down into the ground." Thus Trinity became the first church in New York, and perhaps in the American colonies, to be equipped with an effective lightning rod.

Both Trinity Church and St. George's Chapel were growing rapidly, and the need for a third church was beginning to be felt. Much of the growth was the result of unrest on the part of the younger people of Dutch descent, who were dissatisfied with the services in the Dutch language in the Reformed churches. Although Trinity and the Dutch congregation had been on friendly terms since the beginning, it was indicated that "the greater half of Trinity consisted of accessions from the Dutch Church."

Accordingly, in 1763 a vestry committee was appointed "to enquire and look out for a proper and convenient Lott of Ground" on which a new chapel of ease might be built. The appropriate "Lott" was found at Broadway and Division Street (now Fulton Street), and construction of St. Paul's Chapel was begun.

But the rector did not live to see completion of the new chapel. On August 20, 1764 the Rev. Henry Barclay, who had been ill for some time, died at the age of fifty-three. The funeral service was conducted by the assistant minister, the Rev. Samuel Auchmuty, and burial was in the family vault in Trinity churchyard.

The vacancy was quickly filled by the vestry, who within a week elected Mr. Auchmuty as the third rector. On the first of September, he was formally inducted by mandate of the lieutenant governor, Cadwallader Colden, in accordance with the terms of the royal charter.

The vestry also acted promptly to provide an assistant to the new rector. Their first choice was the Rev. Charles Inglis, at that time rector in Dover, N.J.; but he declined the call on account of the grave illness of his wife. Accordingly, the vestry elected the Rev. John Ogilvie, a Yale graduate and former Indian missionary. A year later, Mr. Inglis was again called as a second assistant, and this time he accepted.

St. Paul's Chapel was now completed, and was opened for worship at a great service on October 30, 1766. It was a handsome building, in a part of the city not yet built up, though the adjoining street had recently been paved and street lights installed. The architect was a Scotsman, Thomas McBean, probably a pupil of Gibbs, who designed the Church of St. Martin's-in-the-Fields, in London, which the chapel somewhat resembles.

Described in a contemporary newspaper account as "one of the most elegant Edifices on the Continent," St. Paul's was rectangular in shape, with the chancel and high pulpit at the east end, topped by a coronet and six feathers, a symbol of British nobility. At the west was a low square tower with a projecting porch open to the river. The portico at the east formed a part of the original design, but the main entrance was by a door in the middle of the south side. The church, later (1802) lighted by huge chandeliers of Waterford glass, contained a pew set apart for use of the royal governor. Above the sacristy at the east end were rooms, one of which served as the parish library; this was to be walled up during the Revolution in order to safeguard its treasures. The distinctive and rather ornate steeple and weathervane, designed by James C. Lawrence, were added in 1794.

With Trinity Parish now consisting of the mother church (Trinity) and two chapels (St. George's and St. Paul's), the clergy staff of the rector and two assistants were kept busy ministering to the three congregations, on a rotating basis. It was soon apparent that a third assistant minister was necessary to care for the growing needs, and on December 23, 1766 the Rev. Samuel Provoost was called, "to officiate in his turn at the several churches on the Lord's Day and at Prayers on Week Days when requested by the Rector."

When Mr. Ogilvie died in 1774, a new assistant minister, the Rev. John Vardill, was appointed, but never entered upon his duties because of the turmoil of affairs on the eve of the Revolutionary War. In his place, the Rev. Benjamin Moore was appointed on February 10, 1775, and another assistant, the Rev. John Bowden, on the same date.

All of these men were soon to be embroiled in the rapidly accelerating crisis leading up to what was, in New York at least, as much a civil war as a revolution against a foreign power. Each of them was to react differently, and Trinity Church, as well as the city and the country, was to be torn apart with controversy. Auchmuty, as rector, was the first to be involved; but Inglis, Provoost, and Moore were equally caught up in the turbulent affairs of church and state—and in due course, each of them was also destined to serve as rector of Trinity Parish. Bowden, suffering from "a weak broken voice, and a tender habit of body," was apparently absent on sick leave much of the time until his resignation in 1777.

ON THE EVE OF THE REVOLUTION

The lightning that struck Trinity's steeple in 1762 was nothing to the bolt that inflamed the colonies three years later, when news reached America of the passage of the Stamp Act. This measure, passed by the English Parliament under King George III, was to go into effect November 1, 1765. Intended to pay the cost of 10,000 soldiers to be sent to America, the Act would require a tax stamp on virtually every legal transaction and on various licenses. Without buying a stamp, colonists would be unable to get a marriage license, buy a newspaper, draw up a will, receive a college diploma, file a lawsuit, purchase an insurance policy, or even buy a drink in a tavern.

Immediately there was an outcry from all classes among the colonists, from Maine to Georgia. In the Virginia House of Burgesses, Patrick Henry made his famous speech denying the right of Parliament to tax the colonies; the cry of "No taxation without representation" began to be heard throughout the land. A New York paper boldly wrote that if the "Interest of the Mother Country and her Colonies cannot be made to co-incide . . . then the Connection between them ought to cease." And on the initiative of the Massachusetts legislature, nine colonies sent delegates to an anti-Stamp Act congress in New York's Town Hall, just down Wall Street from Trinity Church. Described by Delaware's Caesar Rodney as "an Assembly of the Greatest Ability," the congress asked Parliament to repeal the Act forthwith, and asserted the exclusive right of the colonial assemblies to tax their own people. Henceforth, cried Christopher Gadsden of South Carolina, "there ought to be no more New England men, no New Yorkers, . . . but all of us Americans!"

While the congress was in session, a ship arrived in New York harbor with the first consignment of tax stamps. It was greeted by a jeering mob of some 2,000 New Yorkers, and officials did not dare to unload the stamps until late at night, when the crowd had dispersed. Then seven boxes of stamps were taken secretly to the fort, where they were locked up under military protection.

The next day posters appeared throughout the town warning inhabitants against buying or using the stamps. Lieutenant Governor Colden wisely postponed opening the boxes of stamps until the arrival of the newly appointed governor, Sir Henry Moore. As the effective date of November 1st arrived, offices and shops were closed, flags flew at half-mast, muffled church bells tolled, and houses were shrouded in black. On the commons, the Sons of Liberty whipped the crowd into fury as darkness fell, and some surged toward the fort, where troops stood ready to repel them. But the boxes of stamps remained unopened; and a few days later Colden turned them over to the mayor and alderman to await the arrival of the new governor.

Governor Moore arrived November 13th, on a ship bearing a new consignment of stamps; but the governor wisely refused to distribute them. Instead, he opened the gates to the fort and permitted the people to enter as he was sworn into office. Moore then suspended his power to execute the Stamp Act; six months later word was received that the Act had been repealed, and the city rejoiced. Again the people repaired in throngs to the commons, where there was feasting and revelry. Grateful New Yorkers, thinking the storm was over, even decided to erect a statue to George III.

In all the turmoil, the clergy and congregation of Trinity Church found themselves in the midst. The royal governor and the lieutenant governor were of course ex-officio parishioners; Daniel Horsmanden, chief justice of the colony and president of the Governor's Council, was a warden. Several of the vestrymen were merchants who had resisted the Stamp Act. Isaac Sears, the fiery leader of the Sons of Liberty, was a member of the congregation; Robert Livingston was a delegate to the congress that had denounced the Stamp Act, as well as a justice of the Supreme Court.

In spite of the agitation about them, the clergy continued their ministrations in the mother church and the two chapels with diligence and a minimum of friction. On May 21, 1766 the principal clergy of New York, Connecticut, and New Jersey met at the home of Dr. Auchmuty, and formed themselves into a voluntary convention. The rector delivered the sermon at the convention, and at its conclusion "addressed himself to his Audience, and congratulated them upon the Repeal of the disagreeable Stamp Act, and then concluded the whole with Such Advice as our present circumstances highly require should be followed."

No doubt a part of Dr. Auchmuty's "Advice" on that occasion was the reopening of the question of the desirability of a resident bishop for the supervision of the Anglican churches in the colonies; indeed it was widely believed that he had the secret ambition of becoming the first colonial bishop. It is clear that frequent representations were made to both civil and ecclesiastical authorities in England urging that such a bishop be appointed; but without success.

In May 1770 Dr. Auchmuty wrote to Sir William Johnson, a British colonial leader who apparently unofficially acted as representative of the colonists after his return to England:

> The Clergy are much indebted to you, worthy Sir, for your strong attachment to the present happy Establishment in Church and State, and for your animated Letters to the Ministry setting forth the necessity of an American Episcopate, and a proper notice and regard for the American Churches; which, at present, are left destitute of Countenance and support.

In the same letter, Dr. Auchmuty wrote of the political situation in England and the colonies:

> Our great men, instead of being careful pilots, and anxious for the safety of the Nation, are inveloped in false politics's, rack their invention, & exert their utmost abilities to aggrandize themselves, and their families, and suffer, for want of true principles their Sovereign and their Country to be tossed to and fro with every wind of popular discontent, without guiding the Helm with prudence, caution, and Resolution. The Lords Temporal are wholly engrossed in a system of Politic, which must end, if persevered in, in the ruin of themselves,

and their Country; and the Lords Spiritual, while they can unmolested enjoy their opulence, & weight in the Government, pay too little attention to the distresses and injustice that the members of the best church in the world labour under, in America.

One reason that "the Lords Spiritual" refused to listen to the plea for an American bishop was that neither they, nor the Dissenters who mortally feared and hated the idea of the episcopate, could conceive of a bishop with purely spiritual and ecclesiastical powers, and not concerned with civil government and secular affairs. One of the objections of the Nonconformists in America to the Stamp Act, indeed, was the fear that it would lead to ecclesiastical courts, perhaps administered by bishops, as in England, and that they would exercise jurisdiction over the performance of marriages and burials, the setting up of compulsory tithes for church support, and perhaps the forbidding of dissent entirely.

Animated by these fears, the New York Assembly, between 1769 and 1771, four times passed a bill to disestablish Trinity Church, but each time it was voted down by the Governor's Council. Clearly the idea of an established church with an ordered episcopate was a lost cause, even before the Revolution swept away all ideas of an ecclesiastical establishment.

Meanwhile, in 1769 Governor Moore died; he was the last of the colonial governors to receive a state funeral at Trinity. In due course, he was succeeded by Governor William Tryon.

The relative tranquility and unity that marked the rejoicing at the repeal of the Stamp Act was of short duration. On the same day that the Stamp Act was repealed, the English Parliament passed the Declaratory Act, affirming its right "to make laws and statutes of sufficient force and validity to bind the colonies and people of America, subjects of the crown of Britain, in all cases whatsoever." The Quartering Act, requiring Americans to furnish the king's troops with barracks and supplies, was still in effect. And a new series of laws, the Townshend Acts, taxed many colonial imports, including tea. The Americans responded by boycotting British goods. In Boston, citizens disguised as Indians dumped 342 chests of tea into the harbor; a similar raid, on a smaller scale, took place in New York harbor.

The seeds of rebellion were now growing at a rapid pace. In New York, as elsewhere in the colonies, men were being forced to declare themselves and take sides. Those who opposed the new repressive acts were called Whigs, or patriots; those who tried to minimize them and remain loyal to the mother country were called Tories, or loyalists. In Philadelphia, the first Continental Congress met and drew up a declaration of rights and grievances against George III and his government.

New York was represented at the Continental Congress by John Jay, John Alsop, Isaac Low, James Duane, and Philip Livingston. Among the members of the Committee of Fifty-one which selected these delegates, several were vestrymen or pewholders of Trinity, including Edward Laight and Theophylact Bache, Elias Desbrosses, and Miles Sherbrooke. They sent the New York delegation to Philadelphia with a prayer for peace and reconciliation; most of them still hoped in 1774 that a peaceful settlement of the colonists' grievances could be found. But the Continental Congress went beyond what they had expected, and stopped just short of repudiating the royal authority.

As political affairs rapidly approached a climax, the divisions between Whigs and Tories became sharper. Like most organizations, the Trinity vestry was divided in its loyalties. The same was true of the clergy. Although Dr. Auchmuty, the rector, had rejoiced at repeal of the Stamp Act, he felt that things were now going much too fast and too far. "The true principles of a good churchman," he wrote, "are a true regard to the Laws of his God, and, a zealous attachment to his lawful Sovereign."

Of the assistant ministers, Charles Inglis was also an ardent loyalist, while Benjamin Moore maintained a fairly neutral position. Only Samuel Provoost was outspoken in maintaining Whig sentiments. For his pains, some of the parishioners threatened to withdraw their financial support if Provoost remained on the staff; and since the salaries were paid by subscription of the parishioners, and money was in short supply, Provoost was forced to resign in 1771. In one of his last sermons at Trinity he said, "We are fighting for our laws and for our liberties." Provoost retired to a farm near Albany, where he served neighboring parishes and continued throughout the Revolution to support the American cause.

In 1775 the enlarged Committee of Sixty, which contained more than a dozen members of the parish, reelected Jay, Duane, and Alsop, plus three new members, Robert Livingston, Francis Lewis, and Lewis Morris, to the second Continental Congress. This Congress was soon to issue the Declaration of Independence, and to appoint another Anglican, George Washington of Virginia, as commander in chief of the American armed forces.

First news of hostilities reached New York on a bright Sunday, April 23, 1775, when churchgoers were leaving Trinity, St. Paul's, and the other churches and returning to their homes for dinner. Down Broadway, past St. Paul's and Trinity, rode a messenger on a foam-flecked horse, shouting the tidings of battles with the Redcoats at Lexington and Concord. New Yorkers responded with alacrity. Within an hour John Smith and Anthony Lispenard led a crowd to the docks and began unloading troop supplies from a royal ship bound for Boston. Another crowd followed Isaac Sears and his Sons of Liberty to City Hall, where they removed from the arsenal some 500 muskets, and distributed them among the mob.

In the absence of Governor Tryon, who had left for England on leave, the aged lieutenant governor, Cadwallader Colden, called an emergency meeting of the council to restore order. But the council hesitated to call out the militia, for too many of them were sympathetic with the American cause. Surprisingly, there was no further mob action, and New York settled down to a period of uneasy waiting.

However, the patriots were unwilling to leave the city to be administered by the lieutenant governor and his council. Within the week there was formed a Committee of Resistance, with some one hundred members, to carry out the measures of the Continental Congress and the provincial convention. Two vestrymen and at least seventeen members of this committee, which soon assumed effective control of the city, were members of Trinity Parish. They even persuaded Dr. Auchmuty and Mr. Inglis to agree to serve as chaplains to the provincial convention, though their sympathies lay elsewhere.

In June, Governor Tryon returned to New York, only to find that the Committee of Resistance had "assumed the whole power of government" in the city. Moreover, the bulk of the royal troops at the fort were under orders to move to Boston to relieve General Gage. The soldiers departed by sea, but the wagons containing their supplies were seized in the name of the Committee of Resistance, and their contents unloaded by the mob.

On August 23 Marinus Willett and Isaac Sears led a

party of the Sons of Liberty to the Battery to remove its guns. A British man-of-war in the harbor, the *Asia*, sent a landing party ashore to protect the guns, and musket fire was exchanged between the hostile parties, followed by three shots from the ship. The attempt to seize the guns was abandoned, and Governor Tryon was given a bodyguard. But the people could not forget that the British had fired on New York City; they were soon to learn that on the same day George III had declared that the American colonies were in a state of rebellion. Separation from the mother country might still be a subject for debate at the Continental Congress in Philadelphia, but in New York it was a reality as 1775 drew to a close. Late in the year Governor Tryon and the remaining troops abandoned the fort and took refuge on a ship in New York harbor, which for a time became the colony's floating and virtually powerless capital.

4

The Revolutionary Years

1776-1784

For more than a century New Year's Day had been an important holiday in New York. While the city was still styled New Amsterdam, the Dutch burghers had begun the happy custom of holding open house on that day, with friendly and formal calls between neighbors, sleighing in the afternoons, and more hospitality in the early evenings. The English adopted the custom, beginning the day with the ringing of church bells, and enlivening it with cock fights and other sporting events, often ending with a musical evening or gala ball.

But January 1, 1776 was different. Governor Tryon and his staff were aboard the *Duchess of Gordon* in New York harbor; two or three British men-of-war stood by with their guns trained on the city in case of trouble. Many of the citizens had slipped out of the city to join General Washington's forces at Boston; others had taken or were about to take their families to places of refuge up the Hudson or in Long Island, Connecticut, or New Jersey. Such intrepid ones as persisted in their New Year's calls might be met at the door by a householder with his musket at the ready, until their friendly intentions were assured. And the lone individual celebrating at one of the city's numerous taverns did well to avoid the stranger who would ply him with grog, as he might turn out to be an undercover recruiting officer for one side or the other, and the celebrant might well find himself sworn into the Continental army or the king's American regiment before he sobered up.

The effective government of the city was in the hands of the revolutionary Committee of Safety. But despite the sympathy of the committee with the revolutionary cause, when it heard that General Charles Lee, with the famous leader of the Sons of Liberty, Isaac Sears, as his captain and adjutant, was on the march toward New York with 1,200 Continentals enlisted in Connecticut, they protested the troops' entrance to the city, as Captain Parker of the *Asia* had threatened to bombard the town if Revolutionary troops entered it. Undeterred either by the committee's objection or the naval threat, Lee and his men marched in and made their camp in "the Field," the present City Hall Park. "If the ships are quiet," he declared, "I shall be quiet." The ships did remain quiet, and Lee's men were soon reinforced by Lord Sterling and four companies of troops from New Jersey. The Provincial Congress now voted to fortify the city and provide it with a garrison of 2,000 men.

THE BATTLES FOR NEW YORK CITY

Now began the exodus of the loyalists and their families. Despite quantities of floating ice in the harbor, the king's ships drew near the wharves, and landing parties removed many of the public records to the *Duchess of*

Gordon, where Tryon was awaiting relief by General Sir Henry Clinton, who would assume military responsibility. The British still had a journalistic voice in the weekly *Gazette,* edited and published by James Rivington at his shop at the foot of Wall Street. This voice, however, was soon stilled by Captain Sears, who raided the shop, destroyed the press, and carried off the type to be melted down to make bullets for the Continental army.

With New York now, for the time being, in the hands of American troops, the Anglican clergy found themselves in a dilemma. As ministers of the established church, they felt bound by loyalty to the Crown, as implicit in their ordination vows. They were also bound to use the Book of Common Prayer, with its prayers for the king and the royal family. For this many of them were persecuted or dispossessed; Samuel Seabury, later to become the first American bishop, was seized in Westchester and taken under guard to New Haven. It was reported that one Anglican minister in Westchester was carried to Long Island and set adrift in a small boat without oars; when he did not return, his parishioners erected a tablet in memory of their rector who was "lost at sea."

The New York clergy at this time suffered less than most, though they too had their trials. Dr. Auchmuty, Trinity's rector, being ill during the spring and summer, and finding the strain too much for him, retired with his family to New Brunswick, N.J. As the senior assistant, the Rev. Charles Inglis took over the care of the parish; he had taken his wife and three small children seventy miles up the Hudson, where they remained after the rebel troops took over that area. Provoost had left; the other assistants, Moore and Bowden, helped Inglis in keeping Trinity, St. George's, and St. Paul's open as long as possible.

But Inglis soon ran afoul of his erstwhile parishioner,

Capt. Isaac Sears. The occasion was his attempt to engage in a pamphlet war with Thomas Paine, whose pro-Revolutionary pamphlet *Common Sense* was arousing patriots with its challenge "to show a single advantage that this continent can reap by being connected with Great Britain." Inglis wrote a point-by-point refutation in a pamphlet called *The True Interest of America Impartially Stated.* But when the printer announced the pamphlet, a week before its scheduled publication, Captain Sears and two of his men entered the print shop and destroyed both the manuscript and the half-completed pamphlets. Other printers in the city were then sent a threatening notice:

> Sirs, if you print, or suffer to be printed in your press anything against the rights & Liberties of America, or in favor of our inveterate foes, the King, Ministry, & Parliament of Great Britain, death and destruction, ruin and perdition, shall be your portion.

But Inglis had another copy of the manuscript; it was smuggled out of New York and printed in Philadelphia. For this and other reasons, Inglis was heartily disliked by the patriots, though he was not interfered with in the maintenance of the parish, possibly because in April General Washington, himself an Anglican churchman, came to New York and assumed command of the Continental troops.

In May Inglis reported an incident, probably at St. Paul's Chapel, which caused him no little trepidation. On a certain Sunday, he wrote:

> . . . a company of about one hundred armed rebels marched into church, with drums beating and fifes playing, their guns loaded and bayonets fixed, as if going into battle. The congregation was thrown into the utmost terror, and several women fainted, expecting a massacre was intended. I took no notice of

them and went on with the service, only exerted my voice, which was in some measure drowned by the noise and tumult. The rebels stood thus in the aisle for near fifteen minutes, till, being asked into pews by the sexton, they complied. Still, however, the people expected that, when the collects for the king and royal family were read, I should be fired at, as menaces to that purpose had been frequently flung out. The matter, however, passed over without any accident.

Whether Inglis was justified in his fears may be open to question, as the soldiers were probably simply on "church parade," and had no intention of violence. Inglis himself reported that "nothing of this kind happened before or since"; another source indicates that orders were given that the music at "church parade" was to be stopped well before the soldiers entered a church, in order to avoid any such suspicion. But it was customary for the troops to carry their arms into church, as no one knew when hostilities might break out.

Shortly before the arrival of General Washington, an American officer had asked Mr. Inglis if he would omit the prayers for the king if the general attended services at Trinity. Inglis replied in the negative; and although Washington at first lodged at a private house on lower Broadway, not far from the church, there is no indication that he worshiped at Trinity Church or either of the chapels. Later, when his wife joined him, the Washingtons moved into a mansion in Lispenard's Meadows, near the present corner of Varick and Charlton streets, which had been abandoned by the paymaster-general of the British military forces.

At the beginning of the Revolution, New York had a population of 20,000 and was second in size only to Boston. By the middle of 1776, more than half the civilian population had fled; but as Washington's forces numbered nearly 20,000, it was impossible to lodge them all in barracks or abandoned houses, and a large tent city arose in the "outskirts" a mile north of the Battery. As a British attack was felt to be imminent, an elaborate system of forts, batteries, barricades, and trenches was constructed along the shores of Manhattan and on Brooklyn Heights. Nevertheless, surrounded by water as the city was, it was quite impossible to build a truly strong defensive position against a naval power.

On June 29 General Howe arrived from Halifax with more than one hundred vessels which anchored within sight of the city; a few days later his brother, Admiral Richard Howe, arrived from England with a second large fleet. Other vessels arrived from Charleston and elsewhere with more troops, until nearly 500 ships, the greatest expeditionary force the British had ever gathered together, anchored offshore, carrying some 32,000 soldiers, including 9,000 Hessian mercenaries.

During this tremendous buildup of military and naval strength in New York Bay, the second Continental Congress was continuing its deliberations in Philadelphia. On July 4, 1776 the Declaration of Independence was promulgated. The news ran like wildfire through the thirteen former colonies; and at last Americans realized that the die was irrevocably cast. Ahead lay the alternatives of forging a new nation through blood, sweat and tears, or of defeat and utter subjection by the forces of King George III.

Washington had his troops, now numbering men from all parts of the new nation, drawn up on parade grounds to hear the solemn reading of the declaration that was their charter of liberty. Washington himself sat astride his horse within a hollow square in front of the present City Hall, while his men stood at attention and an officer read the historic words.

Later, as bells rang and men cheered, a mob poured into Bowling Green and pulled to earth the statue of George III which had been erected only a few years before. The general reprimanded the few soldiers who took part in this action, but he was glad to order the statue's two tons of lead melted down; from it were cast 42,088 bullets for the Continental army.

With the proclamation of the Declaration of Independence, Inglis and the Trinity vestry—nine of the twenty-two, who remained in New York—decided to close the church and chapels. They were therefore locked up, and the keys left with Mr. Inglis. When officers of Washington's army asked for them, so that their own chaplains might conduct services, Inglis refused; and the Americans did not attempt to force the locks. Shortly thereafter, Inglis fled to Staten Island (where British troops had landed), carrying with him, it was said, plans of the American fortifications for the city and "other intelligence." From that time on, Inglis was attainted as a spy, and he was safe only behind British lines.

The battle for New York City began in August, when the British landed on Long Island. Defeated in the Battle of Long Island on August 27, the Americans retreated to New York. Despite some 1,500 casualties, the withdrawal was completed with the bulk of Washington's army intact. But Manhattan was no longer tenable. The Americans retired further to Harlem Heights, and on September 15 the British occupied New York in overwhelming force. General Howe was knighted for his performance; but again Washington had held his army intact.

THE BRITISH OCCUPATION (1776-1783)

Upon the occupation of the city by British forces, Mr. Inglis returned and resumed his duties. Although his own house had been plundered, he found the church and chapels safe. On Wednesday, he opened one of the churches—the record does not state whether Trinity or one of the chapels—and "solemnized divine service," noting that "all the inhabitants gladly attended, and joy was lighted up in every countenance on the restoration of public worship; for few remained but such as were members of our Church."

The joy was doomed to be short-lived. On Saturday evening, September 21, fire broke out in a wooden tavern on a wharf near Whitehall Street, its origin a mystery. Fanned by a gale from the south, flames spread rapidly northward; before they burned themselves out, a quarter of the city lay in ruins, and thousands were homeless.

Trinity Church, the city's most prominent landmark, was reduced to ashes. Its tall steeple, 175 feet high, resembled a vast pyramid of fire before it crashed in ruins. Besides Trinity Church, the rector's house, the Charity School, the old Lutheran church, and many other fine buildings were utterly destroyed. St. Paul's Chapel, though directly in the line of the fire, was saved because of its relatively flat roof, which enabled men to douse the fire with water. St. George's Chapel, well to the east of the fire's path, was untouched. King's College was damaged but saved with great difficulty.

What was the cause of the fire? Tories and patriots accused each other; some claimed to have seen men spreading the flames; people suspected were bayoneted, hanged, or tossed alive into the smoldering ruins. But despite charges and counter-charges, the investigation set afoot by the British authorities concluded that the fire was accidental. Besides the churches and public buildings, 493 houses were utterly destroyed.

In the midst of the distress occasioned by the holocaust, Dr. Auchmuty returned to his parish, after an arduous and dangerous journey from New Jersey. Refused permission to pass through the American lines, he made the trip alone by night and on foot, despite the precarious state of his health. Returning, he found his church and his home in ruins. "Upon searching the rubble of his late venerable church," it was reported to the Society for the Propagation of the Gospel, "and his large and elegant house, he could find only a few trifles, of little or no value, except the church plate and his own. Providence having preserved him two chapels, he begins to have divine service again regularly carried on, after a suspension of near three months, and his people begin to flock in, so they will soon be filled. . . . His wife and daughters are still in the hands of the rebels, and he knows not when he shall be able to obtain their freedom."

Although Dr. Auchmuty resumed his duties, with the help of Mr. Inglis, his heart was broken, and his health continued to deteriorate. His family was released when British troops advanced into New Jersey, and they returned to New York for a family reunion. But the stress of it all was too much for the rector, and on March 4, 1777 he died of a fever resulting from a severe cold taken at a funeral the previous day.

New York was occupied by the British for seven years, longer than any other American city. When the British troops took over, much of the population had fled, with only about 3,000 civilians remaining. But the British and German troops that were stationed in the city, together with hordes of Loyalist refugees who poured in from the countryside and from other colonies, soon boosted the population to some 33,000. Despite the reappointment of Governor Tryon and constant appeals from Dr. Inglis and other civilians, the city remained under martial law.

The once beautiful city had become "a most dirty, desolate, and wretched place," and after the fire, a quarter of it lay in charred ruins, amid which were tents and shanties hastily erected to try to cope with the housing shortage. Houses large and small were commandeered for officers and officials and their families. Hordes of prostitutes also poured into the city; one "contractor" was reputed to have procured 3,500 women, white and black, to entertain His Majesty's troops. Prices jumped 800 percent; food and firewood were in short supply. Makeshift jails and prison ships housed thousands of captured American soldiers; about 11,000 died on the vessels alone.

Most of the churches were commandeered for one military purpose or another. The Brick church on Beekman Street and the Dutch church on William Street became prisons; the British provost marshal, William Cunningham, on his deathbed confessed that "there were more than two thousand prisoners starved in the different churches, by stopping their rations, which I sold." The Quaker meeting house and the Presbyterian churches were converted into overcrowded hospitals. The French church became a military storehouse. The Middle Dutch church was first a prison, then a riding school, and still later a barracks for Hessian soldiers.

Only the Anglican churches, being a part of the British establishment, were spared for religious purposes. Trinity, of course, lay in ruins, but St. Paul's and St. George's chapels were filled each Sunday with resident and refugee Tories. Moreover the Trinity vestry, remembering the hospitality of the Dutch church in its early days, opened St. George's to the Dutch ministers for two services each Sunday, and later the City Hall was made available for two more Sunday services for Nonconformists.

Shortly before Dr. Auchmuty's death, his wife and family made their way to New York to join him. With great difficulty, Dr. Inglis secured a pass to bring his family back from Kingston, which was in rebel hands. Other wives and families were exchanged, in much the same way as prisoners of war.

Two weeks after Dr. Auchmuty died, the Trinity vestry —or such of it as remained in New York—met and unanimously elected Charles Inglis as the fourth rector of Trinity Parish. With the approval of Governor Tryon, the service of induction was held in the ruins of the mother church, and Inglis took office by placing his hand on one of the charred walls. But for the remainder of the war, and until a new Trinity Church was built in 1790, St. Paul's Chapel doubled as the parish church.

Vacancies in the vestry, occasioned by the leaving of strong Whig vestrymen like James Duane, and by other resignations and deaths, were filled by Tory Anglicans, including David Seabury, whose brother Samuel, later to become the first American bishop, was a refugee priest; Augustus Van Cortlandt; Frederick Phillipse; and Robert Watts. Two vestrymen, Gabriel Ludlow and Thomas Moore, were officers in the Loyalist militia.

The new rector, Dr. Inglis, continued his writing and preaching activities in support of the British government. In a sermon to the Loyalist militia, he declared:

> Never, I will boldly and without hesitation pronounce it, never was a more just, more honourable, or necessary Cause for taking up arms than that which now calls you into the Field. It is the Cause of Truth against Falsehood, of Loyalty against Rebellion, of legal Government against Usurpation, of Constitutional Freedom against Tyranny—in short, it is the Cause of human happiness against Outrage and Oppression.

In a series of letters "addressed to several successive Presidents of Congress" under the signature of "Papinian,"

Inglis pointed out the dangers of an alliance between the new government and France, prophesying that the result would be economic disaster and slavery to France, "the enemy of liberty and Protestantism." In other letters, he defended the role of Major John André in effecting the treason of Benedict Arnold. But at the same time, he was rebuffed by the British in his constant appeals that martial law be replaced by civil government in the beleaguered city of New York.

Inglis' political activities were well known to the members of the new state legislature in Kingston. On October 22, 1779, 53 Loyalists were proscribed by an Act of Attainder passed by that body, declaring the confiscation of their property and death if they were captured. Among the persons listed were Charles Inglis and his wife, Margaret, together with John Tabor Kempe, Miles Sherbrooke, Frederick Phillipse, and Gabriel Ludlow of Trinity's vestry.

The Act of Attainder was a clear violation of due process of law, and as such was condemned by many patriots. John Jay wrote from Spain that "New York is disgraced by injustice too palpable to admit even of palliation. I feel for the honour of my country." Nevertheless, the Act remained in force until after the Revolution, when the adoption of the state constitution forbade such legislation.

The defeat of Lord Cornwallis at Yorktown by Washington's army and the French fleet, October 19, 1781, brought the military phase of the Revolution to a victorious conclusion. But two long years thereafter remained for the occupation of New York by British troops. During this period, New York was a Loyalist limbo, and its civilian inhabitants lived in doubt and fear as to their future. When the British government offered free transportation to Canada for all Loyalists who had lived in New York for a year or longer, thousands took advantage of the opportunity. Others took ship for England; still others made their way quietly to Connecticut or New Jersey to begin new lives under the new government.

For the Anglican clergy, there remained the dilemma of their oath of allegiance to the British Crown. Many of them, however, even those who had been ardent Loyalists, interpreted the king's recognition of American independence as releasing them from their loyalty oaths. Inglis wrote, "The King gives up his claim to my Allegiance; I am therefore at full liberty to transfer it to that State where Providence may place me." Seabury felt the same; he returned to Connecticut where he was soon elected the first bishop of the Episcopal Church.

But Inglis had a special problem when the state legislature refused to withdraw the Act of Attainder and grant a general amnesty, as most states did. Thus his life was safe only so long as he remained under the protection of the British military. As Evacuation Day, set for November 25, 1783, approached, the rector realized that there would be no place for him in the new administration, however willing he might be to swear allegiance to it. Moreover, on September 21 of that fateful year, Mrs. Inglis died, after a short but painful illness.

On November 1, 1783, therefore, Dr. Inglis tendered his resignation to the vestry of Trinity Parish. The resignation was accepted; and in order to provide continuity in the parish affairs, the vestry the same day elected the assistant minister, the Rev. Benjamin Moore, as rector in his place. Mr. Moore accepted the election, and papers were drawn up for presentation to the governor for his approval.

In his farewell sermon at the two chapels, Dr. Inglis assured his parishioners that "were I to remain here, and transfer my allegiance to the new government, I do assure you that I would serve and support that government with the same fidelity that I have served the government under which I have hitherto lived," and he counseled his parishioners to do the same. A few days later, Dr. Inglis and his children embarked on a British transport for England. Four years later he was to be consecrated as Bishop of Nova Scotia, the first Colonial bishop of the Church of England in Britain's overseas possessions.

TRINITY'S OWN REVOLUTION

It had been the intention of the vestry to present the rector-elect, Benjamin Moore, to the British governor for immediate induction. However, Sir Guy Carleton (who was both governor and commanding general of the British troops) had his hands full in preparing for the evacuation of New York, and the ceremony was accordingly not held. With the entry of General Washington on November 25, 1783 a group of "Whig Episcopalians," who returned to the city with the American troops, were quick to challenge Moore's election.

On December 6 a number of these patriot churchmen, including Robert Livingston, James Duane, Marinus Willett, Robert Troup, and John Lawrence, met at Simmons' Tavern, near the City Hall, and promptly issued a declaration "that the late nomination to the Rectorship was improper and unwarrantable." A committee was appointed to confer with those whom they cautiously described as "the Gentlemen exercising the office of Church Wardens and Vestrymen" in order "to consider the Means of preventing the Evils they dread." After some delay, caused by a minor dispute as to the place of meeting, a conference between the Whig Episcopalians and the Tory vestry was held, at which the proposal was made that the vestry should advise Mr. Moore to resign his appointment, and then proceed to the election of a rector who might be agreeable to the Whigs. The Whigs, in turn, would then prevail on the state legislature to confirm the new election and ratify the actions of the vestry. To this proposition the vestry refused to agree, and for a time the two parties appeared to be deadlocked.

The "Whig Episcopalians" now turned to another avenue of approach. In a lengthy petition to the Council for the Temporary Government of the Southern District of New York—an interim body set up by the state legislature—they set forth their grievances, and pointed out the "disagreeable Necessity of either abandoning the mode of worship in which they had been Educated . . . or joining in Prayer with those whose Political Principles they detest, and whose prayers for the success of the British Army all good citizens must thank the Supreme Governor for having rejected." Noting that many of the persons acting as wardens and vestrymen "are disqualified by a law of this State from holding any Place within this State, or voting at Elections," the Whigs asked for a new election of wardens and vestrymen, and that in the meantime they "be vested with all the powers heretofore granted by Charter to the Corporation of Trinity Church, till the Legislature can declare their Sense thereon."

The vestry also attempted to deal with the matter in a novel and radical proposal that the office of Rector be abolished and that there be two ministers in charge of the parish, on the same footing and with equal powers and prerogatives. Vacancies in the vestry were to be filled with "Whig Members," who should designate the clergyman to serve with Mr. Moore in the administration of the parish. This "solution," which would undoubtedly have created more havoc than already existed, was promptly and firmly rejected by the Whig Episcopalians.

The council, which had within its purview all former British property in the city of New York, responded to the Whig petition by the adoption of an ordinance vesting control of the estate of Trinity Parish in the hands of nine trustees, pending further action of the state legislature. Among the trustees were James Duane, Francis Lewis, Lewis Morris, and Isaac Sears—all Whig Episcopalians.

At this juncture, whether by accident or design, the Rev. Samuel Provoost arrived in the city, on February 2, 1784. Three days later, the trustees wrote to Mr. Moore to advise him that "the Reverend Mr. Provoost has been pleased in compliance with our Invitation, to take the charge of the Episcopal Churches in this City, and we have delivered him the Keys. We by no means wish to abridge your usefulness in a Congregation where you have many friends. The object of this Letter is only to apprise you that Mr. Provoost in future will have the direction in the same manner as it was exercised by former Rectors."

To this rather abrupt communication, the gentle Moore made a calm and dignified reply, challenging the right of the trustees to interfere in any but business matters, and concluding:

> Not being permitted to go into the Church but under the direction of the Rev. Mr. Provost (as his name had formerly been spelled) and not being inclined to do anything that may be construed into an implied acknowledgment that my Claim to the Rectorship is annulled, I shall beg leave, for the present, to decline officiating in the Churches until some further *legal* provision is made.

On April 17, 1784 the state legislature passed an act ratifying the charter of Trinity Parish, except for the provisions requiring loyalty to the king and jurisdiction of the Church of England, and appointing a new vestry, all of them Whigs, and nine of them the council-appointed trustees. They included Mayor James Duane and Chancellor Robert R. Livingston as wardens; Francis Lewis and Lewis Morris, both signers of the Declaration of Independence; William Bedloe, first postmaster general of the United States; Isaac Sears, former leader of the Sons of Liberty; Richard Morris, chief justice of the state; Marinus Willett, a general in the Continental army; and other leaders of the state and the new nation. It was probably the most distinguished vestry that ever served Trinity Parish, if service to the new nation be taken as a criterion.

The new vestry promptly took steps to ratify the actions of Samuel Provoost as *de facto* minister in charge since February, and to elect him as rector of Trinity Parish. As the election of the Rev. Benjamin Moore was not acknowledged, Provoost is considered the fifth rector of the parish, the date of his election and induction being April 22, 1784. No formal act of induction appears to have been held, since he was already officiating, and there was no longer a royal governor to whom he had to be presented.

Trinity was entering into a new order; but the old order died hard. Even before Provoost's election, a memorial was sent to the state legislature, containing 376 signatures, objecting to the designation of the new vestry by legal enactment, and asking that one of the two chapels "be allotted to them for the Purposes of Divine Worship, together with a Proportionate Part of the Temporalities of its Church for the support of their Ministers." When it reached the legislature, it was endorsed "Read and referred to a Committee of the Whole," and no further action appears to have been taken. It was the last concerted attempt to restore the old regime at Trinity, or to divide it into two parishes. And that the wounds healed fairly rapidly is attested to by the fact that in subsequent parish elections, several of the former Tory vestrymen were elected to new terms alongside those who had called themselves "Whig Episcopalians."

As for Benjamin Moore, he was later appointed to his former position as an assistant minister, in which capacity he served during the entire rectorship of Mr. Provoost in complete harmony and with no apparent ill-will over the turn of events that had cost him the rectorship.

5

Rehabilitation and the Second Trinity Church

1785-1813

New York City, with 9,000 inhabitants in 1785, faced an enormous task of rehabilitation after the Revolution. Much of the city was still in ruins, with walls of blackened bricks and charred timbers interspersed with jerry-built shanties and tents, where living conditions were primitive and unsanitary, and vice of all kinds flourished. Streets were dark and dank, with wild dogs and pigs fighting over uncovered garbage. Wharves and warehouses were dilapidated; shipping and commerce were crippled.

But recovery was rapid, and in three years the population doubled, making New York second only to Philadelphia in size, with Boston dropping to third place. Trade with Britain and the West Indies being cut off by English regulations, shippers sought new ports and new markets, including the Orient. Ruins were cleared, and new houses and buildings erected, most of them east of Broadway.

The Bank of New York, first in the city and third in the nation, was established by Alexander Hamilton. Trade and industry began anew, and the city began once again to regain something of the prosperity of Colonial days.

From 1784 to 1796, New York served as the capital of the state, and the seat of the first American governor of New York, George Clinton. It was also the capital of the new nation, as the seat of Congress from 1785 to 1790, under the rather nebulous Articles of Confederation which preceded the Federal Constitution. New York indeed was slow in ratifying the Constitution, as the governor and a majority of state legislators were anti-Federalists. As a result, New Yorkers were unable to vote in the election of the first President; indeed, ratification came barely in time for New York to join the Union before it became the scene of Washington's inauguration.

THE FIRST BISHOP

Along with the rest of the city, Trinity Parish faced a monumental task of reorganization and rehabilitation. Many of its most substantial members, Tory officials or sympathizers, had left forever with the exodus of the British army; others, who remained, were dissatisfied with the ousting of Mr. Moore and the choice of Dr. Provoost to take his place. Returning parishioners, who had served with the American forces, found their homes and businesses in ruins, and were forced to spend most of their time re-establishing themselves and their families.

The parish church still lay in ruins, as did much of the property from which Trinity had drawn rents. The new rector found the parish with few liquid assets and burdened with debts. The Charity School also required rebuilding, and a suitable rectory had to be built, all with borrowed funds.

To complicate matters further, the title to the Queen's Farm was again in jeopardy, this time from the state legislature, which threatened to confiscate it as royal property. Fortunately the members and friends of Trinity in the government were able to prevent this catastrophe by insisting that if the title were called into question the matter should be adjudicated in the courts and not determined by arbitrary legislative action.

The dangerous state of the ruins of the parish church required that the walls be torn down immediately, but nothing was done in the erection of a new church until the end of 1785, when the vestry voted "that measures be forthwith taken for the rebuilding of Trinity Church." Commissioners were appointed to propose a plan and to supervise the work, which was to be financed partly by subscriptions and partly by the sale of lots. But actual rebuilding did not begin until 1788, and the work was not completed until 1790.

In ecclesiastical matters, too, Trinity was in much need of reinvigoration. At the request of the rector, two assistant ministers were appointed, Abraham Beach and Benjamin Moore. The appointment of Mr. Moore went far toward appeasing those who resented his ousting as rector. A third assistant, Uzal Ogden, was appointed at the request of "the Society of the Methodists and other members of the Episcopal Church"—an interesting indication that the Methodists had not yet separated from the Anglican Church, though they were soon to do so. To support these additional clergymen, it was necessary for the vestrymen to make a special canvass of church members, so that their meager salaries could be augmented by private subscription.

Moreover, since the Church of England had ceased to exist in the United States, Trinity took the lead in organizing a diocese, consisting of the Anglican parishes in the state of New York. Its rector, Samuel Provoost, was elected the first Bishop of New York, and went to England in 1787 with the Rev. William White of Pennsylvania to be consecrated by the Archbishop of Canterbury and other English bishops. (The Rev. Samuel Seabury had already been consecrated Bishop of Connecticut by the Scottish Non-Juring bishops, as English law prevented the consecration of a bishop in England without requiring him to take the oath of allegiance to the Crown—a law that was changed to make possible the consecration of Bishops Provoost and White, and later Bishop James Madison of Virginia.)

In each of the new states, dioceses were similarly being formed. In 1785 and 1786, a General Convention met, first in Philadelphia and then in Wilmington, Delaware. At these conventions a constitution was drafted for the new Protestant Episcopal Church in the United States of America, and a proposed liturgy, eliminating the prayers for the king, was tentatively adopted. In all of these activities, Dr. Provoost took an active and generally constructive part, though for a time he opposed the acceptance of ordinations by Bishop Seabury, on the grounds that his consecration by Scottish bishops was irregular and of doubtful validity. Fortunately this incipient controversy was settled three years later, when the General Convention made a positive declaration accepting the validity of Seabury's consecration, and uniting all of the bishops in the American church upon an equal footing.

It is interesting to note that while he was in England, Dr. Provoost had a friendly visit with his predecessor, Dr. Inglis, who was awaiting his own consecration as Bishop of Nova Scotia. Inglis also designed the mitre for Bishop Seabury, which has been preserved at Trinity College, Hartford.

Upon his return to New York, Bishop Provoost held his first Confirmation service at St. Paul's Chapel. At this service more than 300 persons were confirmed, mostly adults, and some of them eighty and ninety years old. Most of them had been loyal members of the church all their lives, but had not been confirmed because there had been no bishop in the colonies to perform the ceremony.

Similarly Bishop Provoost began to ordain deacons and priests, the long journey to England for ordination no longer being necessary. One of the first of his ordinands was Richard Channing Moore, later to become a great Bishop of Virginia.

Thus, within three or four years after the evacuation of the British from New York, Trinity Parish was fully organized as a vigorous unit of the new Diocese of New York, with its rector as the bishop of the diocese; and the diocese in turn as one of the nine original jurisdictions comprising the Episcopal Church, independent in its government but in full communion with the ancient See of Canterbury, the center of the Anglican Communion of the Holy Catholic Church. It was truly the beginning of a new and significant chapter in the history of the Church.

INAUGURATION OF PRESIDENT WASHINGTON

Thursday, April 30, 1789, was a red-letter day in the history of New York and of the new nation, and of Trinity Parish as well. For on that day George Washington of Virginia was inaugurated as the first President of the United States; and, following the ceremony, he attended a memorable service of thanksgiving in St. Paul's Chapel, with Trinity's rector officiating.

New York City's population, now 30,000, was swollen by thousands of visitors from all parts of the Union, who had poured into the city by coaches, farm carts, river packets, and on horseback or afoot, taxing all available public and private accommodations. Many of them slept in hastily erected tents in vacant fields from which the rubble of the great fire had recently been cleared.

At nine o'clock the bells of St. Paul's, St. George's, and the other churches of the city rang out to summon the people to prayers for the new president. Crowds surrounded the former City Hall at Wall and Broad streets, now known as Federal Hall, the temporary capitol and meeting place of the newly constituted Senate and House of Representatives. Many climbed to nearby rooftops, and some even scaled the scaffolding of the partly constructed Trinity Church at Broadway and Wall Street; others flocked to the vicinity of the president's mansion on Cherry Street, and lined the route of the procession. It was only with great difficulty that members of Congress were able to force their way through the crowds to take their places in Federal Hall to await the arrival of their popular chief so the ceremonies could begin.

In Franklin Square, near the president's mansion (rented from Samuel Osgood for the purpose), a troop of cavalry and three companies of infantry were deployed. The welcoming committee, led by Sheriff Marinus Willett and the masters of ceremonies, headed by Col. Morgan Lewis, drew up behind the soldiers. A cream-colored coach, decorated with cupids and drawn by four superb horses, with a liveried postillion and two uniformed coachmen, stood at the door to await the distinguished father of his country, as Washington had already come to be known.

At last the door opened, and Washington came out and greeted the members of the committee. He was dressed in a brown homespun suit with metal buttons embossed with eagles, thirteen-starred cuff buttons, white stockings, and a ceremonial sword in a white leather scabbard. His white powdered wig was caught up at the back of his head in a silk net.

A great cheer went up from the crowds as Washington entered his carriage. Colonel Lewis flashed a signal, a band played, the soldiers moved out, and the procession began.

Arriving at Federal Hall, Washington entered, walked to the Senate chamber on the second floor, and was formally presented to Vice President John Adams of Massachusetts. Adams in turn presented him to the members of Congress, the acting secretary of state, John Jay (one of Trinity's wardens), and the distinguished guests, including Bishop Provoost, who had been appointed as the first chaplain of the Senate. "Sir," said the vice president, "the Senate and the House of Representatives of the United States are ready to attend you to take the oath required by the Constitution, which will be administered by the chancellor of the state of New York."

As Washington was led out of the Senate chamber onto the balcony, another great cheer arose from the assembled multitude, and was acknowledged by the president-elect with three bows, after which he sank into a chair, overcome with emotion, and dropped his head into his hands.

When the shouting died down, the red-headed chancellor, Robert R. Livingston (who was also one of Trinity's former wardens), clad in black robes, asked if Washington were ready to rise from his chair.

But then it was discovered that, despite the lavish preparations for the event, no Bible had been provided.

Livingston, like Washington a Mason, and grand master of the New York lodge, hurriedly sent a messenger to the nearby Masonic building to fetch the lodge Bible. When it arrived, it was placed on a crimson cushion held by Samuel Otis, secretary of the Senate.

Placing one hand on his chest, and the other on the Bible, Washington repeated the oath: "I do solemnly swear that I will faithfully execute the office of the President of the United States and will, to the best of my ability, preserve, protect, and defend the Constitution of the United States." Then he bent and kissed the Bible, and added, "So help me, God."

"Long live George Washington, President of the United States!" cried Chancellor Livingston. The crowd took up the cry, the American flag with its thirteen stars and stripes was hoisted to the top of the flagpole, church bells pealed, cannon boomed from the Battery and from ships in the harbor, and a thunderous ovation greeted the new president. Again almost overcome with emotion, Washington bowed to the crowd, stood briefly in dignified acknowledgment, and then retired into the hall, where he delivered his inaugural address to the members of Congress.

The address completed, President Washington left Federal Hall, and was escorted on foot by Robert Livingston, James Duane, Bishop Provoost, and the assembled notables, up Broadway to St. Paul's Chapel, where a special pew had been prepared for him. The bishop read appropriate prayers from the proposed Prayer Book of 1785, and the *Te Deum* was sung. There was no sermon or address. The service was concluded with a simple benediction, and the president was escorted home on foot.

Later in the year, the General Convention of the Episcopal Church, meeting in Philadelphia, adopted an address to the president, expressing their congratulations and personal assurances of loyalty. They also praised him as one "who has happily united a tender regard for other Churches with an inviolable attachment to his own." To this address, President Washington made an appropriate and gracious reply.

A panel on the bronze door of the south porch of the present Trinity Church depicts and commemorates the historic service for President Washington at St. Paul's Chapel.

At St. Paul's Chapel, a pew is still set apart as "Washington's Pew." It is not the original pew, but was rebuilt in the early 1800s, and again in 1960, when it was made to conform as nearly as possible to the original, except that it has no canopy and the original chair has disappeared. Nearby hang replicas of the first United States flag with thirteen stars and thirteen stripes, adopted by Congress in 1777, and of Washington's headquarters flag, also containing thirteen stars on a blue-gray background.

Of even greater interest is an oil painting of the United States coat-of-arms, which may have been hanging next to the original pew at the time of the inauguration service. In 1784 the vestry ordered that a painter be procured to execute the Arms of the United States, and it is rumored to have been completed just in time for the inauguration. Measuring 66 inches by 46 inches, it is probably the first painting of the United States Arms, or at least the oldest one extant.

THE SECOND TRINITY CHURCH

The new Trinity Church, built on the site of the old one, was ready for consecration and use on March 25, 1790. Like the first Trinity, it was rectangular in shape, somewhat shorter (104 feet instead of 148), the same width (72 feet), and with a steeple some 200 feet high, rising from a square turretlike tower. Perhaps in recollection that the steeply pitched roof of the earlier church had hampered the men who tried to extinguish the blaze that destroyed it, the roof of the new church was pitched at an angle of less than 45 degrees, and was surrounded with a low parapet. The windows were pointed in modified Gothic style, and the building was faced with a semicircular portico supported by columns. Built by a local carpenter and two masons, it was a simple and rather boxlike structure, but its tall steeple (even higher than that of its predecessor) gave it a commanding elevation that dominated the surrounding area.

President Washington attended the service of consecration, occupying a special pew set aside for him; other pews were reserved for the governor of the state and members of Congress. By order of the vestry, the president's pew was "properly ornamented," and had a canopy over it. Other pews were sold at public auction, and a contemporary report noted that "such was the desire of having seats in the Church, that many of the pews produced more than Fifty Pounds. The whole amount of the sale was Three Thousand Pounds."

Using the new Book of Common Prayer adopted by the General Convention only a few months before, Bishop Provoost conducted the service of consecration, and the sermon was preached by the Rev. Dr. Abraham Beach, the senior assistant minister of the parish. The "respectable number of people" assembled on the occasion included the clergy of most of the denominations in the city, "and many other persons of distinction."

But although the new church was now ready for use, much remained to be done for its completion. A bell was given by the Lutherans for use until a "ring of bells" was made in England and shipped to New York; a marble slab was placed over the doorway with a suitable inscription; a desk was provided for the clerk, an organ installed, and galleries were built for the scholars of the Charity School. It was some seven years before the church was fully furnished, and even then it scarcely equalled the elegance of the former church with its crimson damask and its "gilt Busts of Angels winged"—but it was perhaps more in accord with the rather simpler tastes of the citizens of the new republic.

New York was growing, and new streets were being laid out in the vicinity of Trinity Church. As many of these were on land given by Trinity for the purpose, the vestry was given the privilege of naming them. Thus the parish itself was commemorated in the names of Rector, Church, and Chapel streets, and its early rectors in Vesey and Barclay streets. Provoost, Moore, and Beach also had streets named after them, as did vestrymen Duane, Jay, Harrison, Laight, and Desbrosses. Watts Street was named after John Watts, the last royal recorder of the city of New York, whose bronze statue now stands in Trinity churchyard. And some years later, the name of the street directly behind the church was changed to Trinity Place.

The Episcopal Church was also growing, and Trinity and its two chapels could no longer accommodate all its members. But it was hard for the members and vestrymen to relinquish the claim of Trinity to be the sole parish church of the community. When in 1793 certain members built a new church on the north side of Ann Street, between William and Nassau streets, the vestry protested vigorously; and for some years Christ Church was denied representation in the diocesan convention.

However, a few years later, the vestry itself took the

initiative in establishing a new church on land given by Mr. Stuyvesant for the purpose. In 1795 the vestry pledged themselves to raise a substantial sum of money toward erection of the new church, named St. Mark's-in-the-Bowery, and subsequently gave the munificent gift of thirty lots for its endowment. St. Mark's was an independent parish from its foundation in 1799.

Other parishes, all aided by Trinity, were founded in the first decade of the nineteenth century: St. Stephen's in 1805, St. Michael's (Bloomingdale) in 1807, Grace Church and St. James' in 1809. In addition to financial aid, each church received an endowment of land from Trinity, with the provision that the donee remain an Episcopal church. Grace Church was built by Trinity and provided with an organ, at a cost of nearly $60,000.

In 1811, St. George's Chapel became an independent parish. Thus by that time there were eight parishes in Manhattan, with Trinity no longer claiming control of the others, but continuing to assist them with grants of land and money. Even the former rival, Christ Church, was provided with four "lots of ground" by Trinity for its endowment. And when St. George's burned down in 1814, Trinity rebuilt the church at a cost of $45,000.

Other churches outside New York City were also generously aided by Trinity, which was rapidly becoming known as the Mother of Churches. Among these were the Episcopal churches at Ballston, Duanesburgh, Hudson, Poughkeepsie, Rye, Jamaica, Brooklyn, Staten Island, Flushing, Goshen, Newtown, Johnstown, Albany, Peekskill, Stamford, Westchester, Highlands, Salem, Constantia, Fishkill, and New Rochelle; as well as the Presbyterian and Roman Catholic congregations in New York City. By the end of 1800 the value of these gifts outside the parish was close to $100,000, despite the fact that Trinity itself had been heavily in debt for several years after the Revolution.

Bishop Provoost, a fine classical scholar and botanist, though not a great preacher, administered the parish with great skill, and his wise policies did much to heal the scars of the division that had rent the parish after the Revolutionary War. As bishop he set the new diocese in a sound mold, insisting upon the rights of the laity to share at every level of the church's organization. He was not a great missionary, and rarely visited parishes outside the immediate vicinity of New York City; but as shown by the gifts of the parish to other churches, he helped to establish many new parishes, especially in Long Island and up the Hudson River. Like the other bishops of the day, he had to give his first attention to the parish of which he was rector, and was dependent upon that parish for most of his financial resources.

But in later years, Bishop Provoost was beset with domestic difficulties and infirmity. When in August 1799 his wife died, he decided to resign his parish and diocese. First, however, he was instrumental in calling as assistant at Trinity a young and vigorous clergyman, John Henry Hobart, who might give added strength to the clergy staff. That accomplished, in 1800 the bishop formally presented his resignation as rector of Trinity, and shortly thereafter sent Bishop White, the Presiding Bishop of the Church, his resignation as Bishop of New York.

On the nomination of Bishop Provoost, Dr. Benjamin Moore, whose election in 1784 had been nullified by the turn of events, was unanimously chosen by the vestry as Trinity's sixth rector. A year later, Dr. Moore was chosen by the diocese as the second Bishop of New York. He was consecrated in St. Michael's Church, Trenton, N. J., on September 11, 1801.

The remaining years of Bishop Provoost's life were spent in strict retirement at his home on Greenwich Street, New York. He devoted himself to literary and scientific studies, and took no active part in affairs of the parish or the diocese, except in 1811, when he participated in the consecration of Bishop Hobart. He died September 6, 1815, at the age of seventy-three, and was buried in Trinity churchyard. About forty years later, his remains were moved to the plot of his grandson, David Colden, in Trinity Church Cemetery.

Dr. Moore, like his predecessor, was a fine scholar, having served as professor of rhetoric and logic in Columbia College (as the former King's College had been renamed), and for a time during the Revolution as acting president of the college; and later as its president, from 1802 to 1811. His entire ministry was spent in Trinity Parish. As bishop he continued Provoost's policies, and under his leadership the church expanded along the Hudson between Westchester and Albany, and a start was made on missionary work in the western part of the state.

As before, Trinity's generous gifts helped to finance the founding and maintenance of many of the new churches, as the diocese itself had few financial resources. Among the churches thus aided during the regime of Dr. Moore were those at Bedford and New Castle, Brookhaven, Setauket, Ballston, Cooperstown, Duanesburgh, Hampton, Hudson, Manlius, Poughkeepsie, Rye, Coldenham, Jamaica, Hamilton, Lansingburgh, Waterford, Troy, Otsego, Phillipsburgh, Brooklyn, Flushing, Hempstead, Schenectady, Goshen, Hyde Park, Milton, Newtown, North Salem, Huntington, Johnstown, Yonkers, Catskill, Islip, Unadilla, Bloomingdale, Charlton, Paris, Albany, Aurelius, Stamford, Westchester, Athens, Fairfield, Fishkill, Geneva, Rensselaerville, Utica—all in New York—

and several parishes in Connecticut, New Hampshire, Vermont, and New Jersey. Aid was also given to several new parishes in New York City, and to various missionary and cultural societies, as well as to Trinity School, as the former Charity School was now known. Truly Trinity continued to merit its reputation as the Mother of Churches.

At the turn of the century, although there were several parishes of the Episcopal Church in New York and Brooklyn, Trinity Parish was by far the strongest and largest. Indeed by 1802 there were so many applicants for pews in Trinity and its two chapels that the rector was authorized by the vestry "to hire a room for public worship in the neighborhood of Brannon Street (now Spring Street), with benches for the accommodation of a congregation." From this developed St. John's Chapel, built at the edge of a swamp, where snakes abounded, but soon surrounded by the residences of wealthy and fashionable New Yorkers. Consecrated by Bishop Moore in 1807, it introduced an arrangement later called "the Hobart chancel." The altar was on a slight elevation, above it the prayer desk, and still above that, the pulpit, reached by a door from behind.

Members of Trinity Church and its chapels included many of the leaders in the politics and society of the city; but there was also a substantial cross-section of business men, small merchants, and workers. The parish also felt a responsibility for the poor, including Negro slaves and freedmen.

It was a time for the founding of all kinds of societies for missionary, educational, and charitable work. Among those sponsored or aided by Bishop Moore, and largely promoted by his young assistant, John Henry Hobart, were such organizations as the African Episcopal Catechetical Institution, the Education and Missionary Society, the

Free School Society, the Society for the Cultivation of Sacred Music, the Society for the Promotion of Religion and Learning in the State of New York, the Widows' Society, and the Society for the Propagation of the Gospel. The considerable collection of books comprising the library in St. Paul's Chapel was transferred to the New York Protestant Episcopal Literary Society and formed the nucleus of the New York Society Library on University Place.

Bishop Moore was considered a good preacher, and somewhat of a "high churchman," by the standards of the day. As a bishop, he showed interest in the extension of the Episcopal Church northward along the Hudson River, but ill health and the duties of the rectorship, together with a disinterest in traveling, led him to confine most of his episcopal visitations to New York, Brooklyn, and the immediate vicinity.

Much of the administration of the parish was in the hands of his able assistant, the Rev. Dr. Abraham Beach. Dr. Beach's long term of service, dating from 1784, contributed much to the continuity of policy throughout the rectorships of Bishops Provoost and Moore, and gave him an acknowledged leadership in the many institutions and organizations that centered in Trinity Parish. Other able assistants were the Rev. Thomas Y. How, appointed in 1808, and the Rev. Mr. Hobart, who also served as secretary of the diocese of New York. Another assistant, the Rev. Cave Jones, appointed in 1801, rendered faithful service for a number of years, but later became involved in an unseemly controversy with Mr. Hobart, marked by bitter feelings and pamphlet attacks on both sides, leading to the dismissal of the Rev. Mr. Jones in 1811.

During Dr. Moore's rectorship, Grace Church on Broadway was instituted as a separate parish, with generous aid from Trinity, and St. George's Chapel also became an independent parish. Other new parishes, mostly begun with Trinity's aid, were Christ Church; St. Michael's, Bloomingdale; St. Stephen's; St. James', Hamilton Square; and St. Ann's, Brooklyn. The Lutheran congregation of Zion Church was united to the diocese, and its pastor ordained by Bishop Moore. Other parishes to the north of the city were also established, and their churches consecrated by Bishop Moore.

Trinity Church itself continued with a communicant strength of about 1,000. A return from the parish for the year October 1, 1803 to October 1, 1804 listed 378 baptisms, 115 marriages, and 400 burials. St. Paul's Chapel continued as a chapel of ease, and St. John's Chapel, built by Trinity at a cost of $172,833, attracted a considerable congregation from the well-to-do families living in its neighborhood. It is interesting to note that the organ alone cost $8,000—no inconsiderable sum in those days. Its original cost was $6,000; but a ransom of $2,000 had to be paid to the British, who captured it on the high seas on its way from Philadelphia, in one of the instances of naval harassment preceding the War of 1812.

In 1811 Bishop Moore was stricken with paralysis, and Dr. Beach, appointed assistant rector, became the effective head of the parish. Dr. Moore was confined to his room thereafter, until his death in 1816, at the age of 66. Unable to carry on either his parochial or episcopal duties, he also asked for the election of an assistant bishop; and the diocesan convention elected his parochial assistant, John Henry Hobart, to that position. Thus Dr. Hobart found himself for a time in the curious position of being Dr. Beach's subordinate, as assistant minister, and his superior, as the Assistant Bishop of New York. But the two men were close friends and had worked together for many years, so no conflict of authority between them appears to have arisen.

Dr. Beach was one of the ablest clergymen in the organization of the new national church after the Revolution. He did much to bring about the cooperation of the clergy in the various states, both by correspondence and by meetings, and as president of the House of Clerical and Lay Deputies in the General Conventions of 1801, 1804, and 1808. His friends twice nominated him as Bishop of New York—in 1801 and again in 1811. On the latter occasion he refused to be a competitor to his associate, Dr. Hobart, but many votes were cast for him nevertheless.

Dr. Beach was a loyal and gentle soul, a fine priest, a good administrator, and truly one of the founding fathers of the newly independent Episcopal Church in the United States. He retired from his parochial ministry in 1813, and thereafter lived at his farm on the Raritan River until his death in 1818, at the age of eighty-eight.

6

Hobart, Bishop and Rector

1813-1830

One of the brightest stars of the Episcopal Church in the early nineteenth century was John Henry Hobart. Born in Philadelphia in 1775, of New England stock, he was baptized and confirmed by Bishop White at Christ Church, attended the University of Pennsylvania and the College of New Jersey (Princeton), where he later became a tutor and instructor after a short and unsuccessful venture into business. But his real vocation was the ministry, and in 1798 he was ordained deacon, also by Bishop White. While still a deacon, he became secretary of the House of Bishops at the General Convention of 1799, and the following year he declined a call to the rectorship of St. Mark's-in-the-Bowery, New York, going instead to the small parish of St. George's, Hempstead, Long Island. But his ability had attracted Bishop Provoost, who in one of his last acts before resigning the rectorship in 1800 appointed him an assistant minister at Trinity Church, and shortly thereafter ordained him to the priesthood.

It must be admitted that in the early 1800s the state of

The First and Second Churches

the church, both nationally and in New York, was at a low ebb. Episcopalians were on the defensive; their pre-Revolutionary dependence on the English church and state made it imperative that they consolidate and unite their own parishes and prove their loyalty to the new nation. The early bishops, who were also either parish rectors or presidents of colleges, had little time to devote to missionary enterprises, and the founding of new parishes was largely left to local initiative. Suspicious of "enthusiasm," they alienated the Methodists (who had begun as a society within the church), and left the evangelization of the frontier largely to them and to the Presbyterian and Independent churches.

Services, held in most Episcopal churches both morning and afternoon on Sundays, were rather arid, with the priest reading Morning and Evening Prayer, or the ante-Communion, and the paid clerk making responses, with little congregational participation. Even in Trinity Church, regarded as relatively "High Church," the Holy Communion was celebrated only on Christmas, Easter, Whitsunday, and a few other Sundays during the year, and with a minimum of ceremonial. Though Trinity and its chapels had organs, the music was confined mostly to the singing or chanting of psalms from a book that has been described as "a dreadful mixture of said and sung verses."

Half a century later, in a debate in the House of Deputies, Dr. Benjamin Haight recalled the laxity of those days:

> What did you do in Trinity Church fifty years ago? You saw at the end of the church a high pulpit, underneath it a large reading desk, and under that a clerk's desk. How was the service conducted? The organist died only a few years ago who

played the first chant to which the *Venite* was sung in Trinity Church. The services—were they conducted by the whole body of the people as now? The clerk did the responding with his loud sonorous voice, and the people sat back and quietly looked on. How was Baptism administered? There was no font in Trinity Church. Back by the door in a pew was a shelf, and there was a basin. Public baptism was a thing scarcely known. Owing to the miserable customs that prevailed in the city, brought over from London, the baptisms were done in private. . . . In Trinity Parish the clergyman never went to the Lord's Table except on Communion Sundays.

Of those Sundays, Dr. Morgan Dix, in a sermon in 1867 on "Church Progress in Fifty Years," wrote:

After the sermon, which was preached in a black gown—that emblem of sin and death—the congregation was dismissed with a collect. . . . The clergyman then left the church, and went into the vestry-room, while almost all the congregation withdrew. By and by he reappeared, and the service (Holy Communion) proceeded, without one note of music except the metre hymn, which was generally started by some courageous sister in the congregation.

Hobart, in his thirty years of ministry as priest and bishop, was to make a profound impact upon the church of his day, not only at Trinity and in the Diocese of New York, but throughout the country. With the watchword of "Evangelical truth and Apostolic order," he was to bring to the church a higher concept of its mission and ministry and better standards of preaching, teaching, music, and congregational participation in worship. But in so doing, he was to become a highly controversial figure, and to make enemies as well as devoted friends among the clergy and laity alike. In the parish history, Dr. Dix thus described Hobart:

In personal appearance, he gave the impression of vigor and ability. Below the average stature, his figure was well knit and muscular, his head large, his voice strong and flexible. Near-sighted from his youth, he always wore spectacles of more than ordinary power; these in his portraits inevitably attract attention by their size and their great tortoise-shell rims. In consequence of his defective sight, he dispensed as much as possible with manuscript, committing his sermons to memory, and preaching with rapidity and energy. Like most men of lively temperament, he had intervals of depression; but generally it was said of him that his presence in a room was like a ray of sunshine.

Such was the man who became an assistant minister of Trinity Parish in 1800 (at the age of twenty-five), Assistant Bishop of New York in 1811, assistant rector on the retirement of Dr. Beach in 1813, rector of Trinity and Bishop of New York in 1816.

HIS YEARS AT TRINITY

As assistant minister, Hobart took his full share in the ministry of the parish, and was particularly active in forming and guiding the many devotional and educational societies sponsored by Bishop Moore. He also found time for a great deal of writing, some controversial but much of it of a devotional and spiritual nature. Two of his best books, *A Companion for the Altar* and *A Companion for the Festivals and Fasts,* were published in 1804. Based upon the Book of Common Prayer, they recalled many to the treasures of the church and appreciation of its sacraments. The former, the first and for many years the only devotional and Eucharistic manual of the church, went through many editions and brought new standards of personal devotion to thousands of lay people. The latter was a strong defense of the church as "a society established by God to which He had annexed all the privileges and blessings of the Gospel covenant." Between them, they were a powerful influence in his promotion of Hobart's standards of Evangelical faith and Apostolic order, as were his sermons and the editorials in the *Churchman's Magazine*, which he began to edit in 1805 and which became the first church periodical of considerable general circulation.

Hobart's preaching brought a new dimension to Trinity's pulpit, and had a profound influence on many of the congregation. To those accustomed to lengthy, impersonal, and often abstruse sermons, carefully written out and read with little inflection, Hobart's seemingly extempore sermons, delivered in an earnest and often fiery manner, imbued with the substance of personal piety and strong conviction, sounded a new and electrifying note. Many followed him from the parish church to one of the chapels when he was scheduled to preach there, and perhaps would go to still another place to hear him again in the afternoon.

Among those profoundly influenced by Hobart's sermons, and by his example and personal counsel, was Elizabeth Bayley Seton, wife of a local merchant and daughter of Dr. Richard Bayley, New York's first public-health doctor. Already active in the Widows' Society, Mrs. Seton enlisted the help of her sister-in-law, Rebecca Seton, and, under Hobart's guidance, took up the numerous projects of charity that the young assistant encouraged. So much did they give of themselves to ministry to the poor, the sick, and the dying that their friends called them "Protestant Sisters of Charity." The name was prophetic, for later, after her conversion to Roman Catholicism, Mrs. Seton became the founder of the American Sisters of Charity. More than a century later Mother Seton was to receive beatification, the first step in the official procedure to recognize her as a saint. But her letters, the record of her good deeds, and the entries in her spiritual journal show very clearly that, largely under the influence of Hobart, she attained a great measure of sanctity while still an Episcopalian. Perhaps if the spiritual climate of the church in her day had been favorable to the religious life, she might have founded her religious order within the traditions of Anglicanism; but it was to be another half century before the religious life was restored to the Anglican Communion, both in England and in the United States.

When Elizabeth's husband, Will Seton, was stricken with a serious disease, she took him to visit business friends in Italy, in the hope of restoring his health. The voyage took nearly seven weeks, and when the ship arrived at Leghorn, it was clear that the disease was a highly contagious one. Seton, with his wife and their small daughter, was confined to a cold and drafty *lazaretto*, where they were quarantined for a month. While Will grew steadily worse, Elizabeth ministered to him day and night. Together they read the daily offices from the Book of Common Prayer and passages from the Bible, and the mother and daughter played games and jumped rope to keep warm. In the midst of it all, Elizabeth could write:

Looked round our prison and found that its situation was beautiful. Comforted my William all I could, rubbing his hands, and wiping his tears and giving words to his soul, which was too weak to pray for itself. Heard Ann read, while I watched the setting sun in a cloud. After both were asleep, read, prayed, wept, and prayed again, until eleven, at no loss to know the hours. Night and day four bells strike every hour, and ring every quarter.

William Seton died shortly after release from quarantine, and was buried in the English cemetery at Leghorn, with an English chaplain reading the burial office from the Prayer Book.

Elizabeth and her daughter remained in Italy for many months, as the guests of her husband's business friends, the Filicchi, who became her own dear friends. Devout Roman Catholics, they took her to many churches, where the beauty of color, light, and liturgy contrasted sharply with the formality and drabness of the church services to which she had been accustomed.

Upon her return to New York, Mrs. Seton was torn between her loyalty to the Episcopal Church and the greater richness of devotion that she had found in the Roman Catholic Church in Italy. Although armed with a letter to the Roman Catholic Bishop Carroll, and almost persuaded to transfer her allegiance to the Church of Rome, she went to Dr. Hobart for his advice. Hobart, sympathetic with her doubts, but firm in his convictions, did his best to persuade her that the Episcopal Church was as truly Catholic as the Roman, and suggested that she let all controversy rest until her agitated mind was settled and her soul quieted. This advice she tried to follow, but she no longer felt at home in the church in which she had been baptized and raised. She could find no peace in the Episcopal Church, and at last she went to the tiny St. Peter's Church on Barclay Street, and there in 1805 she submitted herself to the Roman Catholic Church.

It is interesting to note that the Roman Catholic Church apparently did not require her to be rebaptized, even conditionally. A century later, when Rome began to take steps to canonize her, they came to Trinity to seek the record of her baptism; but Trinity's records had been lost in the fire that destroyed the first Trinity Church during the Revolution. However, a record was found of her status as a communicant, and on that basis the validity of her baptism was conceded. Thus Trinity Church can lay claim to some considerable share in the spiritual nurture of the first native-born American to achieve recognized sainthood in the Roman Catholic Church.

BISHOP OF NEW YORK

Upon the retirement of Dr. Beach in 1813, Hobart, already Assistant Bishop of New York, became also assistant rector of Trinity. In both capacities he was virtually in charge of the diocese and the parish, respectively, because of the illness of Bishop Moore; and on the death of Bishop Moore in 1816, he succeeded to both positions. As bishop, he was also in charge of the Episcopal churches in Connecticut after the death of Bishop Jarvis in 1813, and until his successor, Thomas Church Brownell, an assistant at Trinity, was consecrated Bishop of Connecticut in 1819.

With such a wide territory to administer, and with the poor methods of travel in those days, Hobart was frequently out of New York City on episcopal visitations and missionary journeys. Not content to confine his efforts to the well-settled strip along the Hudson and Long Island Sound, he journeyed throughout the two states, concentrating on the western part of New York State, where there were only two or three churches at the outset of his episcopate. Before his death, the Episcopal Church was established in almost every New York county, and in Rochester and Buffalo there were two parishes.

As diocesan resources were almost nonexistent, Bishop Hobart depended largely upon the generosity of Trinity for the financing of these far-flung ventures. Trinity's vestry responded to the many appeals that came in an increasing flood from congregations, new and old, throughout the state, until the parish itself, despite its extensive real-estate holdings, became hard pressed for ready cash. Demands for increased salaries to sextons, clerks, organists, and other employees further depleted the parish resources, and brought the finances of the corporation to a low ebb. For the first time in its history, Trinity had to borrow money from the banks, and, as an extreme measure, sold all securities acquired during the preceding years.

Eventually, the vestry was compelled not only to decline all new requests for assistance, but even to defer meeting obligations already incurred. But before this point was reached, Trinity had made generous gifts to establish or maintain some seventy-five parishes during the period from 1800 to 1830, at a cost of more than a million dollars in cash and land values. Truly the name of Mother of Churches was well deserved.

Hobart's missionary activities as bishop of the diocese did not lessen his interest in maintaining and expanding the services and activities of Trinity Church and its chapels. He had a genius for selecting some of the ablest clergymen of the day to serve as his assistants, and to maintain the schedules of services on Sundays and holy days at a high level of dignity and concern, though without any excess of ritual. Among these assistants were William Berrian, who was to be his successor as rector; Benjamin T. Onderdonk and Jonathan M. Wainwright, who were to become bishops in the Diocese of New York; Thomas C. Brownell, who became Bishop of Connecticut;

George Upfold, later to be Bishop of Indiana; William H. DeLancey, first Bishop of Western New York; and George Washington Doane, later Bishop of New Jersey. It might well be said that during Hobart's rectorship, Trinity Church served not only as the *de facto* cathedral of the Diocese of New York but as the training ground for future bishops of the Episcopal Church.

Religious education, both of children and adults, was one of Bishop Hobart's prime interests. The basis of all such education, he believed, was the Bible and the Book of Common Prayer. Accordingly he organized the Bible and Common Prayer Book Society, for the publication and distribution of these two basic books, and urged the formation of similar societies in every parish. "Both these volumes," he wrote in a pastoral letter, "exhibit divine truth, the one as the original code, which contains the various commands of the Most High, and which alone as the law and testimony speaks with supreme authority; the other as the invaluable digest, in which the truths and precepts of the sacred volume are arrayed in lucid order, set forth with simplicity, embellished with the graces of diction, and animated by the purest fervours of devotion." But when the interdenominational American Bible Society was established in 1816, he opposed the cooperation of churchmen in that organization, which was largely under Presbyterian auspices, as posing the danger "of compromising their position, or of relaxing in any measure a spirit of attachment to the distinctive principles of their own Church."

As to the education of children in religious principles, Bishop Hobart, assisted by Mr. Berrian and Mr. Onderdonk, at first followed the practice long established in Trinity, of gathering the children at the altar rail, once a month, to hear them recite the catechism and to give them further explanation and training. To this he added a series of books known as *The New York Catechism*, intended to help in home instruction and family prayer.

Bishop Hobart followed with interest reports of the Sunday school experiments of Robert Raikes in England, and similar efforts being undertaken in New York. Accordingly, in February 1817 he called a meeting to form "The New York Protestant Episcopal Sunday-school Society," under the auspices of which a Sunday school was started in St. John's Chapel with 120 children, who had been "collected through the diligence of committees appointed for that purpose, in the short space of three days." Within five months, the school had grown so rapidly that it had to be divided into departments; with 241, of whom twenty were Blacks, in the male department, and 144, of whom twenty-six were Blacks, in the female department. Later the system was extended to the whole parish, and to other churches in the city.

Although Trinity now began turning down many of the innumerable appeals for financial assistance, one application met with particular favor, because of Trinity's long-continuing concern for the education and welfare of Negroes, both slave and free. For nearly a century, the parish had paid special attention to the catechetical instruction of Blacks, often employing a catechist or assistant minister especially for this purpose. In 1818 the "African Episcopal Catechetical Institution in the City of New York," which had grown out of these efforts, asked for a grant of land as a site for a building. The petition was favorably considered, and the vestry appropriated $3,000 to provide a schoolhouse and place of worship. This was the beginning of St. Philip's Church, which soon became an independent parish but continued to receive an annual grant from Trinity for many years.

Another generous grant was made at about the same time to Zion Church in Mott Street, a former Lutheran congregation which had become an Episcopal church. On August 31, 1815 the church was totally destroyed by fire. Twice the Zion vestry appealed to Trinity for help in rebuilding, and twice their appeal was refused. Unable to satisfy its creditors, the property was sold under bankruptcy procedures, but fortunately was bought by a group of Episcopalians in order to save it for the church. Rebuilding had already begun, but help was needed in the form of a loan of $10,000 to assure completion of the building. To this appeal Trinity responded, even though the sale of three lots on Warren, Church, and Chambers streets was required to raise the money.

Bishop Hobart was also tremendously concerned with the training of men for the ministry of the church. Early in his ministry he organized a private class for candidates, many of whom afterward attained eminence in the church. When the General Convention met at Trinity Church in 1817, its chief work was the passage of a resolution approving the establishment of a General Theological Seminary, and Hobart was appointed one of three bishops on a committee to make the necessary arrangements. But Hobart was not enthusiastic over the project, as he preferred diocesan seminaries, which might be more effectively controlled by the bishop of the diocese. Nevertheless, the seminary was begun in New York in 1819, with a faculty of two and a student body of six. At first it met in a small room at St. John's Chapel, but with the coming of winter, and the failure of the chapel to provide firewood to heat the room, it was transferred to a room in a girls' school.

After this cold reception, the General Convention in 1820 moved the seminary to New Haven, where Bishop

Brownell gave it a warmer welcome. Bishop Hobart promptly founded his own diocesan seminary, and later added a branch at Geneva, N.Y. Both were short-lived, but the latter became Geneva College—later renamed for its founder as Hobart College. In 1821 a New York layman, Jacob Sherred, left $60,000 to go either to a general seminary, if established in New York, or to a diocesan one. A special General Convention was called to settle the disposition of this legacy. In a compromise the General Theological Seminary was moved back to New York and combined with the diocesan seminary. Bishop Hobart now supported the combined institution, and even found time to serve as its professor of Pastoral Theology and Pulpit Eloquence.

For a time Trinity Parish was again the host of the General Theological Seminary. Twenty-three students assembled on February 13, 1822 in the vestry room (now heated) of St. John's Chapel. Later they moved to quarters prepared for them in the adjacent building of Trinity School. A solemn service of inauguration of the newly combined seminary was held in Trinity Church on the evening of March 11. The church was crowded with clergy and trustees, professors and students, and a large congregation. "I have hardly room to give you an account of the address which the Bishop delivered," wrote one of the participants—a statement that may well be believed, for it is recorded that Bishop Hobart's sermon on that occasion lasted an hour and twenty minutes.

Meanwhile, the General Seminary received a magnificent gift from a Trinity parishioner, Clement Clarke Moore, son of Bishop Moore and a professor at the new seminary. This was a splendid tract of land from the Moore estate, containing about sixty usable city lots from Ninth Avenue to the Hudson (North) River, between the present 20th and 21st streets. On this site in 1827 was erected the first of the seminary's buildings, a pseudo-Gothic rectangular pile of stone. Truly the seminary might be grateful for this gift from the talented churchman who wrote:

> 'Twas the night before Christmas
> When all through the house
> Not a creature was stirring,
> Not even a mouse.

Bishop Hobart prided himself on being a high churchman; indeed several of his diocesan charges were devoted to a defense of that position. The church, he felt, was a divine organism, and essential to its life was the threefold ministry of bishops, priests, and deacons. Anglicanism, he believed, was the best exponent of this position, at least in the Western world, and he defended it against what he felt to be the shortcomings of Protestantism and the excesses of Rome. In this he antedated the revival known as the Oxford Movement, which is commonly dated from Keble's famous 1833 sermon in England on National Apostasy.

Hobart also emphasized the importance of the Holy Communion, and of proper preparation for it. His instructional and devotional manuals were all directed to this end. But he was not interested in what later came to be known as ritualism or in vestments; for the conduct of services he wore the customary black rochet and chimere of Anglican bishops, and for preaching, a black gown. He advocated the ante-Communion service as the normal Sunday worship; that is, the Communion service through the Gospel, concluded with a sermon and blessing, except when the rest of the Communion was to follow. Thus he must share responsibility for the unedifying custom, which persisted into the early twentieth century, whereby most of the congregation left the church during the singing of a hymn after the offertory, leaving only a handful of communicants to receive the Blessed Sacrament when the rest of the Communion service was celebrated.

Yet what the Episcopal Church owes, under God, to John Henry Hobart can hardly be overestimated. His work began a new era in the church, when men again recognized its divine and apostolic origins. His missionary zeal initiated a great period of church expansion, and his preaching set a high standard. No longer was the Episcopal Church on the defensive, as it had been since the Revolution, but was ready—somewhat belatedly, to be sure—to take its share in the evangelization of the rapidly expanding frontiers of the nation.

In time the ceaseless energy of Bishop Hobart and his extensive travels began to undermine even his rugged constitution. His diocese covered an area of some 50,000 square miles from the Canadian border and the shores of Lake Erie to the eastern end of Long Island. From New York City, Albany could be reached by steamboat; beyond that point, the bishop had to rely on canal boats, stagecoaches, horseback, or walking. Once, on a visitation, he traveled nearly 4,000 miles, confirming, ordaining, and consecrating new churches. On another occasion, he traveled to Detroit, and to Wisconsin—visiting in the latter state the Christian Oneida Indians who had been transferred there from New York.

In the early autumn of 1830, while on a visitation to the western part of his diocese, Bishop Hobart was taken ill with an attack of the "bilious fever" that had often troubled him on his travels. He had conducted a confirmation service at St. Peter's Church, Auburn, N.Y., and was staying in the home of an old and dear friend, the Rev. J. C. Rudd, rector of the parish. Although the illness was not at first considered serious, he was prevailed upon to cancel plans for further travel. One of his sons was sent for, to accompany him back to New York City. But after a few days it became apparent that the bishop was dying. Dr. Rudd administered the Holy Communion, and the bishop made the responses clearly. At sunrise on Sunday, September 12, 1830, at the age of fifty-six, the end came.

The body was taken by canal boat and barge to New York, where it was met by the clergy and vestry of Trinity and other parishes in the city. Borne on men's shoulders, with six presbyters as pallbearers, the corpse was carried on foot to Trinity Church, followed by ministers of all faiths, the students of Columbia College and of the General Theological Seminary, and civic dignitaries. As by chance they passed a military company, the ranks were parted and the soldiers stood with reversed arms while the procession passed. The funeral in Trinity Church was attended by the acting governor, the mayor, and a large congregation. He was buried beneath the chancel of Trinity Church. The inscription on his monument described him as the "faithful and valiant Soldier of Christ, who, on all occasions, stood forth the able and intrepid Champion of the Church of God."

Among the voluminous and often lengthy tributes paid to the memory of John Henry Hobart, rector and bishop, none was more memorable than that of Arthur Cleveland Coxe, historian of the Diocese of New York and later himself a bishop: "He lived and died like an Apostle." Bishop Hobart, champion of the doctrine of Apostolic Succession, would have relished that sincere tribute.

7

The Third Trinity Church

1830-1849

The sudden death of Bishop Hobart left both Trinity Parish and the Diocese of New York without leadership. Both the parish and the diocese had grown to the point where it was widely recognized that one man could not serve effectively both as bishop and rector. But Trinity, despite the depletion of its revenues, was still the richest parish in the diocese, and had for so long underwritten most of the diocesan expenses that other churches were reluctant to accept their share.

On October 7 and 8, 1830, therefore, the convention of the Diocese of New York met at St. John's Chapel. With near unanimity, the delegates elected the Rev. Dr. Benjamin T. Onderdonk, an assistant minister of Trinity Church, as Bishop of New York; he was consecrated in the same chapel on November 26.

Trinity's vestry met three days after the diocesan convention to choose their new rector. Their unanimous choice was the Rev. Dr. William Berrian, who had served as an assistant minister at Trinity since 1811. He was inducted the following day, and immediately entered upon his duties.

TRINITY'S RESPONSES TO NEW DEVELOPMENTS

For the support of the episcopate, it was agreed that an endowment of $100,000 was required. The Trinity vestry offered to contribute $30,000 to the fund, provided that the other $70,000 be raised in other parishes within three years. Meanwhile, an allowance of $1,000 a year was to be given to cover the bishop's travel and other necessary expenses. But the diocese was slow in raising its share, and for some years Trinity actually had to provide for most of the expense of the episcopate, as well as the salary and expenses of its rector. It was not until 1836 that the diocese was able to fulfill its share of the agreement; meanwhile, Bishop Onderdonk retained his connection with Trinity and shared to such extent as he could in the services and other ministrations of the parish. Other assistants, appointed by the new rector, were Edward Higbee, Henry Anthon, and Jonathan Mayhew Wainwright.

The population of New York City was growing rapidly. In the ten years from 1820 to 1830 it had increased from 123,000 to 202,589. Many of the new residents were immigrants of the poorest class, and New York was rapidly becoming the polyglot metropolis it was to remain. The opening of the Erie Canal in 1825 had also brought a notable increase in the commerce and importance of New York, the water gateway to the expanding west.

So great was the need for ministry to the growing population that the churches were called upon to enlarge their missionary resources. The newcomers from abroad were mostly Roman Catholics, many of them Irish. They soon outgrew the little St. Peter's Church on Barclay Street, near Trinity, and the first St. Patrick's Cathedral was dedicated on Mulberry Street. New Protestant churches were built, and older ones expanded.

Episcopalians responded to the new needs by establishing in 1831 "The New York Mission Society," later to become the Episcopal City Mission Society. Bishop Onderdonk was president of the new society, which had "lay managers" consisting of prominent vestrymen of Trinity and other parishes. Funds were raised and a former Dutch church purchased and established as the Church of the Holy Evangelists, to minister among the people in the crowded and neglected area east of Broadway. The vestry of Trinity strongly supported this first united missionary endeavor of the New York parishes. Thus began the involvement of Trinity in the work among native and foreign-born Americans on the lower east side, which was to be so great a concern of the parish for the next 150 years and more.

The church was also expanding nationally, into the new territories of Ohio, Illinois, Kentucky, Wisconsin, and beyond. The Domestic and Foreign Missionary Society had been inaugurated by the General Convention in 1820, and in 1835 the convention declared that the entire membership of the Episcopal Church constituted the membership of the society. New dioceses in the west and southwest were being rapidly established, and the society sent missionaries as far afield as Florida, Missouri, and Texas—the last named, when it became a republic, being the first "foreign" missionary field of the Episcopal Church.

On October 31, 1832 St. Paul's Chapel was the scene of the consecration of four bishops in a single service—Bishops John Henry Hopkins of Vermont, Benjamin Bosworth Smith of Kentucky, Charles Pettit McIlvaine of

Ohio, and George Washington Doane of New Jersey. Of this service, unique in the history of the church in the nineteenth century, Dr. Morgan Dix later wrote (in the Trinity parish history):

> The consecration of the four bishops in St. Paul's Chapel was an event of the utmost importance in the history of our branch of the Church in this country; the signal for an advance along the whole line, and the expression of a resolve to extend far and wide the knowledge of the Gospel as we have received the same. It closed a period of uncertainty and hesitation, and inaugurated an era of earnest missionary work, east and west; it was the outcome, under God's Providence, of the work of the great Bishop Hobart, in asserting the cause of the Church, repelling the assaults of her jealous adversaries and rivals, and proclaiming her principles fearlessly and without reserve.

Trinity Church itself was enlarged, a memorial to Bishop Hobart installed, and a new organ planned. The organ, however, was placed in St. John's Chapel in 1840, the parish church being at the time under reconstruction.

More important than the new organ, however, was the coming to Trinity of a truly great musician, Edward Hodges, a Doctor of Music of Cambridge University. Dr. Wainwright was instrumental in bringing Dr. Hodges to New York, and in 1839 the rector appointed him as parish organist and as choirmaster at St. John's Chapel. Hodges found the music of Trinity "unimaginative," and the choir to which he was appointed consisted of six persons, largely untrained, and one "supernumerary."

Hodges rebuilt the choir at St. John's, and gave stirring organ recitals on the new organ, to which large numbers of appreciative listeners flocked. Later he became an instructor of music in Trinity School, and sixteen musical scholarships were established to furnish the church with well-trained boy choristers. He also taught music at the General Theological Seminary, and thus helped to raise the standard of music in the whole church.

PLANNING AND BUILDING THE THIRD TRINITY CHURCH

But Trinity Church now found itself in new and grave difficulties. Heavy snows in the winter of 1838-1839 caused the roof of the church to sink several inches, and an investigation in the spring indicated that the whole church was in danger of collapse. A special committee of the vestry reported that repairs and improvements would cost $30,000; the vestry approved the plans and authorized the committee to carry them out.

Before the repairs had proceeded very far, it became apparent that the building had been too poorly built to be susceptible of repair, and the vestry reluctantly concluded that the edifice should be torn down and an entirely new church built. Demolition was begun in August 1839, and soon the second Trinity Church lay in ruins.

Philip Hone, sometime mayor of New York, an ardent member of Trinity and later vestryman, wrote in his diary:

> We are vagrants now on Sundays. Poor old Trinity being razed nearly to the ground, and a new church to be erected on the same spot, which will require two or three years to complete, we shall be compelled during that time to hire a pew in one of the uptown churches, or quarter upon our friends. . . . I found, on my return to the city, a shapeless heap of ruins on the spot where my imperfect devotions have been performed for the last thirty-seven years. It occasions melancholy reflections to see the dark mass of ruins still overlooking the magnificent temples of mammon in Wall Street, and to think of the

changes which have occurred during the time the venerable spire which is now removed has thrown its shadow over the place "where merchants most do congregate."

May I not also see in this dilapidation a type of my own decay and speedily approaching removal? When I first went to Trinity Church I was young, ardent and full of hopes, capable and industrious, and I should now be ungrateful not to acknowledge that in most cases my hopes were realized and my industry rewarded; but the storms within the last three years have beaten upon me, the timbers are decayed, the spire no longer "like a tall bully lifts its head," and the vestry has no funds to rebuild me.

Thus the second Trinity Church, consecrated in 1790 by Bishop Provoost in the presence of George Washington with brave hopes for the future, was reduced to rubble after a half century of service in the fastest-growing city of the new nation; and the painful work of reconstruction had to begin again. But this time the vestry was determined to employ the best architect available, and to rebuild with stone and careful workmanship that would endure for many generations, as the House of God towering over the busy structures of the nation's growing financial center.

The vestry lost no time in authorizing and planning for a new church, but the actual construction took considerably more than the two or three years contemplated by Mayor Hone. It was actually two years before the cornerstone was laid, and nearly seven years before the new church was ready for occupancy.

The vestry wisely chose Richard Upjohn, then of Boston, to draw plans and supervise the erection of the church. Only thirty-seven years old, Upjohn was an Englishman who had come to the new world in 1828, arriving at Manlius, N.Y., with "three silver dollars in his pocket."

He moved to Boston, where he set himself up as a draughtsman and attended Trinity Church in that city. There he came under the favorable notice of the Rev. Jonathan Wainwright, rector of that church until he came to New York as assistant minister of Trinity Parish in 1837. It was apparently Dr. Wainwright who recommended Upjohn, first as draughtsman for the planned repairs to Trinity and then as architect of the new building. His work at Trinity was to establish his reputation as the ablest church architect in this country.

Mr. Upjohn's plans called for a chancel much deeper than was then customary, a nave of five bays, and a spire 275 feet high, surmounted by a cross—an imposing structure of Gothic architecture far in advance of any yet built in this country. Some of the vestry objected to the deep chancel, others to the cross instead of the customary weathervane; but in the end, the architect prevailed, and his plans were fully approved.

The cornerstone was laid on June 3, 1841, bearing the names of Benjamin Tredwell Onderdonk as bishop, Richard Upjohn, architect; James Thom, sculptor; James Vandenburgh, master mason; and Samuel Martin, master carpenter. Aided by these skilled craftsmen, Upjohn built slowly but thoroughly, to produce the third and present Trinity Church. Its tall spire, topped by the cross, was long to dominate the skyline of New York, and to serve as a landmark for incoming ships. Today, of course, it is surrounded by taller buildings, and the rector, from his twenty-fifth-story office behind the church, can look down upon the church and its spire; but such a contingency could hardly have been foreseen when it was built.

All New York followed with interest the erection of this magnificent structure, "the pride of Episcopalians and the glory of our city," to quote Mayor Hone again. At last, although the new organ was not fully ready, the consecration of the church was set for Ascension Day, May 21, 1846. Then occurred an episode which was really a tempest in a teapot, but which for a time threatened to mar the opening services. Invitations to the clergy were sent out by the committee on arrangements, requesting that the visiting clergy march in procession wearing surplice and scarf. Now the surplice had become a badge of "high churchmanship," and feelings on churchmanship ran high in those days. Nine of the Episcopal clergymen of the diocese therefore joined in declining the invitation, making public a letter stating: "We are unwilling to sanction such innovation or to accept an invitation based upon such a condition." Even the daily press took part in the ensuing controversy.

Nevertheless, the service of consecration was conducted as scheduled, with the Rt. Rev. Samuel A. McCoskry, Bishop of Michigan, officiating in place of the Bishop of New York, and preaching the sermon. Mr. Hone, himself a member of the committee on arrangements, described the ceremony in his diary:

> The clergy, the rectors, wardens and vestrymen of the several Episcopalian churches, the members of the Theological Seminary, the present and former mayors, the scholars of Trinity School, and invited guests assembled at ten o'clock at Mr. Bunker's in Broadway and marched in procession to the church. At eleven o'clock the grand and solemn assemblage preceded by the Rt. Rev. Bishop McCoskry, who officiated as Bishop of the Diocese during the suspension of Bishop Onderdonk, entered during the impressive chanting of one hundred and fifty clergymen in white surplices and scarfs, followed by a most dignified and respectable body of laymen.
>
> The consecration service was performed by the Bishop assisted by a number of prominent ministers; and the splendid

vaulting of the solemn temple resounded with the notes of the grand organ and with the sounds of praise and adoration from the voices of the devout assemblage.

In the leisurely custom of the day, the service lasted from eleven in the morning until three in the afternoon; it included the office of consecration, Morning Prayer, Holy Communion, and sermon. Dr. Hodges played the organ, despite its "very imperfect and incomplete state," including an anthem and other selections which he had composed for the occasion.

The new church presented an opportunity for a more dignified service, and Dr. Berrian and his assistants were quick to take advantage of it. Profoundly influenced by the Oxford Movement, with its emphasis on the catholicity of the church, he had already laid plans for expanding and enhancing the services at Trinity Church. Morning and Evening Prayer were to be said daily in the church, and a more prominent place to be given to the Holy Communion. This was to be celebrated monthly in the mother church and the chapels, on successive Sundays; and not less than four clergymen were to participate in the administration of the sacrament "whenever practicable." Moreover, the ministry of the church and chapels was to be directed beyond the immediate membership for the benefit of the surrounding people. Dr. Berrian noted that "as the lower part of the City has been deserted by the fashionable and wealthy inhabitants, but a large part of the population of the poorer classes remain, and will remain, and probably even increase, Trinity Church, then, being the only place of worship of any denomination below John Street, would seem to be discharging only a bounden duty, while at the same time it would unquestionably secure for itself the approbation of all the devout members of our communion, by taking the pastoral care as far as possible of the poor in this part of the City."

To aid in this work, the vestry authorized an additional assistant minister, and two deacons to work with them. It was a recognition that Trinity was no longer a comfortable, closely knit parish church, but a Christian outpost in a migratory and constantly shifting population of differing religious and national backgrounds to whom the church had a genuine responsibility for evangelism and pastoral care. This was a mission of which Trinity was to become increasingly conscious in the years ahead.

The 1840s and 1850s were a time of great controversy in the Episcopal Church, growing out of the English *Tracts for the Times.* These advocated a Catholic view of the church, not unlike the teachings of Bishop Hobart, but going beyond in the field of what came to be called "ritualism"—actually an attempt to recover the emphasis on color and dignity in the vestments and conduct of services that had been lost in the reaction of Anglicanism to the Roman Catholic counterreformation. The *Tracts* had a wide circulation in the American church, and aroused bitter antagonism among Evangelicals and low churchmen. Controversial references to the principles for which they stood, and which came to be known as Anglo-Catholicism, were unfortunately often marked by intemperance and bigotry on both sides.

There is no need to go into details of the controversies of those days, except insofar as they affected the work of Trinity Parish and the Diocese of New York. So far as the parish was concerned, the wisdom and moderation of Dr. Berrian, together with the foundations laid by Bishop Hobart, led the parish to weather the storm with a minimum of internal strife and to emerge in a sounder and healthier condition. But the chief victim of the unhappy controversy, so far as New York was concerned, was its bishop, Benjamin Onderdonk, who, though relieved from duty at Trinity in 1836, continued to be closely associated with the parish, which was also his principal source of income.

Bishop Onderdonk was generally in favor of the viewpoint set forth in the *Tracts,* and indeed on several occasions commended them to the clergy and laity of the diocese, in his convention addresses, and in his teaching at the General Theological Seminary, where he held the chair of ecclesiastical polity and law.

The issue came to a head in controversy over the ordination of a brilliant student at the seminary, Arthur Carey. When it came time for Carey's ordination, his sponsor, the Rev. Hugh Smith of St. Peter's Church, New York, refused to sign his testimonials on the ground that Carey's opinion, influenced by the *Tracts,* was more extreme than he had thought, and presented a statement of his reasons to Bishop Onderdonk. Carey thereupon turned to Trinity Parish, and secured the necessary testimonials from Dr. Berrian.

The bishop, anxious to clarify the matter before ordaining Mr. Carey, invited Dr. Smith and his supporter, Dr. Henry Anthon, of St. Mark's Church, to assist at a special examination of Carey before himself and six of the leading presbyters of the diocese, including Dr. Berrian. After the examination, Smith and Anthon were dissatisfied, but the others expressed the opinion that the candidate's answers to their questions were satisfactory. The bishop thereupon ruled that, as the matter had been satisfactorily adjudicated, he would proceed with the ordination.

On July 2, 1843 the bishop, assisted by Bishop Ives of North Carolina, began the service of ordination to the diaconate in St. Stephen's Church, New York. With the two bishops in the chancel were Professor Haight, of the seminary, who presented the candidates, Dr. Berrian, the rector of Trinity, and the Rev. Joseph Price, rector of St. Stephen's. When the bishop reached the point in the ordination service where he formally asks the congregation "if there be any of you who knoweth any impediment or notable crime" on account of which any candidate should not be ordained, Dr. Smith, wearing his gown, rose up in the aisle and read a formal protest to the ordination of Carey. When he finished, Dr. Anthon stepped beside him and read a similar protest.

But the bishop was not unprepared for the unseemly interruption. "Majestic, indignant, and determined," according to one observer, he read his own statement, indicating that the charges made by the two presbyters had been investigated "with the valuable aid and counsel of six of the worthiest, wisest, and most learned of the presbyters of this diocese, including the three who are assisting in the present solemnities," and that "there is consequently no reason for any change in the solemn service of the day." Bishop Ives then began the ordination litany, and the two protesting clergymen left the church.

The matter was, however, not allowed to rest there. Carey himself unfortunately did not live to exercise for long the ministry to which he had been ordained; in ill health, he died on a voyage to Havana, where he had hoped to recuperate. But at the instigation of Smith and Anthon, the trustees of the General Seminary appointed a committee to investigate the teaching in the seminary. On hearing its report, the trustees voted, 26 to 25, to inform the House of Bishops that the seminary had never been "in a more healthful condition." A minority report however also went to the bishops, and the resulting investigation by the House of Bishops upset seminary routine for several years before that institution was acquitted of teaching strange doctrines.

The aftermath for Bishop Onderdonk was more serious.

Unable to touch the bishop on doctrinal grounds, some of his enemies began to collect various charges which they thought reflected seriously on his moral character. When the diocesan convention refused to listen to these accusations, they persuaded three Evangelical bishops to present charges against Onderdonk to the House of Bishops. On these charges, flimsy though some of them were, the bishop was found guilty, and sentenced to indefinite suspension from the ministry—a punishment from which he was never released. Dr. Dawley writes, in *The Story of the General Theological Seminary*:

> The Bishop of New York, maintaining his innocence, returned home to live in quiet seclusion, exhibiting a spirit of Christian charity and submission that won the admiration of all save his most vengeful enemies, until the day of his death fifteen years later. To try to estimate the part played in Onderdonk's disgrace by the passions of controversy is now almost useless. That ecclesiastical partisanship was an important element in the sad affair has long been admitted. It is with singular appropriateness that the serpent of slander is depicted under the feet of the effigy of the Bishop that lies in Trinity Church.

The suspension of Bishop Onderdonk was a great blow to the Diocese of New York, which was thus left without a leader. Moreover, there was no legal way of filling the vacancy, as the canons of the church had not provided for such a contingency. The matter was resolved in due course by the election in 1852 of the Rev. Jonathan M. Wainwright, another assistant minister of Trinity Parish, as Provisional Bishop of New York.

8

Turbulent Metropolis and the Civil War

1850-1865

By 1850 New York had become a thriving and turbulent metropolis. Lloyd Morris, in *Incredible New York*, notes that strangers "were awed by the splendor of its hotels and theaters, its costly and magnificent stores."

They were astonished by the incessant torrent of traffic, the day-long, night-long surge and roar of more than five hundred thousand people. To many of them, New York seemed a city of crowds and carnival—breezy, recklessly extravagant, perpetually bent on pleasure. The bright gaslights of bars and restaurants and hotels threw a glare over Broadway until well toward dawn. The rumble of omnibuses and the clatter of hackney-coaches was never stilled. New York was a city where men made such incredible fortunes that a new word, "millionaire," was on everybody's lips. Two things gave it a quality, a flavor that was unique, and New Yorkers were proud of both. Nowhere else was the tempo of life as fast. And the only permanent characteristic of New York was continuous change. From week to week, almost from day to day, the look of the city was constantly being transformed.

New York was becoming a city of contrasts—great wealth and ostentatious display, on one hand; dire poverty, corruption, and crime on the other. Plush hotels and restaurants, like the St. Nicholas Hotel on Broadway and Broome Street, or Delmonico's Restaurant, were the scenes of lavish parties; magnificent homes were built with ballrooms in which members of an exclusive "society" attended balls and cotillions surpassing those of European royalty. Yet a stone's throw from Broadway, along Worth Street and the Bowery, were filthy streets and alleys with overcrowded and dirty tenements, where drunkenness, crime, and immorality were rampant.

AN AGITATED DECADE

In the midst of this hodge-podge, Trinity, with its beautiful new church, tried to pursue its even course. Many of its wealthy parishioners had moved uptown, and had transferred to newer parishes. Grace Church, largely founded by Trinity but quite independent of it, became the recognized center for wealthy society; its sexton doubled as master of ceremonies for parties of the socially elite. St. Paul's Chapel, too, found itself in a growing business district. Only St. John's Chapel remained in a fine residential area.

Trinity, beset by the problems of shifting population, tried to meet the situation in two different ways. On the one hand, as we have seen, it began tentatively and at first not very successfully, to reach out toward the poor in its neighborhood. On the other hand, it began to plan for a new chapel, farther uptown where many of its parishioners had moved.

But the parish was still in debt and beset by financial problems, aggravated by the cost of the new church. Gen. John A. Dix, who became a vestryman in 1849 and later warden, introduced a series of resolutions providing for a plan whereby the expenditures of the corporation should be limited to its income, and further that the church and its chapels should abolish the system of pew rents. He favored the building of a new chapel, as soon as available funds would permit, but on the understanding that thereafter the funds of the parish should be used, "as far as may be practical, in the education and religious instruction of the poor of the city." At first his views met with little support; but eventually most of them were adopted. Not only was financial disaster averted, but within the decade the income of the parish was largely restored—though it was estimated that Trinity, whether through generosity or poor management (or a combination of both) had given away something like two-thirds of its original patrimony.

A suitable site for the new chapel was found and purchased on the north side of 25th Street, between Broadway and Sixth Avenue. Richard Upjohn was commissioned to draw up plans for the building. But on the insistence of General Dix, the vestry voted that the chapel should not be built until the parish debt had been reduced to $300,000 and that the expense of construction should, "as far as practicable," be limited to $40,000. By July 14, 1852 the comptroller was able to announce that, when certain real-estate sales were completed, the state of parish finances would permit the construction of the chapel.

But when the itemized specifications for the chapel were submitted to the vestry, it was found that the estimated cost would be $79,000; subsequent changes brought the costs even higher, and in the end the expenditures for the site and building totaled $230,000. Nevertheless, contracts were let and the work of construction on what was now named Trinity Chapel began. Commenting on the decision, Dr. Dix in his parish history drily remarked: "The persuasive power of architects and the docility of building committees must always be taken into account, when estimates for new structures are under consideration." He does not indicate what the total cost of the chapel was; but it was completed in 1855, and turned out to be a beautiful church, with handsome quarters for the rector attached.

Trinity Chapel contained, moreover, a splendid organ, built under the supervision of the parish organist, Dr. Hodges, who wrote: "If I can only be trusted by this people I think I can make a most delightful organ effect there." And so he did, especially with an anthem that he wrote for the occasion; but it was almost his last act as organist, for he was taken ill shortly after. Dr. Hodges took a leave of absence and went to England for a year, and then returned to live in virtual retirement. In 1863 he formally resigned his post and returned to England, where he died in 1867.

Trinity Chapel was consecrated on April 17, 1855 by the Rt. Rev. Horatio Potter, who had succeeded Dr. Wainwright as Provisional Bishop of New York, assisted by the Rt. Rev. Henry Whitehouse, Bishop of Illinois. Nearly one hundred clergymen were present, together with the rector and clerical staff of Trinity Parish, members of the vestry, and a large congregation. Bishop Potter preached the sermon.

George Templeton Strong, the noted diarist, was present in his capacity as vestryman, and described the occasion in his journal:

The services were well conducted and impressive; church packed full, of course. I was there at nine and found people assembling. . . . The entering procession was imposing; sextons of the church and chapels with very big staves gilded and colored in the early decorated style; the "parochial" churchwardens with lesser staves (like the pointers used by lecturers to indicate and demonstrate their diagrams), which the committee had licensed them to "bear" on their solemn written request. I wanted to give them letters-patent authorizing cocked hats, also. Lots of clergy in surplices. Happily, it was a fine day and the distance walked by the procession very small, so they did not have to wear their hats and present the appearance of a holiday turnout of cartmen in clean frocks. The string of fifty or sixty priests and deacons, and as many divinity students, passed into the chapel under my nose as "we" received them on the chapel porch, and I must say that I was not favorably impressed by my review of their physiognomies. . . . Here and there was a nice, manly, earnest face, now and then, among the elder clergy, one that showed energy and cleanness. But they were mostly a sad set. Why does that profession attract so few men of mark, moral vigor, and commanding talent? . . . The music was tolerable. The multitude of voices gave much dignity to the chants and other pieces in which the congregation joined.

Strong had high regard for Dr. Berrian, and for several of the other clergy, but he observed that "the prevailing type was that of the commonplace fourth-rate snob." Coming from one whom many regarded as a first-rate snob, the opinion must be evaluated accordingly!

With the mother church and three chapels now in operation, it became necessary to enlarge the clerical staff of the parish again, and to assign the clergy to the several churches, instead of having them serve in rotation. The organization when completed was as follows:

Trinity Church: The Rev. Drs. Benjamin I. Haight and Frederick Ogilby.

St. Paul's Chapel: The Rev. Dr. Francis Vinton and the Rev. Morgan Dix.

St. John's Chapel: The Rev. Sullivan H. Weston and the Rev. John Freeman Young (later to be Bishop of Florida).

Trinity Chapel: The Rev. Drs. Edward Y. Higbee and John Henry Hobart (son of the late bishop).

In 1856, a year after the establishment of Trinity Chapel, the rector, Dr. Berrian, reported on the state of the parish:

> The condition of the Parish, with its present effective force and under its new arrangements, is exceedingly gratifying. Notwithstanding so great a number of parishioners have removed to the upper part of the city, the attendance at Trinity Church still continues to be large; it has materially improved at St. Paul's Chapel, it is well sustained at St. John's; and Trinity Chapel is often filled to its utmost capacity.

Continuing, he gave statistics for the parish in the previous year: 33 adult baptisms, 400 infant baptisms, 114 marriages, 751 burials, 176 confirmations; with 1,100 communicants, and 901 children in the Sunday schools. The aggregate of the offerings was $16,430.84. Total services in the church and three chapels was "about 2000," with the Holy Communion administered weekly in the parish by rotation in the several churches.

Despite Trinity's generosity to other parishes and missionary work, which had reduced her own resources to a danger point, the parish was subjected to two bitter attacks on its financial integrity in the mid-1850s. The first of these took place within its own household, at the diocesan convention of 1855, held, as usual, in St. John's Chapel. It grew out of a demand that the support of the clergy in country parishes should be entirely at the expense of Trinity Parish, on the ground that the property of Trinity, the mother parish of the diocese, really belonged to all Episcopalians in the state of New York. For the same reason the report of the committee on the salary of the provisional bishop, showing a very small response from the other parishes, led to a demand that the whole burden of the bishop's support should be laid upon the Trinity corporation. Dr. Dix notes in his parish history:

> With sarcasm and innuendo, and in impassioned speeches, these wild views were ventilated, by most respectable and worthy gentlemen, both of the clergy and laity, many of whom in after years deeply regretted what they had said. Over those scenes it is well to draw the veil; they are forgotten; and it would be unkind to recall them to a full report of what occurred. They were, however, on the line of an agitation at that time proceeding with ever-increasing acrimony. So sudden and unexpected was the attack that the representatives and friends of the parish in the convention made little or no response.

The parish was better prepared for a further attack the following year, in which a strong effort was made to have the state legislature interfere in the affairs of Trinity. The claim was made that since the original charter of Trinity had made a grant to "the Inhabitants of the City of New York," control of Trinity's resources should be in the hands of the public and not of the rector, wardens, and vestrymen of the parish. Upon the agitation of this question in the state Senate at Albany, a resolution was adopted to submit certain questions to the vestry of Trinity Parish, as a basis for possible legislative action. The vestry, through the parish comptroller, William E. Dunscomb, in due course supplied the information requested, but appended to it a strong protest, "not acknowledging the power of the senate to exact such information," and noting that "if there should be at any time any cause for complaint against this corporation, the courts are open, and are adequate to afford a remedy."

Upon receipt of this document, the Senate appointed a special committee of investigation, which visited New York "for the purpose of examining the report." Four "hearings" were held by this committee in December, 1856, but only witnesses selected by them were allowed to testify. Dr. Dix reports:

> Many witnesses were summoned to appear, eleven of them being clergymen, of whom only three were assistant ministers of the parish. Among the laymen summoned was the Comptroller of the corporation. A summary of the testimony taken at that time shows that the committee was following a preconceived plan, as only answers to questions already prepared by them were allowed, and no voluntary statements were admitted. The sessions were held with closed doors, and there appears to have been no effort to call friends and members of Trinity Church.

Having completed their investigation, the committee presented a report to the Senate, together with the draft of a proposed Act to amend the Act of 1814 establishing Trinity's charter. Dr. Dix continues:

> The committee gave it as their opinion that the property of the Corporation was held in trust for all the inhabitants of the city of New York; they also charged the Corporation with partiality in grants and extravagant expenditure within the parish, and arraigned it for not building free churches for the general use of the citizens of the metropolis. The report, upon its face, was so partial, that even those senators who cared little or nothing for Trinity Church thought that it needed further consideration, and it was recommitted.

Trinity now asked for and obtained an opportunity to be heard and to call witnesses on behalf of the corporation. At this hearing, the corporation was represented by two able attorneys, Amasa J. Parker and Orlando Means, and was able to call a distinguished list of witnesses in its behalf. These included the bishop, the rector, several of the parish clergy, and lay members of the vestry and of the parish.

At a subsequent hearing, the senior warden, Gen. John A. Dix, presented detailed figures and a long communication, as well as verbal testimony covering all the points at issue. His testimony included a masterful presentation of the whole background and history of the parish, and refutation of the arguments of partiality, prodigality, and parsimony made by the opposition.

As a result of these hearings, the committee submitted an amended report, in which, however, "none of the allegations of misuse and abuse of the trust were withdrawn." The debate on this amended report was long and bitter. At last a substitute bill was offered by the original proponents, providing that all Episcopalians should be regarded as corporators of the parish, but that the property should remain in the custody of the corporation. The substitute was finally passed by a vote of 19 to 12, and sent to the Assembly, where it died with the adjournment of the legislature. Dr. Dix concludes:

> Thus, providentially, was averted a great evil, not only to the parish of Trinity Church, but to all churches in our communion; for no more radical measure could have been imagined, nor one better calculated to affect injuriously the rights and interest of corporations in general. The case for the Church was managed with great skill, wisdom, and dignity, and from that day to the present, . . . there has been no renewal of that bold and unjustifiable assault.

The financial panic of 1857 caused great distress in New York, as in other cities in the United States, and eventually in England and elsewhere. Unemployment in New York City rose to between 30,000 and 40,000, and many families faced near-starvation. On October 10 of that year, George Templeton Strong noted in his diary:

> We seem foundering. Affairs are worse than ever today, and a period of general insolvency seems close upon us. . . . Depression and depletion are going on without any sign of limit and promise to continue till we reach the zero point or universal suspension.

Despite Trinity's own stringent financial situation, Dr. Berrian and the parish clergy did what they could to alleviate distress, especially through its mission house in the Bowery. On October 13 Dr. Morgan Dix, who went there every day to minister to both the temporal and the spiritual needs of the poor, wrote in his diary:

> We began to feel the pressure of the panic today in the increased number of applications for relief. About half past 3 o'clock I received the startling news that 18 of the banks of the city had suspended specie payments. Wall Street was in a situation of the most unparallelled excitement, innumerable crowds blocking it up and a strong police force on duty.

The next few days there were tremendous runs on all banks, and by the 15th, in Strong's words, Wall Street was "blue with collapse." Banks refused payment in gold or any metallic coin, and many became insolvent. Mills and factories shut down, and many payrolls went unmet. At the mission house, Dr. Dix recorded:

> Among those who came in was a man who talked very gloomily indeed, saying that he could get no work, had a wife

and children at home whom he could not see starving. He had talked a great deal with other men about the times, and they thought there was only one thing they could do by and by if the worst came to the worst: he would as soon be shot down as starve. Dr. Vinton talked to him very earnestly about the necessity of keeping the peace and resisting all inducements to riot, but we all felt gloomy enough, knowing that this man represented a large class.

By November 2 Dix and the other clergy of the parish were themselves feeling the pinch:

> Applied to the Treasurer of the Vestry for my salary [he wrote] and learned to my confusion that none of the salaries of the clergy can be paid, there being no funds at all at his disposal. Took counsel with the other clergy whom I met, but we remained without relief at all. I now have not the monies to pay my board and lodging, now due for 4 weeks.

The unhappy situation lasted until December 14, when the banks at last resumed payment. Meanwhile, the poor suffered; and as there was no system of public relief, Trinity and other churches did what little they could to give emergency assistance. Even after the banks had been able to achieve some measure of financial stability, there was no help for the masses of unemployed, and it was a winter of acute suffering for the poor of the city. As late as March 8, 1858 Dix noted that "the poor appear to be even more helpless than ever as regards obtaining employment."

By September 1858 conditions in the city were more normal. Trinity Church was the scene of a gala celebration of the successful completion of the trans-Atlantic cable, conducted by the rector, Dr. Berrian, and his assistants. The service inaugurated a three-day gala civic celebration, with bands, illumination, a torchlight procession, dinners, receptions, and fireworks.

THE VISIT OF THE PRINCE OF WALES

Despite rising concern about slavery, an important presidential election, and threatened secession of southern states, New York was thrown into a frenzy of anticipation in 1860 by the prospect of its first visit from the scion of a reigning royal family. During the summer, Queen Victoria had sent the young Prince of Wales, Albert Edward (later King Edward VII), on a state tour of Canada. President Buchanan invited the prince to visit the United States, and the queen graciously accepted, provided the prince could travel incognito under the name of Baron Renfrew. The disguise, if such it was intended to be, was a thin one, and no one was the least fooled by it, but it did have the effect of simplifying protocol.

Peter Cooper, one of New York's most distinguished citizens, called a meeting of community leaders to invite the prince to the city. After prolonged discussion, it was decided to invite the prince to a banquet; but when a delegation went to Canada to present an engrossed invitation to the royal entourage, it was indicated to them that His Royal Highness—"nineteen, slim, handsome, and deplorably frivolous"—would greatly prefer a ball, since he was having quite enough of state banquets. Returning to New York, the committee reported the change in plans, and leaders of "Society"—with a capital S—were delighted. A list of 400 gentlemen was drawn up to receive and dispense invitations—ten invitations to each, upon payment of $70.00 per invitation. Each invitee was subject to further scrutiny by the committee, to be sure that none but the socially elite (plus Mayor Wood and civic officials who hardly qualified for that category) were admitted to the Academy of Music, where a special dinner room was constructed. Ordinary citizens were permitted to view the decorations on the day after the dinner.

The prince arrived on a fine October day, and was welcomed by crowds estimated at 300,000 who lined the streets from Bowling Green to the Fifth Avenue Hotel, to cheer as he passed by in an open carriage drawn by six horses. The Duke of Newcastle reported to Queen Victoria that the crowds were "worked up almost to madness, and yet restrained within the bounds of the most perfect courtesy." After various municipal ceremonies, he was entertained with a torchlight parade by the fire department. Next day Prince Edward had breakfast with the mayor, and then was taken on a tour of the city.

But the highlight was the ball on the night of October 12, and for that the social leaders pulled out all the stops. Many said it was so brilliant and beautiful that they would remember it all their lives; and the ladies who danced with the royal guest were quite overcome with joy. The prince apparently enjoyed himself to the full; indeed, as the poet Edmund Stedman wrote:

> It was even said that his great delight
> Established etiquette scorning
> Would be not only to dance all night
> But—once escaped from Newcastle's sight—
> To go home with the girls in the morning.

Whether the prince indeed "escaped from Newcastle's sight" to spend the rest of the night "on the town" is not officially recorded, but a rumor that he did persisted for many years after the notable event.

At any rate, by Sunday, two days later, the prince was ready for a more sedate occasion, attendance at the morning service in Trinity Church. Again an immense throng lined Broadway to catch a glimpse of royalty, and the church, with admission by ticket only, was packed. Unfortunately the rector, Dr. Berrian, was ill, but the two senior assistants, Drs. Francis Vinton and Frederick Ogilby, acted as hosts in his absence.

The two wardens, William E. Dunscomb and Robert Hyslop, each bearing a staff of office, met the royal party and conducted them to their seats as the organist, Henry S. Cutler, played a prelude on the great organ. Officiants included Bishops Potter of New York, DeLancey of Western New York, Odenheimer of New Jersey, and Talbot of the Northwest, assisted by the parish clergy, with Dr. Vinton preaching the sermon. His text, rather ambiguously, was from the Book of Daniel: "Then the presidents and princes sought to find occasion against Daniel concerning the kingdom; but they could find none occasion nor fault; forasmuch as he was faithful, neither was there any error or fault found in him."

The service was mainly choral; and for the occasion the men and boys of the choir appeared for the first time in surplices—a rather daring innovation for the time. However, as Dr. Dix observed: "Once on, they were never removed, for the sight of the secular costume could not again be endured by persons who had seen the effect of the proper ecclesiastical habit. And so it fell out that we were indebted to one of the royal family of England for the advantage and enjoyment of our surpliced choir."

On the occasion, the prince was well supplied with Prayer Books. A special copy of the Book of Common Prayer was presented by the vestry; it was "bound in red morocco, of royal octavo size, and magnificently embellished; the gold clasp alone, on which was engraved the prince's plumes with the motto '*Ich Dien,*' having cost $250.00." Not to be outdone, Drs. Vinton and Ogilby gave the prince a pocket-sized Prayer Book, "richly bound in brown Russia leather, secured with silver clasps adorned with the Royal Arms, and having the edges of the leaves embossed with gold, silver, and ultramarine." For this attempt to upstage the vestry, the two assistants were later severely reprimanded by that body.

Dr. Vinton concluded his sermon with a prayer for the Queen, the Prince of Wales, the Prince Consort, and all the royal family; adding:

> Let the lesson on this sermon be to each and every one—Be thou pious and faithful; be thou a man, a man of honesty, industry, uprightness and prayer; be thou a whole man—a man of true integrity of character, a Christian man, a Churchman.

Thus admonished, and with the blessing of the bishop, the prince and the royal party took their departure through the doors leading to Broadway, where a strong detachment of police held back the throngs who again cheered the prince as he rode away in his carriage.

THE CIVIL WAR YEARS

New York was a divided and tumultuous city during the Civil War years. Although Abraham Lincoln had been cheered in a campaign speech at Cooper Union, which he later noted as the turning point in his campaign for the presidency, there were many interests in the city that were favorable to the South. New York was still the center of the slave trade with Africa, though it had been illicit since 1820. It was also the chief shipping port for arms and munitions to the South, and New York bankers had advanced to Southerners some $150,000,000 in long-term crop loans. Many of the city's politicians openly or covertly favored the South; indeed, as war loomed ever nearer Mayor Fernando Wood had the audacity to send a message to the city council recommending that New York itself secede from the Union and declare itself a free city.

On the other hand, New York was second only to Boston in the demand of many of its citizens that slavery be abolished, and that a hard line be taken toward the southern states that were threatening secession. Harriet Beecher Stowe had electrified the nation with her book, *Uncle Tom's Cabin*; and John A. Dix, a New York Democrat and secretary of the treasury (as well as the father of Trinity's assistant rector) ordered: "If anyone attempts to haul down the American flag, shoot him on sight."

The attack on Fort Sumter, S.C., on April 12, 1861, little more than a month after Lincoln's inauguration, brought home the fact of civil war to the nation and the city. Thereafter no one could remain neutral; and the departure of New York's Seventh Regiment to reinforce the defense of Washington brought the grim facts home to the nation's metropolis. With the National Guard regiment, as chaplain, went the Rev. Dr. S. H. Weston, an assistant minister of Trinity Church. And from the pulpit of the Rev. Henry Ward Beecher, fiery pastor of Plymouth Congregational Church in Brooklyn, came the shrill demand: "Give me war redder than blood and fiercer than fire!"

No such warlike pronouncements came from the traditionally nonpolitical pulpits of Trinity and its chapels; but the fact of war had to be reckoned with.

On the third Sunday after Easter, eight days after the fall of Fort Sumter, Dr. Morgan Dix, assistant rector of Trinity Church, preached a sermon in St. Paul's Chapel on the Way of God in the Storm. "Brethren," he said, "you can bear us witness that the clergy of the Church are slow to turn their eyes from the study of the word of God and the ministration of the offices of the Church, toward the ways of the outer world. But we too are men, and we must feel as men; and when it is right, we may speak what we feel."

Recalling that it was in this very church that George Washington, just inaugurated, "bowed as a child before the invisible presence of the Lord of lords and King of kings," Dr. Dix called for "the spirits of loyalty, and patriotism, and good faith, and sacred love of country and of law, to stand within these walls, and rule our hearts and minds." He continued:

Here, then, friends and brethren, let us acknowledge the supreme power and glory of the mighty God; and here let us place in His hands the destinies of the nation. Here let us settle it in our minds that there be worse evils in the moral and social world than any storm that may arise and blow out of them. Here let us consider that it is far better to suffer than to be disgraced; that it is better to strive against evil than to succumb to it effetely; that loyalty and unity of heart are virtues for which no transient prosperity could make up to us if haply they were lost; that when the soul of a people moves as it does, thank God, today, with one strong impulse toward that which is just and right, that soul is growing every hour to true nobility and to worthiness of its mission. . . . Here, also, let us offer, for those of our noble-hearted men who have gone away and are to go, to give to their country and their government the best they had to give—their presence, their manly strength, their blood, and if it must be so, their lives—let us offer for them the warmest of Christian prayers from the very deepest places of our souls; and then let us remember that He who holds all issues in His hands, will, in His good time, give back to His people the blessing of peace; and when it is right that we should have it, and when it is so secured as that there shall be no more ground for unrighteous and unbrotherly agitation and controversy, then—but not till then—let us hope that it may come.

Dr. Dix was exercising the leadership that had fallen from the hands of the aged and ill Dr. Berrian, who had had to retire from active duties in the parish. From the time of the death of Mrs. Berrian in April 1860 the rector's health steadily declined, and he was virtually confined to the rectory. On November 7, 1862, in the midst of a storm with driving hail and snow, Dr. Berrian died. In his memorial sermon, Dr. Dix described him as "a man, not of this age and generation, but of the past."

The vestry lost no time in electing Morgan Dix as rector, and the following day he was inducted in the ancient ceremony that is unique in Trinity Parish, dating from Colonial days. George Templeton Strong thus described it in his diary:

> Tuesday at two o'clock we "inducted" the Rev. Morgan Dix according to our corporate usage. The vestry met in the robing room of Trinity Church, came to order, resolved to induct incontinently, and then marched down the north aisle with the Rev. Morgan Dix at our head and all the sextons at our tail, through the north porch and round the tower to the front or "principal" entrance, which was locked. There (William E.) Dunscomb as warden delivered the key to Dix, with a formal declaration that he thereby transferred the church to his charge as rector. The keys of the chapels were in like manner delivered, and then handed by Dix to the sextons. He unlocked the church door, and we marched back to the robing-room, feeling that we had done something rather striking and effective. The curious crowd that gathered on the sidewalk of Broadway outside the church railings to inspect this mystical process probably supposed we were testing some new patent impregnable anti-burglarious lock. . . . This witnessed our connection with churchmen of 1697, and through them with ages longer past, and so rather impressed me. Dix's election seems pretty generally approved.

Of Trinity's "war activities," Dr. Leicester C. Lewis later wrote in the parish history:

> Trinity's contribution to the blood, sweat, and tears of those dark days was made for her by the men of her flock who served and died under their country's colors, by the tireless work of her women, who gave their time and utmost efforts to the relief of the wounded and the suffering and paid their tribute to the dead. We have records of days of humiliation, fasting, and prayer in the parish when darkness overshadowed the country, and days of thanksgiving and solemn *Te Deum* when the sun shone through the war clouds. We have accounts of organized activities to aid the war effort; there are preserved sermons, printed by authority, preached on special occasions, but of more direct involvement in the war there is little to record. How could it be otherwise? The Church was stirred to its depths by the fears and the hopes that surged through the community. She shared them with all the citizens of a temporal world, but she carried on in the troubled days of war with her message of witness to Him whose kingdom is eternal.

In October 1862 the General Convention met in St. John's Chapel, as it had so often before. It was a crucial time in the history of the Episcopal Church, because political secession had inevitably caused a split in the church as well. The southern dioceses had organized themselves into a "national" church, adopted a new constitution, and revised portions of the Prayer Book to adapt it to the political changes. Only the northern dioceses were represented at this convention; but the Rev. Francis Vinton of Trinity, as chairman of the committee on arrangements, provided seats for the absent dioceses as well, and in the House of Bishops the full roll was called. Despite a belligerent opening sermon by Bishop McCoskry of Michigan, and some vigorous debate on political lines, the General

Convention took a mild attitude toward the absent brethren, and so laid the groundwork for reconciliation three years later. Thus the Episcopal Church wisely managed to avoid the permanent split between northern and southern churches, which separated many Protestant denominations for more than a century after the restoration of political union.

On two occasions New York City itself became virtually a battleground.

On July 11, 1863 the drawing of names for induction under the newly enacted Draft Act began in the city. The next day riots began, with mobs attacking the draft centers, the arsenal on Seventh Avenue, police stations, and eventually banks, hotels, newspapers, shops, and private residences. For a week property was burned and looted, and blood flowed freely in the city streets. It was estimated that some 50,000 to 60,000 rioters took part in what amounted to an insurrection; some individual mobs ran as high as 10,000 persons. The police were unable to cope with the situation, and federal troops had to be brought into the city, many of them straight from the battlefield at Gettysburg.

For some reason, the fury of the mobs turned against the city's large Black population; scores of Negroes were hanged from lampposts, hundreds were shot or stabbed, and the Colored Orphan Asylum was attacked and burned.

Behind St. John's Chapel was a garden surrounded by a wall, which separated it from a section of the city inhabited by Blacks, many of whose children attended the chapel Sunday school. Someone tipped off Dr. Dix that a mob was preparing to attack the Negroes there, and to burn down the chapel. At his request, troops were dispatched to the area, forming a defense perimeter which doubtless prevented a bloody massacre.

Total casualties in the draft riots were never known, as the mobs smuggled many victims out of the city and buried them secretly at night. Deaths among the police and soldiers alone numbered over 1,000. More than a hundred buildings were burned down, and 200 others damaged and looted. Property losses were estimated at between $1,500,000 and $5,000,000.

All in all, the Draft Riots marked the darkest chapter in New York's history—and the damage was done not by the enemy but by its own citizens, though there were naturally rumors that Confederate agents had masterminded it, or at least taken advantage of the breakdown of law and order to aggravate the situation.

The other instance of the war coming to New York was definitely a Confederate plot to burn down the city. This took place in November 1864 when eight Confederate agents, each armed with ten fire-bombs, tried to set off as many fires as possible at the same time. The St. Nicholas Hotel was badly damaged, and several other hotels, the Winter Garden Theater, and Barnum's Museum were set on fire; but most of the bombs did not perform very efficiently and scores of small blazes were quickly extinguished. Nevertheless it threw a great scare into the city, and the *Herald* was quite right when it observed that the city had "undoubtedly had a most wonderful escape."

Despite the war, two events of considerable ecumenical importance to the church took place during these years.

On March 13, 1864, after some initial hesitation, Dr. Dix preached the sermon at an interdenominational service at the Baptist Broadway Tabernacle. For an Episcopalian to participate in such a service was virtually a unique event in those days of denominational rivalry, but Dr. Dix accepted the invitation, with permission of the bishop, after being assured that on this occasion the "Episcopal Service" (Morning or Evening Prayer) would be used.

Dr. Dix took the occasion to preach on church unity, and set forth a "working hypothesis" for an approach to such unity. He proposed the Holy Scriptures, with an authoritative interpretation; the Creeds; the threefold ministry; and the rites or sacraments of the church as a basis for mutual study.

This was apparently the first time that such a fourfold pattern was proposed for Christian unity, and it attracted little attention at the time. Twenty-two years later the General Convention in Chicago, with Dr. Dix as president of the House of Deputies, adopted a similar platform, which was reaffirmed two years later by the Anglican bishops in the Lambeth Conference. Known as the Chicago-Lambeth Quadrilateral, this declaration has ever since been considered the basic pattern of the Anglican Communion for Christian unity.

The other notable ecumenical occasion took place in Trinity Chapel, on March 2, 1865, when apparently for the first time, the Divine Liturgy of the Eastern Orthodox Church was sung in an Episcopal Church. The occasion was the arrival of a Russian priest in New York, sent to minister to the growing number of Slavonic people in the city. Bishop Potter gave his permission for the service, but declined to attend it himself. However, other Episcopal clergymen did participate, and the service created much interest, as well as some opposition. The parish history quotes a contemporary account from the *New York Post*:

Trinity Chapel was crowded, and a large number of the Clergy of the Episcopal Church were present. In the Chancel were Bishop Southgate, formerly Missionary Bishop Resident at Constantinople, Rev. Dr. Dix, Rector of Trinity Parish, and Rev. Dr. Thrall (a member of the Russo-Greek Committee, appointed in the General Convention of 1862). Outside of the Chancel were other Clergy of Trinity Parish, and the Rev. Dr. McVickar, the oldest Presbyter in the Diocese of New York.

From sixty to seventy members of the Orthodox Communion (i.e., the Greek Church) occupied seats near the Chancel, and followed the service with close attention, making the sign of the cross and inclinations of the head at the proper points.

The Choir, which sang admirably, was composed of picked singers who volunteered their services, and were rehearsed under the direction of Rev. Freeman Young, who brought the music from Russia. . . .

The long-drawn-out and exhausting Civil War was at last coming to an end. After nine months of siege, on April 3, 1865, Petersburg, Va., was taken by the Union forces, and Lee fell back on Richmond. When the news reached New York, it was quickly followed by a false report that Richmond had also fallen, though actually that did not take place until a week later. Dr. Dix, who was conducting prayers at Trinity when the news was received, notes in his diary:

New York went off at once into fits. There was an immense gathering in Wall Street, at which between 5,000 and 10,000 people sang the Doxology, and the bells of Trinity clattered and clanged as fast as three raw hands could make them go, for the bell-ringer, Aylcliffe, was absent from town. All business ceased, and could not be resumed all day.

George Templeton Strong added: "I walked about on the outskirts of the crowd, shaking hands with everybody, congratulating and being congratulated by scores of men I hardly know even by sight. Men embraced and hugged each other, *kissed* each other, retreated into doorways to dry their eyes and came out again to flourish their hats and hurrah. There will be many sore throats in New York tomorrow." The next morning a 100-gun salute was fired at the foot of Wall Street, and Broadway was "a river of flags."

When the news of Lee's surrender at Appomattox on April 12 reached New York, there was more celebration, muted this time because of a hard all-day rain. But Strong reported: "Guns have been firing all day in spite of foul weather." He adds:

> To Trinity Church at half-past twelve. A meeting of business men yesterday resolved on a *Te Deum*, and arrangements for a service of thanksgiving had accordingly been made, as far as they could be made on such short notice. . . . Service began a little after one o'clock. The church was then jammed to its utmost capacity, and (I am told) there was a dense crowd at its doors. It was an irregular, special service, conforming to no rubric, but the great assemblage joined in it heartily. The "Lesson" was the Beatitudes. Vinton made a very short and a very judicious little address from the pulpit, enforcing the duty of forgiveness and charity. In alluding to the President, he used terms that do his insight credit: "Wise, merciful, resolute, Christian." . . .

Unfortunately, tragically, Lincoln was not to live to exercise his wisdom and mercy toward the defeated South. On the evening of April 14, Good Friday, he was shot in a box at Ford's Theater in Washington; he died early the next morning without regaining consciousness.

From the heights of delirious joy, New York, with the rest of the North, was plunged into the depths of sorrow. Shops were closed and draped with black cloth; flags were lowered to half-staff.

A special meeting of the Trinity vestry assembled on Saturday afternoon. Says Strong: "A series of resolutions was read, drawn by the Rector. They were masculine and good, and they were passed *nem. con.*, though Verplanck and Tillou were in their seats—Copperheads [southern sympathizers] both." He adds:

I looked at the record of our action when Washington died sixty-six years ago. It was a mere resolution that the church and chapels be put in mourning. Our resolutions of today went, naturally, much further. I record to the credit of Gouverneur Ogden, whom I have always held cold-hearted and selfish, that he broke down in trying to read these resolutions, could not get beyond the first sentence, and had to hand them back to the Rector. There was a little diversity of opinion whether we should put our chancel into mourning tomorrow, being Easter Sunday, or postpone it a day longer. We left it to the Rector's discretion.

Next day Strong described the Easter service:

Trinity was never filled so full, not even last Tuesday. The crowd packed the aisles tight and even occupied the choir steps and the choir itself nearly to the chancel rails. The outer doors, by the by, were in mourning, and the flag on the spire edged in black pursuant to my suggestions yesterday. Within the church, the symbols of public sorrow properly gave place to those of Easter. When we came to the closing prayers of the litany, Vinton proclaimed: "I bid you all unite with me in prayer for all of the bereaved and afflicted families of this land, and especially for that of Abraham Lincoln, late President of the United States, recently destroyed by assassination," and read the proper prayer for those in affliction. He then prefaced the usual prayer for a sick person by a like bidding "for the Secretary of State [Seward] and the Assistant Secretary of State, now in peril of death from wounds inflicted on them by an assassin." The effect of these formulas introduced into the service was telling. . . . Vinton's sermon . . . blended the Easter sentiment with that of public grief most skillfully, or I should rather say by presenting suggestions of deep-lying truths that harmonized them. . . ."

The war was over. The president was dead. It was time to turn to the work of reconstruction, under the leadership of a new president, Andrew Johnson. And for Trinity Parish, it was time to gather up the fragments and to reorient its ministry to the needs of the postwar society.

9

The Postwar Years and Rapid Growth

1866-1880

New York City came out of the Civil War more prosperous than ever, but with even more marked disparity between the rich and the poor. The population had dropped from approximately 813,000 to 727,000, but it soon began to renew its upward climb, which was to reach two million by the end of the century. Moreover, the city and county government, under the machinations of "Boss" Tweed, were to reach new depths of corruption, largely through manipulation of the hundreds of thousands of foreign-born. As James Bryce wrote: "Plunder of the city treasury, especially in the form of jobbing contracts, was no new thing in New York, but it had never before reached such colossal dimensions."

POSTWAR GROWTH

It was also the beginning of what came to be known as the age of the moguls—financial wizards whose wars for

The Sanctuary of Trinity Church

control of railroads, shipping companies, banks, and other business enterprises made them multimillionaires at the expense of the workers, small merchants, and ordinary people.

In a small way, Trinity Parish was one of the early victims of the wars of the giants. Cornelius Vanderbilt, whose unofficial title of "Commodore" derived from some of his early coastwise shipping ventures, had gained control of the New York Central Railroad, extending from New York to Buffalo, and was engaged in an effort to eliminate rivalry by adding its main competitor, the Erie, to his transportation empire. But first he needed a freight terminal in midtown Manhattan, and for that purpose he determined to acquire St. John's Park, which ran along Hudson and Varick streets, facing St. John's Chapel, and belonged to the Trinity Corporation.

The story of St. John's Park is an interesting one, marking one of the earliest examples of community planning and zoning in the city's history. As early as 1799, Trinity exchanged some pieces of the Church Farm property with Anthony Lispenard. This area, known as Lispenard Meadows, was a wild tract of land, with underbrush and bulrushes surrounding sluggish ponds draining into a canal that later gave its name to Canal Street. Snakes abounded, as did woodcock and all manner of wildlife, and the ponds were used only by skaters who frequented the spot in winter.

On this unpromising land, the vestry in 1802 determined to build a new chapel of ease. After several sites were tried and abandoned as impractical, a site was selected on slightly higher ground, on the east side of the adjoining Hudson Square, and on it was built a handsome Georgian church with a high steeple that the vestry named St. John's Chapel.

Attention was then turned to clearing and draining Hudson Square, and laying out plots to make it an attractive residential area. At the center of the newly created community, there was designed an "ornamental square without any buildings thereon," for the exclusive use of the residents of the community. With the chapel facing on it, the common land was known as St. John's Park. Title was retained by the corporation and the plots were sold on the ground-lease principle for ninety-nine years. Strict zoning requirements were set up. Houses were to be of fine brick trimmed with good stone and topped with slate roofs. No building could be more than 30 feet high and commercial enterprises were excluded. Each owner of a lot, and his family, had the right of access to the park, cultivated and maintained at the expense of the community, which had exclusive use of the well-kept garden spot.

During the ensuing half century, this garden community became the home of many prominent New Yorkers, among them the widow of Alexander Hamilton, members of the Morton, Delafield, Van Renssalaer, Lorillard, and other families whose names were prominent in New York annals. John Jacob Astor, one of the first new millionaires, had his home there, as did John R. Livingston, a member of Trinity's vestry. The rectory adjoining the chapel was occupied successively by Bishop Hobart, Dr. Berrian, and Dr. Dix.

By the 1860s, however, the city had encompassed St. John's Park and its surroundings were increasingly commercial. Many of the owners were anxious to sell their property and move to the new residential area along Fifth and Madison avenues, but to do so required consent of the rector and vestry; as long as Dr. Berrian lived, no such consent was forthcoming. After his death, Dr. Morgan

Dix, seeing the handwriting on the wall, realized that the days of St. John's Park were numbered.

Thus, when Cornelius Vanderbilt offered the vestry a cool million dollars for the property, the offer was one that could not be resisted—or, at least, was not resisted. Trinity was in hard straits financially and the proceeds would enable the vestry to use $600,000 to reimburse the owners for their loss in equity and to retain $400,000 to reduce the parish debts and ease the financial crisis.

George Templeton Strong, who was absent from the vestry meeting that decided to accept the Commodore's offer, took a dim view of the transaction. "I fear this will stir up a perilous storm of abuse and misrepresentation against us," he wrote. "Forty flagrant lies will be told about the transaction and thirty-nine of them will be firmly believed except by a minority of rational people." His prophecy proved to be largely correct.

Nevertheless, the sale was consummated in 1867. The ink on the deed was scarcely dry when workmen invaded the park and turned its beauty into desolation. Soon the garden spot was gone; in its place stood an ugly three-story freight terminal, surmounted by a huge bronze statue of Commodore Vanderbilt which was to dominate the scene for sixty years until 1929, when the "hideous group of molten images," as Strong described it, was removed and placed before the Grand Central Terminal, where it remains to the present day.

Trinity's financial position was greatly improved by the expiration in 1866 of a long-time ground lease dating from pre-Revolutionary days. The property involved covered some twenty-six acres, originally consisting of rolling hills, woods, and swampy lowlands with small value except as farmland. However, Abraham Mortier, paymaster of the British forces in New York, considered it a good place for a country estate. He negotiated with the vestry to give him a ground lease for ninety-nine years, beginning May 1, 1767, the heirs to remove or sell any improvements at the termination of the lease. Ground rent was to be £2 an acre for thirty-three years, £3 an acre for the next thirty-three years, and £4 an acre to the termination of the lease.

Mortier did not enjoy his country estate for long, though he remained in New York until the evacuation of British troops following the Revolution. After the Revolution, the ground lease was acquired by Aaron Burr and, in turn, it was bought by the first John Jacob Astor early in the nineteenth century.

By 1866 the property, which had once consisted of the fields and well-tended lawns of a country estate, comprised some 355 lots in twelve blocks of city streets, lying between Brannon (Spring) Street and Hamersley (W. Houston) Street, and westward from about modern Sixth Avenue to Greenwich Street. Forty-nine houses stood on this valuable city property, yet Trinity's total income from the ground lease was only $269.00 a year.

With the expiration of the lease, now held by William B. Astor, Trinity was in a position to buy some of the houses and require demolition of others. By agreement with Mr. Astor and a wise exercise of these options, the vestry received, in 1867, a net income from this property of $138,586, with a similar or increasing annual amount in succeeding years.

Prior to the settlement of the Astor lease, Trinity Parish had been running an annual deficit of $25,000 to $30,000. Its cumulative debt in 1865 had been $805,200. Now, the parish was in a position to make substantial payments on the debt and to expand its work, particularly among the poor in lower Manhattan, from which most other churches had departed. A part of that expansion was the addition to the Trinity parochial system of three new chapels: St. Cornelius', St. Chrysostom's, and St. Augustine's.

Among the new chapels, St. Cornelius', on Governors Island, was unique. It was a military chapel, ministering to the needs of the army personnel stationed on that island in New York harbor.

The history of St. Cornelius' goes back to 1844 when the Rev. Dr. John McVickar, a professor at Columbia College, accepted a part-time appointment as civilian chaplain at Fort Columbus (later known as Fort Jay). Despite the fact that Dr. McVickar was fifty-five at the time of his appointment and continued to hold a full-time teaching position, he held his military chaplaincy for eighteen years (1844-1862). He was very faithful in his duties, often under considerable hardships. Living on Manhattan, he had to be rowed in a small boat to the island each Sunday, in all sorts of weather, as there was no ferry service to the military post.

Dr. McVickar not only conducted services at the post every Sunday, but also devoted the rest of the day to giving instructions and counseling to the soldiers and their families. At first his ministrations were conducted in a large room used during the week as the business office of the post, but in 1847, with the permission and encouragement of Major-General Winfield Scott, he drew plans and supervised the construction of a frame church to be the post chapel. No government funds were available, but Dr. McVickar contributed generously from his own earnings and raised additional amounts by personal appeals to his friends and interested churchmen in New York. The small church, which cost about $2,500, was consecrated as the Chapel of St. Cornelius the Centurion by Bishop DeLancey of Western New York on April 19, 1847.

Dr. McVickar continued his one-man ministry to Governors Island and to the recruit depot at Bedloe's Island until a year after the outbreak of the Civil War. At that time the army began assigning military chaplains to its more important posts or requiring that any civilian chaplain reside on the post. As Dr. McVickar was unable to meet this requirement, he was reluctantly obliged to resign his ministry to Governors Island.

After the close of the war, in 1868, the army discontinued its chaplaincy post on the grounds that, since Governors Island was within the boundaries of New York, the churches of that city ought to carry on their service to the military.

As Trinity Church was one of the closest to Governors Island, the rector and vestry made a proposal to the War Department to maintain a clergyman at the post at their own expense on the condition that the Chapel of St. Cornelius be placed at their disposal for the purpose. The government was to furnish quarters and fuel for the clergyman and other facilities normally given to chaplains. On these terms, St. Cornelius' became a chapel of Trinity Parish and the parish assigned the Rev. J. B. C. Beaubien as vicar and chaplain. This arrangement, unique among army posts, continued for nearly one hundred years, with a new and more adequate chapel being built by Trinity in 1906. In later years, the agreement was modified to the extent that the army appointed a military chaplain, always a priest of the Episcopal Church, who was thereupon appointed honorary vicar by Trinity.

Trinity's second new chapel began as an outgrowth of

Trinity Chapel in West 25th Street. The clergy of that chapel, particularly the Rev. Cornelius E. Swope, felt the need for extending the ministrations of the church to the rapidly growing section of the city north of the chapel and began a small mission in temporary quarters among the poor on 32nd Street. The mission attracted the attention of the vestry, which appropriated $775 in 1866 to help move it to more suitable quarters on West 34th Street. After a further small appropriation for furnishings and a visit to the mission by the rector, the vestry decided to put up a permanent church for the mission, now known as St. Chrysostom's Chapel. Accordingly, in 1868 the architect, Richard M. Upjohn, was commissioned to draw plans for a chapel and $66,000 was appropriated for it.

Work was begun on the new chapel, located on the southwest corner of Seventh Avenue and 39th Street, and the first service was held in the unfinished building on November 7, 1869. The Rev. Thomas H. Sill was appointed vicar and the work prospered from the outset, although the chapel was not completed and consecrated until October 30, 1879. The sermon on that occasion was preached by Dr. Neely, then Bishop of Maine. By that time, the area was fast filling up with theaters and the Metropolitan Opera House covered the entire block across from the chapel. Nevertheless, under the devoted leadership of Mr. Sill, who served as vicar for forty-five years, the chapel continued a truly notable ministry among the ever-changing population of that area.

The third of the new chapels was a missionary one, St. Augustine's, located near the Bowery. It grew out of the work among immigrants already being conducted by Trinity in that area, using various rented halls. The first services under the name of St. Augustine's were held in

1869. The Rev. Mr. Beaubien was transferred from Governors Island to be in charge of the chapel, assisted by students from the General Theological Seminary.

Many of the residents of the area of St. Augustine's were Irish and there was great friction between the Roman Catholics and those considered Orangemen. In 1870 the uneasiness broke out into open rioting and bloodshed and an attack on the chapel was feared. Dr. Dix wrote in his diary:

> Shortly after 3 P.M. Mr. Beaubien came to tell me of the threatening look of things in the Bowery and that St. Augustine's was to be attacked. Sent a letter to Governor Hoffman by him. About 4 P.M. my maids came in; they saw with their own eyes the bloody scene on 8th Avenue, cor. of 24th Street, and the streets strewn with dead and wounded. I then went over to St. Augustine's and stayed about an hour, but there seemed no danger. Returned to dinner; and at 8 P.M., as there were rumors that more trouble would begin at dark, I went across to the Bowery and the Mission Chapel; but finding no sign of disturbance, returned to the rectory at 9 P.M.

In 1875 the vestry determined to build a permanent church for St. Augustine's, which had outgrown its rented quarters. Land was purchased on East Houston Street, between the Bowery and Christie Street, for $80,000 and work was begun on a mission house and chapel to cost $120,000. The new edifice was consecrated on November 30, 1877 by the bishop of the diocese, assisted by the clergy of Trinity Parish. The Rev. Dr. Arthur C. Kimber was now in charge of the mission work and the Irish neighborhood was rapidly becoming German. The Germans were succeeded by Italians, who were later inundated by Jewish immigrants. Thus, the ministry of the chapel was a constantly changing one in an effort to keep up with the rapidly shifting population.

In addition to the three new chapels, the growth of St. John's Chapel made alterations and improvements necessary in 1868. Accordingly, the choir of that chapel was enlarged, the organ was partially rebuilt, and additions to the schoolhouse were made.

Trinity Parish now had, in addition to the mother church on Broadway and Wall Street, six active chapels, strategically located on both east and west sides of the city and extending from 39th Street on the north to Governors Island south of the Battery. Its clergy staff numbered more than twenty. It was, in effect, like a small diocese within the larger bounds of the Diocese of New York and was a principal supporter of diocesan missionary enterprises as well. The parish also continued to assist a considerable number of other churches and institutions, though on a somewhat reduced scale because of its own financial difficulties.

In general, the parish was healthy and growing, with a strong sense of missionary responsibility. George Templeton Strong, from his vantage point as a vestryman, deplored the constant "applications from anemic little city parishes," and observed: "Our clergy are generally a feeble folk. I don't think any of the first-grade assistant ministers of Trinity Parish earns a quarter of his salary." Of one of them, whose salary and allowances came to $10,000 a year, he wrote that he was "a positive deadweight upon the parish. His sermons are enough to make one turn 'Positivist' or Swedenborgian or anything else, and I do not know of his doing parochial work of any kind, but perhaps he does."

Morgan Dix was a leader in the Catholic revival in the

Episcopal Church. During his rectorship, the clergy of Trinity Parish were vested in traditional Eucharistic vestments, daily celebrations of the Holy Communion were held, the altars were decorated with flowers and vested in ecclesiastical colors, and the choirs wore cassocks and cottas. For preaching and Morning and Evening Prayer, Dr. Dix wore surplice and stole, instead of the black gown and bands worn by his predecessors. Under his leadership, Trinity Parish became recognized as the principal exponent, at least in New York, of moderate Anglo-Catholic ceremonial, but without the frills and extremes that sometimes characterized the Catholic revival elsewhere. At Trinity and its chapels, the ideal was to render all services "decently and in order," with the beauty of color and lights, but with the restraint of simplicity and good taste.

The time had come, too, for the revival of religious communities of men and women, under the threefold vows of poverty, chastity, and obedience, and in this movement the rector took a leading part. Although a bachelor, Dr. Dix himself took no such vows, but he encouraged the establishment of religious orders, especially of women, and was happy to incorporate the service of Sisters into the life of Trinity Parish.

It was not Dr. Dix, however, or another recognized Anglo-Catholic leader, who took the first steps toward the introduction of the religious life in the Episcopal Church. Dr. William Augustus Muhlenberg, rector of the Church of the Holy Communion in New York City and a leading Evangelical churchman, was the first priest of the American church to encourage the foundation of a Sisterhood, primarily for work in his own parish and in St. Luke's Hospital, of which he was a founder. But Dr. Dix served as one of a committee of five priests appointed by Bishop

Potter to study and report on the feasibility of establishing a more inclusive religious community for women along traditional monastic lines and, as a result of this study, the Community of St. Mary was founded in 1865. On February 2 of that year, in St. Michael's Church, the first five Sisters of this order were professed, with Bishop Potter officiating and eight priests, including Dr. Dix, participating. A year later, the bishop appointed Dr. Dix as chaplain of the community, of which the talented Harriet Starr Cannon became the Mother Superior. Dr. Dix wrote and compiled a rule of life and book of instructions for the community, and for many fruitful years he served as their devoted chaplain and spiritual adviser. He also defended the community from the misunderstandings and antagonisms that inevitably arose from this reintroduction of the Catholic religious life into a church that was regarded by many, even of its own members, as a Protestant communion.

In 1873, at the request of Dr. Dix, the Mother Superior assigned three of the Sisters to work in Trinity Parish. They took charge of the house on Varick Street, near St. John's Chapel, which had formerly been the rectory, and was thenceforth known as Trinity Infirmary or Hospital. Here they worked for many years, ministering to the sick and poor.

Despite their good work and the quiet, unassuming nature of their ministry, the Sisters of St. Mary continued to be the objects of attack by many who considered religious communities as evidence of "Romanism" invading the Episcopal Church. Much of this criticism was quieted when, in 1878, several of the Sisters were sent to Memphis to minister to the sick and dying in a terrible epidemic of cholera that struck in that region, with scenes of horror reminiscent of the Great Plague in London. During a single month, three of the Sisters died of the plague while ministering to its victims, an act of martrydom that went far to still the criticisms of these devoted women who had laid down their lives in the service of the stricken victims, regardless of race, creed, or condition.

Because of the increasing numbers of Germans in the area, Trinity in 1876 began a special German branch of the Sunday school and, a year later, added to its staff a German priest, the Rev. Martin Albert, a former Evangelical missionary to India. A special chapel was assigned to Pastor Albert (as he was known) in Trinity parish house, where he held German-language services on Sundays and weekdays. Similar services were held in St. John's Chapel and, in time, a strong German congregation was built up. However, many of the younger generation preferred to worship at the English-language services and, as the economic status of the German-Americans improved, many of them moved away from the slums to better homes elsewhere. Nevertheless a number of families continued to return to Trinity or one of its chapels for Sunday services, even when living at great distances from the church. The German congregation at the mission house continued for more than thirty years, until the retirement of Pastor Albert in 1909.

Arthur H. Messiter, Mus. D., described by Canon West as "another Englishman in the great succession of Tuckey and Hodges," became Trinity's director of music in 1866, at the age of thirty-two. One of his great services to the parish was the beginning of a splendid library of church music; another was the introduction of the *Trinity Parish Psalter*, replacing an earlier work by a predecessor, Henry S. Cutler. The new book was compiled by the four organists of the parish and introduced a higher standard of music for the Sunday services. These were normally

Morning Prayer, often with the Litany, followed by the sermon and Ante-Communion. Later, the full service of Holy Communion became the norm for the 11 o'clock Sunday service.

In 1870 Dr. Messiter inaugurated what he called "the boldest innovation yet made in the services of Trinity Church, namely the introduction of an orchestra for accompaniment, which was effected on Ascension Day." Messiter had experimented the previous year with the use of a harp to accompany the choir, and the success of this experiment led to the full orchestral service which was to become traditional at Trinity on Ascension Day, also observed as the anniversary of the consecration of the present church in 1846.

On this occasion, the orchestra and choir rendered Gounod's *St. Cecilia Mass*—a work described by Dr. Messiter as "grave, dignified, and generally ecclesiastical." (Canon West, recounting the incident, had a different opinion: "There is a certain quality about Gounod which is like soothing syrup; it corrupts while it comforts.") The service was rendered with some difficulty of coordination, since the choir was in the chancel and the orchestra in the gallery at the back of the church, but the performance, Messiter recorded, "was a complete triumph."

George Templeton Strong, who had encouraged the orchestral plans, wrote in his diary in May 1870:

> Our experimental Ascension Day orchestra at Trinity succeeded beyond my hopes. . . . There were twenty-eight in the orchestra, of which sixteen played string instruments, and the whole orchestra was judiciously reinforced by bass diapasons of the nave organ. Of course the brass was too strong; the trumpet and trombone glared through the violin work as does a conflagration through lace window curtains. The choir and orchestra kept together wonderfully well, considering their re-

moteness from each other. . . . It was the first time anything like an orchestra has accompanied an Anglican church service in New York. May it not be the last.

It was by no means the last such occasion. Indeed, so well was the venture received that it was decided to have an orchestra for the major festivals of Christmas, Easter, and Whitsunday as well. That arrangement lasted only until 1877, but the orchestral accompaniment for the Ascension Day service has continued to the present day. In later years the orchestra played in the crossing, not an ideal situation, but better than before. Since 1968, when choir stalls were removed and the altar transferred to the crossing, both choir and orchestra have been accommodated in the chancel, thus achieving an ensemble never before possible. As Dr. George Mead has noted:

> Many musical hazards were eliminated and some other dangers as well. The day finally had passed when, with a conductor beating time in the crossing at the Offertory, there was an off chance that one of the vestrymen, as he marched up to the chancel, might be struck on the head with a baton—a near thing in the experience of two organists.

Dr. Messiter introduced other innovations into Trinity's musical repertoire, one of them being an annual service with the combined choirs of the mother church and the chapels. He edited an edition of the Hymnal in 1893 and had it adopted in the parish; later it was widely used throughout the Episcopal Church. In July 1897 he retired as musical director of the parish after a distinguished service of thirty years. He was succeeded by Victor Baier, Mus. D., who had started his musical career as a choir boy at Trinity in 1872 and had served as assistant organist under Dr. Messiter, whose style and taste he continued.

Dr. Baier continued as organist of the mother church until his death in 1921.

But this is getting ahead of the story, in the interest of continuity in the account of Trinity's music. We, therefore, return to the history of the parish in the 1860s and early 1870s.

On a brief war-time holiday in upstate Saratoga, a favorite resort of the rector, Dr. Dix recorded in his diary a surprising event, since the entry is dated September 8, 1863:

> Great excitement occurred in the evening when a horseless buggy, propelled by steam, scurried up and down the main street, amid mingled applauses and jeers. It went like fury (*could* go a mile a minute) and made little noise and hardly any smoke. One man, regarding it contemptuously, said that you would never catch him a-setting there stuck up in front of that blamed old tea-kettle! This remark appearing to exhaust the subject, no more was said.

During this period, Trinity Parish was fortunate in having a number of clergymen of unusual ability on its staff. In a single year, 1867, three of these were consecrated to the episcopate.

Daniel Sylvester Tuttle, who was later to serve for twenty years as Presiding Bishop of the Church, was one of these. A son of the parish, Tuttle served as superintendent of the Sunday school at St. Paul's Chapel while attending the General Theological Seminary, and continued at that post after his ordination to the priesthood in 1863, though never formally appointed an assistant minister. At the age of twenty-nine, he was elected Missionary Bishop of a vast jurisdiction including Montana, Idaho, and Utah. He had to wait a year to attain the canonical age of thirty before being consecrated to that office. The service took place on May 1, 1867, at Trinity Chapel, with the combined choirs of the chapel and the mother church participating.

In the same year, on January 25, Henry Adams Neely, assistant minister assigned to Trinity Chapel, was consecrated in that chapel as Bishop of Maine. And on July 25 John Freeman Young, assistant minister assigned to St. John's Chapel, was consecrated at Trinity Church as Bishop of Florida.

At about this time, Dr. Dix was urged to accept nomination as Bishop of Massachusetts, but he refused to let his name be considered. Throughout his ministry, Dr. Dix declined to consider any call that would take him away from his beloved Trinity, including an offer of appointment as professor of ethics and moral philosophy at Columbia (of which, however, he served as trustee), and calls to parishes in Norwich, Conn., Baltimore, and Milwaukee.

The senior assistant minister was Dr. Edward Y. Higbee, whom George Templeton Strong praised as "by far the most eloquent and impressive preacher I have ever listened to." He died December 10, 1871, at the age of sixty-two, and his funeral at Trinity Chapel attracted an overflow attendance that bore testimony to the respect and affection in which he was held.

An equally great loss was sustained when Dr. Francis Vinton died on September 29, 1872. At the time of Dr. Dix's election as rector, Dr. Vinton had been the regular preacher at the parish church, and the rector left him in that position, remaining himself at St. Paul's Chapel. It was Dr. Vinton who introduced the Holy Communion at Trinity on every Sunday and Prayer Book holy day, with the celebrant wearing traditional Eucharistic vestments and with dignified but not extreme Catholic ceremonial.

After Dr. Vinton's death, Dr. Dix took his proper place at the mother church, assisted by Dr. Frederick Ogilby and one or two junior ministers. Dr. Benjamin Haight, now the senior assistant minister, took charge of St. Paul's Chapel, with Dr. James Mulchahey as his senior assistant.

At this time, in addition to the Sunday schools, each of the chapels (except St. Cornelius') had a well-equipped day school, but the school at Trinity Church itself was hampered by inadequate facilities. The parish, therefore, bought lots on New Church Street (now Trinity Place), directly behind the parish church, for something over $67,000 and in 1871 built a fine, well-equipped school there. The building also served other purposes, notably for choir rehearsals and as headquarters of the American Guild of Organists. There the school continued for nearly half a century; after World War I, it was sold for $175,000 and became a part of New York University.

The parish was growing rapidly, both in numbers and in spiritual vitality. Baptisms and confirmations in the mother church and its chapels led the whole diocese during the 1870s. Dr. Dix records an Easter festival at St. John's Chapel at which, in a single service, there were sixty or seventy baptisms, with two priests administering the sacrament simultaneously. A week later he records that the bishop confirmed fifty-eight persons at Trinity Chapel.

" 'O Cupid, king of gods and men', what have I heard today!" So began George Templeton Strong in his diary entry for January 16, 1874. What he had heard, in a roundabout way, was that "Morgan Dix is engaged to Miss [Emily] Soutter, Mrs. Ned Bell's younger sister."

Mr. Strong might well be surprised. For one thing, as warden and comptroller of Trinity Parish, and a close personal friend of Dr. Dix, he might have been a little miffed to hear the news at second or third hand. For another, he did not know the young lady, though "her sister, Mrs. Bell, is charming and kindly, with the special attractiveness that belongs to the best Southern women, or women of Southern descent."

Others were surprised, too, for Dr. Dix was forty-seven years old and had long been considered a confirmed bachelor, if not one vowed to celibacy. The bride-to-be was only twenty-three, but Mr. Strong generously observed that, in his opinion, "the disparity of age is nothing." Later, when he came to know the young lady, whom he found "intelligent and interesting rather than pretty," he gave her and the marriage his strong approval.

The marriage took place June 3, 1874 at the home of the bride's mother on East 17th Street. Bishop Potter officiated; the ceremony was a simple one attended only by a few invited guests, principally the clergy and vestry of the parish and their wives. Strong observed that "Morgan Dix looked like a beatified saint and, as it were, phosphoresced from brow to boots." The vestry granted the rector six months' leave of absence and a gift of $5,000. The couple thereupon departed for a trip to Europe. On their return in November, Strong recorded an anecdote about his rector:

> While in London, he went to the illustrious Poole's to order some clothes. The urbane salesman said, "Certainly, sir, with great pleasure, sir; but then we don't take orders, sir, from strangers, sir, without some kind of reference, sir." "Oh-ah—of course, very proper," said the Rev. Morgan Dix, and produced from his pocket a letter of introduction from Bishop Potter to the Archbishop of Canterbury. The salesman hummed and hesitated and then said: "Yes, sir, a most flattering endorsement, sir. It would carry great weight, sir, in clerical circles, sir, but it won't do here, sir." So the Rev. Mr. Dix had to go into the city and get a letter from his banker.

While Dr. Dix was away, the General Convention was again held in St. John's Chapel. As comptroller of the host parish, Strong noted that the convention would cost Trinity "not less than $8,000—feed included." Later he observed: "The General Convention thinks its oysters too small. So I assumed the responsibility of ordering bigger oysters and, also, of issuing them daily instead of every other day. Anything to inspire the Council of the Church with the spirit of peace and harmony, which is the fruit of good living and eupepsia." Alas, the convention went down in history as one that was torn by churchmanship controversies, despite the fact that, as Strong noted at its conclusion, its members had "devoured, absorbed, ingulphed, ingested, bolted, gobbled, munched, masticated, ingurgitated, deglutinated, and, I hope, digested and assimilated 80,000 oysters." He also observed resignedly that the hospitality committee "expects the long-suffering corporation of Trinity Church to pay its deficit of some $7,000 (hotel bills)."

The following year, George Templeton Strong was taken seriously ill. He was granted a leave of absence as comptroller, and General Dix assumed the post, supposedly on a temporary basis, but, on July 21, 1875 Strong died. His funeral at Trinity Church was attended by a great gathering and we are told that "the choir, remembering with affection its patron, sang Croft's service with notable excellence."

The year 1876 marked the one-hundredth anniversary of the Declaration of Independence and was celebrated throughout the country as National Centennial Year. Trinity's part in the observance was a great service on July 4, at which the Bishop of New York was present and the sermon was preached by the rector. Following the sermon, the choir, under the direction of Dr. Messiter, sang a solemn *Te Deum* to music written by Sir Arthur Sullivan. As an unexpected accompaniment, at noon, just as the choir reached the words "Heaven and earth are full of the majesty of Thy glory," guns from the forts and men-of-war in the harbor roared in a mighty salute. As the parish history notes, the heavy artillery continued "in an accompaniment like muffled thunder far along the course of the all-but-inspired words of that grandest of all hymns of the Church."

Sisters of another Anglican order were added to Trinity Parish in 1876. These were members of an English order, the Community of St. John Baptist, some of whom had come to this country in 1874 to open work of a settlement type on lower Second Avenue, which later grew and became the Holy Cross Mission. Dr. Dix turned to these devoted women to undertake similar work under the auspices of Trinity Parish.

About March 1, 1876 Sister Edna, C.S.J.B., perhaps with another Sister, took up residence in a tenement house on Greenwich Street, adjoining the Home for Aged Women which the rector had started a few years before. The Sisters began a systematic visitation of the many tenements in the neighborhood, bringing many to baptism or confirmation and reporting or referring any needing medical aid or poor relief. The people among whom they worked were mostly immigrants, mainly Germans, English, and Irish, but including Norwegians, Swedes, Danes, French, Spaniards, Scots, and a scattering of "Africans."

A year later the Sisters, now three in number, were more suitably housed on Morris Street, near the tip of Manhattan, where the Home for Aged Women was also moved and a mission house established. They had the aid of a devoted physician, Dr. L. S. P. Fitch, and more serious cases were sent to the Trinity Infirmary on Varick Street.

For the year 1877 the Sisters of St. John Baptist listed

4,520 home visits, 12 adult and 175 children's baptisms, and 117 confirmations. They continued their tireless work until 1880, when they had to withdraw from Trinity Parish to meet other commitments.

THE ASTOR MEMORIAL

In November 1875 William B. Astor had died. Son of an immigrant who had made a fortune in the fur trade, Astor had increased his wealth by real-estate dealings and, by 1855, was listed as the wealthiest of New York's millionaires. He left some twenty million dollars to his son, John Jacob Astor, a vestryman of Trinity since 1865, who was in turn to increase the family wealth during his lifetime to something over one hundred million dollars.

John J. Astor and his brother, William Astor, decided to erect a magnificent memorial to their father in the form of a handsome marble altar and stone reredos for Trinity Church. The rector and vestry approved the plan and appropriated an additional $40,000 for necessary structural changes to add choir and robing rooms behind the wall against which the reredos would be erected. Frederick C. Withers was engaged as architect, both for the memorial and for the other improvements. Because of the great weight of the stone, it was also necessary to lay massive new foundations under the chancel and to erect scaffolding from floor to ceiling. Thus the church had to be closed for a period of time in early 1877 and parish services were again temporarily transferred to St. Paul's Chapel.

When the Rt. Rev. Horatio Potter, Bishop of New York, dedicated the new memorials on June 20, 1877, parishioners and the public, for the first time, saw the splendid reredos and altar.

The reredos occupies nearly the whole width (35 feet)

of the chancel and is carried up to the sill of the large seven-light window, topped by a triangular arch enclosing a statue of the risen and reigning Christ and surmounted by a stone cross. The main part of the reredos, constructed of Caen stone elaborately carved, depicts the twelve apostles. Under them are panels showing scenes in the life of our Lord. In the center, under a large multifoiled arch, is a striking representation of the Crucifixion in high relief. On the left of the cross stand St. John and the Blessed Virgin Mary. Kneeling, and embracing our Lord's feet, is Mary Magdalene; on the right is the other Mary and the Centurion. Underneath are carved the words: "Behold the Lamb of God." Panels showing the Resurrection and Ascension are sculptured above the central scene. Under the cornice of the main bays is inscribed in raised letters: "To the glory of God and in memory of William B. Astor this reredos is erected, A.D. 1877." Angels with uplifted wings, playing musical instruments, crown the four buttresses.

Beneath the reredos is the 11-foot altar of pure white statuary marble, with symbolic emblems and a head of our Lord in the center and symbols of the four evangelists at the ends, flanked by two kneeling angels. The super-altar is of red Lisbon marble, with the words "Holy, Holy, Holy" inlaid in mosaics. Above it is a scene of the Lord's Supper, after the fresco by da Vinci.

The writer of the parish history notes:

> The reredos of Trinity Church is the focal point of the edifice to which all eyes turn. It is remarkable as one of the first of its kind in this country built on such a large scale. Enrichment of the sanctuary by such traditional structure would probably have met with much opposition in earlier times before the Oxford Movement turned Churchmen's minds toward the value

of beauty in the fabric of churches. However that may be, the design of the reredos fits perfectly into the general scheme of Trinity's architecture; its rich carvings glow in the quiet setting of the church, which without it might well seem a little somber.

For nearly ninety years thereafter, a large cross stood on the altar, on which the Holy Sacrifice was offered at all principal services in the church. With the remodeling of the chancel in 1968 and the erection of a new altar at the crossing, the old altar fell into disuse and now remains bare. Thus the changes in liturgical custom render the old obsolete, at least for a period of time, but who knows when the old may again come into its own and be made new? Meanwhile the magnificent reredos still stands to the glory of God and continues as a unique and beautiful feature of Trinity Church.

In the latter years of the decade of the 1870s, death claimed two of Trinity's most distinguished clergymen and its senior warden and comptroller, the rector's father.

Dr. Frederick Ogilby, at the age of sixty-four, was relieved of his preaching duties in 1877, but continued as superintendent of the Trinity day school, which had been under his direction from its inception. He died March 25, 1878, after twenty-three years of service in the parish.

Dr. Benjamin Haight was also retired in 1877, at the age of sixty-eight, and died on February 21, 1879. Besides his manifold duties in the parish, Dr. Haight had served as a professor in General Theological Seminary, as secretary of the diocesan convention for twenty years, and as a prominent deputy to the General Convention in 1868, 1871, and 1874. He was known as a master of debate and a brilliant speaker and preacher.

John A. Dix died on April 21, 1879, at the age of eighty-one. He had had the remarkable distinction of serving as a commissioned officer in two wars half a century apart—as an ensign in the War of 1812, and as a major-general in the Civil War. A practicing attorney, he had served in civil life as secretary of the Treasury, minister to France, and governor of New York. In Trinity Parish, he was a vestryman from 1850 to 1876, and again in 1879, warden from 1876 to 1878, and comptroller in 1872 and again from 1875 until his death.

HOAX OF THE CENTURY

In the year 1880 Washington's birthday fell on a Sunday. It was a day for civil and military observances and for commemoration in the churches of the Father of His Country. No one was surprised, therefore, when a small group of aged veterans of the War of 1812 filed into St. Paul's Chapel just before the opening of the morning service and took their places in and about Washington's pew—no one, that is, except the Rev. Dr. James Mulchahey, who was about to begin the service. On inquiry, he found that the veterans had been promised that the rector would preach an appropriate sermon for them on the occasion, but the rector was not in sight and his assistant had no knowledge of such an appointment. Embarrassed, Dr. Mulchahey welcomed the veterans, explained that there had been "some oversight," and hastily adapted his sermon to bring in some reference to the brave soldiers of 1812.

If there was what, in modern terminology, would be called a "communications gap" between Drs. Dix and Mulchahey, it could be explained by the harassing experiences that the rector had undergone during the previous four days, which had doubtless driven the Sunday appointment right out of his head. Dr. Dix did remember his appointment at the afternoon service in Trinity Church, where he delivered a patriotic sermon to some sixty Civil War veterans and a large congregation.

Dr. Dix's harassment had begun the previous Wednesday, and was to continue for more than a month, to the ultimate delight of the readers of the daily press. But, at the time, no one outside the rectory knew anything about it—no one, that is, except "Gentleman Joe," the instigator of one of the monumental hoaxes of the nineteenth century.

It all began in a small way. In the Wednesday morning mail, the rector received a letter from the Acme Safe Company saying that a representative would call in response to his inquiry. Dr. Dix wrote a courteous reply, indicating that there must be some mistake, as he did not need a safe and had sent no inquiry. Nevertheless, the salesman arrived, hard on the heels of the letter, and Dr. Dix had some difficulty in convincing him of the error.

The salesman was not the only caller that day. He had scarcely departed when a faculty member of a girls' school arrived, affirming that the school would be an ideal place for the twenty young parish wards about whom he had written. Pressed for further information, the teacher produced a postcard inquiry signed "Rev. Morgan Dix," but obviously not in his handwriting.

Before the day was over, Dr. Dix had a score of other callers, all apparently summoned by postcard, offering him such things as a pair of matched bay horses, a wig for his head (which was well covered by his own hair), and dancing lessons for twenty-five Sunday school teachers. The afternoon mail (for those were the innocent days in which mail was delivered more than once daily) offered him dozens of bargains in locks, stoves, kitchenware, and other items, all in response to alleged inquiries about large-scale purchases for parish use.

The next few days the stream of callers and the deluge of mail continued, indeed increased. Among the callers were four organ dealers, three purveyors of farm equipment, and other salesmen, some from as far away as Boston and Philadelphia. The rector, who insisted on seeing each person himself and not leaving servants to turn them away, became increasingly exasperated and annoyed—as did the salesmen, who found it hard to believe that their prospect had not sent inquiries to their firms. Mail now poured in not only from New York, but from cities as far away as Detroit, Chicago, and St. Louis. Each thanked him for his inquiry and offered merchandise ranging from breakfast food to steam engines. The rector was not amused but he kept his troubles to himself. It was no wonder that he forgot his Sunday commitment to the Veterans of 1812, though his father, until his death a year previously, had been their acknowledged leader.

Sunday was a day of respite from his tormentors, but on Monday the tempo increased almost geometrically. That day brought to the rectory door some twenty-eight dealers in old clothes to buy discarded garments from Mrs. Dix's wardrobe—each having been summoned by postcard. He collected many of these cards and noted that on each a definite time was specified, spaced at intervals of fifteen minutes. Despite the cold and snow, many of the poor itinerant dealers camped outside with their wagons and pushcarts, attracting a gaggle of children and curious passersby. In the afternoon, fourteen pawnbrokers turned up and the crowds grew so great that Dr. Dix finally resorted to a new and little-used invention, the telephone, which the vestry had recently had installed for his convenience. He spun the little crank and asked the operator to connect him with the police. A squad of bluecoats soon arrived and dispersed the crowd.

Next to arrive was a prominent physician, who had been summoned by a messenger to treat the rector for an epileptic fit. Other doctors arrived until far into the evening, each having been called to treat the rector or his wife or daughter for some imaginary ailment. (Author's query: How could you get even one doctor to make a house call today on a vague message from one who was not a long-time patient?)

The mail became more personal and embarrassing. A manufacturer offered to clothe all the Sisters of St. Mary in whalebone corsets. And several clergymen, including at least one bishop, wrote to know why the rector had criticized them for not answering previous letters, which they denied having received. Each of these required a tactful and courteous answer.

But then came a letter from an alleged classmate, signed with initials that Dr. Dix did not recognize, stating that a friend who "professes to know all about your private affairs" had been sending the letters and would desist for $1,000 if Dr. Dix would place a notice in a newspaper personal column reading: "Gentleman Joe—all right. M.D."

This appeared to be a serious attempt at blackmail. Dr. Dix had no "private affairs" that had to be concealed, and neither did he consider yielding to the implied threat. Instead he called his carriage and took the letter to the post office and gave it, with all the postcards he had been able to get from his callers, to the local postmaster. The latter called in James Gayler, superintendent of city delivery and a former special agent. They promised to get on the trail and try to find "Gentleman Joe." They also advised Dr. Dix to consult an attorney and to notify the police, both of which he did.

Returning to the rectory, Dr. Dix ran the gauntlet of some forty shoe dealers, prepared to submit bids for fitting shoes to the poor children of the parish, only to find himself faced with a new problem. Fourteen clergymen of neighboring parishes had accepted his supposed invitation to a luncheon to meet the Bishop of Exeter—who, so far as Dr. Dix knew, was on the other side of the Atlantic. Patiently, Dr. Dix explained his predicament and served his visitors tea, since Mrs. Dix could hardly prepare a more generous repast with no advance notice.

After this, there was a short respite, while the police and postal inspectors pursued their separate and fruitless inquiries. The Post Office officials even went to the length of posting plainclothes guards at every mailbox along Fifth Avenue, to unlock the box and examine every postcard mailed by a citizen, however innocent he might appear.

And, of course, by this time the newspapers were in on the hoax and it was a secret no more. Every detail was published and, when the mysterious callers resumed their activities, large crowds awaited them outside the rectory. Police blocked off 25th Street and a 24-hour guard was posted to protect Dr. and Mrs. Dix and their child, who they feared might be kidnaped. Nevertheless, on one memorable day, Dr. Dix had fifty callers, including a tattoo artist, four lawyers to advise Mrs. Dix on a divorce, and an undertaker to measure the rector for a coffin.

After many false leads, the authorities eventually tracked down "Gentleman Joe" in Baltimore. He turned out to be a former Sunday school teacher at Trinity Chapel, who had been dismissed for immorality many years before. The dismissal had been by an assistant minister and Dr. Dix did not even know the man, who called himself E. Fairfax Williamson, and claimed (falsely) to be a member of the famous Fairfax family of Virginia. He denied having a grudge against Dr. Dix, and said, "I seem to have eccentricities at times, which are too much for me to understand. . . . I suppose it may have been a practical joke."

Williamson voluntarily returned to New York where an unsympathetic judge, who did not appreciate practical jokes, sentenced him to three and a half years at hard labor. He died of ulcers in the Sing Sing Prison Hospital after he served only eight months of his sentence.

A Trinity Congregation at Worship

10

Trinity Extends Its Outreach

1880-1900

Until 1880 the support of Trinity Mission House and other medical, missionary, and social service activities among the poor had been funded from normal parish funds, supplemented by receipts from an annual appeal to the congregations of the mother church and chapels. Dr. Dix felt, however, that the members of the congregations should have more personal involvement in this important work. In a great missionary sermon, he pointed out the vast field that lay at the very doors of the church among the 25,000 poor, foreign-born, and unchurched men, women, and children of lower Manhattan. He appealed for volunteers and for funds adequate to rent a better and larger mission house and to expand the neighborhood missionary activities that were meeting with a good response.

> The congregation of Trinity Church [he said] might make itself felt as a real, vital power in this parish and in this city. It might afford an example of what can be done by a band of

warm-hearted, devout, thoughtful men and women who are drawn to each other by that highest of bonds, the love of Jesus Christ; who respect and regard each other and are a united household; who wish to work together for definite ends and objects, under a sense of individual responsibility, and with the same interest in the practical charities of the church as that they now feel in her service and worship. That is the point at which we should aim, and so I do not ask for *yours*, first, but for *you*.

In response to the rector's challenge, a group of distinguished parishioners met at the rectory on 25th Street on January 27, 1880 to form a committee on ways and means. Two weeks later a larger group of forty parishioners founded the Trinity Church Association, dedicated to the support and extension of various parochial and charitable works downtown under the auspices of Trinity Church.

The original group of forty gradually grew to an average of 125, among them members of the Roosevelt, Astor, Auchmuty, Cutting, Gorham, Swords, Delafield, Stewart, Glenn, and other families famous in the history of the city. They not only gave generously of their financial means but took an active part in directing the various activities. In the words of Canon C. T. Bridgeman, historian of the association, "Trinity's congregation came alive as a vital force for community good and the furtherance of the Church's mission."

The original program, as outlined in 1880, marked the course that the association was to carry out in the ensuing years:

1. Financial support for a proper mission house, located on State Street until a permanent home was built in 1887 at 211 Fulton Street.
2. Provision of a dispensary under a competent physician at the mission house.

3. Training facilities for young girls under the Sisters at the mission house.
4. Quarters for guilds and organizations for young men and boys.
5. Opening of a summer rest home, originally at Far Rockaway and later at Trinity Seaside Home, Great River, Long Island.
6. Facilities for popular lectures and entertainments for the downtown residents; this was made possible when the Fulton Street property was established.

To these were added various projects in course of time: a kindergarten, a relief and unemployment bureau, a monthly magazine, an Americanization program, and other services. All were supported by the association itself, a lay organization under direction of the rector, without recourse to vestry funds.

When the Sisters of St. John Baptist had to withdraw from the work at the mission house because of other commitments, the Sisters of St. Mary undertook the parochial work and that of the clinic and infirmary. They also had charge of furnishing of the altars at Trinity and St. Paul's, taught Sunday school, instructed girls and women for confirmation, directed guilds, and assisted the clergy of the parish in every way possible. The able and efficient Sister Superior of Trinity Mission House for twenty-five years was Sister Eleanor, C.S.M.; with her, at the mission house, lived three or four other Sisters assigned from time to time by the Mother Superior at Peekskill, New York, where the main convent was located.

THE NEW TRINITY MISSION HOUSE

The mission house on Fulton Street was a six-story fireproof building, well designed for its purpose. The dispensary was installed in the basement, with its own entry. The first floor contained reception and meeting rooms and a people's chapel, later named St. Christopher's. On the second floor was the kindergarten, with the Sisters' oratory above. The upper floors were given over to guild rooms, Sisters' quarters, rooms for "house children" in domestic training, dining rooms and kitchen.

The growth of Trinity's activities made it necessary to construct new and improved office facilities and quarters for the clergy assigned to duties in the lower part of the city. The building used for these purposes at the westerly end of the graveyard of St. Paul's Chapel had long been considered obsolete, but could not be enlarged or rebuilt because a part of it was leased to the city and used as a firehouse. In 1885 arrangements were made to transfer the fire apparatus to a building of its own on Vesey Street and the old building was then torn down.

On the same site, a new building was erected with adequate accommodations for offices for the rector and comptroller and parish house facilities, with living quarters for the unmarried clergy of the parish. The building was a handsome one, designed by the architect Charles Haight and erected at a cost of $150,000. It fronted on the churchyard with a pleasant outlook, but the rear was only a few yards from the new Sixth Avenue elevated railroad, with its noise and smoky trains, then operated by steam power. Nevertheless, the building was to continue in use into the twentieth century. It finally had to be torn down in 1926 when the city widened Church Street and condemned a part of the property for the BMT subway.

A truly ecumenical event took place at Trinity Church in the autumn of 1880, when the Rt. Rev. Eduard Herzog, Bishop of the Old Catholic Church in Switzerland, visited New York. The Old Catholics were a considerable body of Dutch, German, and Swiss churchmen who broke away from the Roman Catholic Church after the First Vatican Council in 1870, in protest over its declaration of the infallibility of the Pope. In 1874 the House of Bishops of the Episcopal Church appointed a committee to keep up a "fraternal correspondence" with the Old Catholic bishops, and it was doubtless as a result of this correspondence that Bishop Herzog visited Episcopal churches in this country.

Two entries in the diary of Dr. Dix record what was undoubtedly the first instance of intercommunion between the Episcopal and Old Catholic Churches, which were not to enter into a formal relationship of full communion until half a century later (1934):

> Sunday, September 19th. In the forenoon went to Trinity: preached from Romans 5: 3, 4, 5, and celebrated. Bishop Herzog came down with Dr. Nevin, and a German deacon, and was present at our service and received the Holy Communion at my hands. He wore a cassock and short surplice trimmed with broad lace, and a handsome embroidered white stole, with a gold chain and pectoral cross around his neck.
>
> Sunday, October 10th. This was a great Historical day for the Church: Bishop Herzog was celebrant at Trinity: the first time he has celebrated anywhere out of his own communion. He was assisted by the Bishop of Albany and Dr. Nevin. The only parts of the service which he took were the absolution, the Canon and the Benediction. He wore a silk chasuble, white, with a cross handsomely orphreyed, albe and cope with deep lace, pectoral cross and chain, amice, crossed stole. His manner was intensely reverent. Immense congregation present, among whom were the Bishops of Virginia and Florida and a great many clergy. Morning Prayer was said by Messrs. Douglas, Hitchings and Frisby. It was a great epoch in our History.

Dix had high regard for and close friendship with the Rt. Rev. Horatio Potter, Bishop of New York since 1855, when Dix had come to Trinity as an assistant minister.

When the aging bishop called for a coadjutor in 1883, Dr. Dix was somewhat embarrassed to find himself nominated to the position, as the Anglo-Catholic candidate, while the bishop's nephew, Henry Codman Potter, was the nominee of the Evangelicals, or low churchmen. The younger Potter won the election and, even before his uncle's death in 1887, he was in active charge of the diocese. Dr. Dix gave the same loyalty to the new bishop that he had to the old one and their friendship was equally cordial. Bishop H. C. Potter, for his part, "made a scrupulous effort to be thoroughly non-partisan, and his administration of the diocese was marked by a breadth and tolerance that were unusual for the time," wrote Dr. William W. Manross. Dix worked closely with both bishops as president of the diocesan standing committee, a position which he held from 1868 until his death.

In the autumn of 1886 Dr. Dix went to Chicago to attend the 35th General Convention of the Episcopal Church, the first one held in the middle west. It was the fourth General Convention at which he had served as a deputy and he had frequently been mentioned or nominated for the presidency of the House of Deputies. At Chicago he was elected as president on the first ballot in a field of four candidates. Thereafter, at four successive triennial Conventions, he was re-elected by acclamation to this highest national office open to a priest or layman of the church. Although Dr. Dix was again chosen by the Diocese of New York as chairman of its clerical deputation in 1901, held in San Francisco, he did not attend that convention or subsequent ones.

At the time of his death, the *Churchman* made the following editorial comment:

It is as president of the House of Deputies in the General Convention, to which New York made him seven times a delegate, that Dr. Dix became a national figure in the American Church, universally regarded with a respect that was akin to veneration, yet had in it also something of affection. His gracious dignity, his noble presence, his judicial impartiality, his unfailing command of parliamentary situations, however tense or complex, set a standard for the emulation of his successors which has already become a tradition.

Morgan Dix was the second clergyman of Trinity Parish to be elected president of the House of Deputies, Dr. Abraham Beach having served in that capacity for three terms in the early years of the nineteenth century. Another member of the parish, this time a layman and member of the Trinity vestry, was to serve three terms as president in the mid-twentieth century, making Trinity the only parish in the country to contribute three members to the presidency of the House of Deputies, for a total of eleven terms.

Despite his activity in diocesan and national church affairs and the growing recognition of his leadership in the Anglo-Catholic movement and in social service projects, Dr. Dix devoted most of his efforts to the parish, of which he had now been rector for twenty-five years. In his address at a service in November 1887 Dr. Dix gave some striking statistics to emphasize the growth of the parish during the past quarter-century:

In 1862 there were in the parish nine clergy; in 1887 eighteen. In 1862 there were 371 baptisms; in 1887, 1,158. In 1862 there were 206 confirmations; in 1887 there were 488. In 1862 the communicants numbered 1,227; and in 1887 there were 5,535. In 1862 there were 99 marriages; in 1887, 268. The burials in 1862 were 128; and in 1887, 100. In 1862 the children in the schools numbered 2,770; in 1887 there were 7,071. In 1862 the contributions of the parish were $22,000; in 1887, $91,000. The contributions of Trinity Church alone were $2,189 in 1862 and $47,000 in 1887.

In addition, the rector noted, three new chapels—St. Cornelius', St. Chrysostom's, and St. Augustine's—had been added to the parish system. The new mission house on Fulton Street marked the growth of the parish in social service. Truly the parish had good reason to rejoice at the record of growth, not only in numbers but in maturity and realization of its mission to the underprivileged as well as the well-to-do.

In the same year, two unusual services connected with foreign royalty were held in Trinity Church. On May 22, 1887 Queen Liliuokalani of the Hawaiian Islands, a devout Anglican, attended the Sunday service, occupying the same pew in which King Edward VII, while Prince of Wales, had sat in 1860. And, on June 19, an elaborate service was held to commemorate the fiftieth anniversary of the accession of Queen Victoria. The church was crowded, largely with people of English origin, and the Rev. D. Parker Morgan, rector of the Church of the Heavenly Rest, preached an appropriate sermon.

No account of New York City in this period would be complete without some record of the Great Blizzard of 1888. It began on Sunday, March 11, following the mildest winter in seventeen years. The forecast was "Cloudy followed by light rain and clearing," and the Sunday papers were filled with advertisements for spring merchandise. The day began in accordance with the forecast. The temperature rose to 40 degrees at noon and, shortly after, a light rain began to fall. But then the temperature began to drop, the rain developed into a downpour and turned to sleet, then snow, driven by winds of near-hurricane force. By Monday morning streets were blocked, railway service came to a halt, and the horse-cars were taken off the streets. The elevated also ground to a halt and passengers had to be removed from the trains by volunteers with ladders, who charged them whatever the traffic would bear.

Dr. Dix wrote in his diary:

> We saw few people out; many falling in snow drifts; locomotion about ceased. Carriages could not get through the streets, which in many places were drifted 6 feet deep or more; and, most remarkable of all, the dead had to be kept unburied, as it would have been impossible to get them to the cemeteries. Not a vessel left the port and not a train from any quarter could reach the city.
>
> There was something awful in the noise of the gale and in the whole appearance of the city. At night many of the lights gave out. Even birds flew boldly into houses for shelter and safety; one came into our own; a shy [bird] took refuge in the park and was brought in and fed. . . . I spent the whole day, almost, writing a sermon for Sunday. The children were overjoyed, as their teacher could not come; it was an extemporized and unexpected holiday and so the more delightful.

The storm continued all day Monday and the wind drove the snow into drifts thirty feet high in places. "A man standing at a Broadway and Ann Street window watched in disbelief as a snowbank grew before his eyes until it covered the fence around St. Paul's Chapel." On Tuesday the storm had abated, but walls of snow blocked all the streets west of Seventh Avenue. The church and chapels were mostly inaccessible; the vestry meeting was called off when only three men showed up, and Dr. Dix "kept the house all day Tuesday." He recorded that "our deep sunk area at the rear of the rectory [on W. 25th Street] was on a level, with the church ground beside it 10 feet above. The snow drifted in front of the house must have been 6 feet deep. . . . The accounts in the morning papers gave such a chronicle as never read before; and as yet we have not begun to receive the intelligence of the innumerable disasters which must have occurred. . . . We had a terrible panic about the approach of another snow storm but it did not come."

It was not until Thursday that the vestry was able to have an adjourned meeting at 187 Fulton Street and Dr. Dix recorded it as "one of the most important ever held. A large scheme was approved looking to outlays of $1,250,000 and it was ordered that land for a chapel west of the park should be bought" for the future St. Agnes' Chapel.

A notable service, of national significance, was held at St. Paul's Chapel on April 30, 1889. The nation was celebrating the centennial of the inauguration of George Washington as the first president, and the current president, Benjamin Harrison, was the guest of the city for the occasion.

President Harrison arrived by ferry at the foot of Wall Street on Monday, the 29th. After an address of welcome by Hamilton Fish, the president and his entourage went in procession to the Equitable Building, while the bells of Old Trinity played a selection of national airs. On his arrival at the arcade, a battalion of artillery presented arms and the massed choirs of Trinity Church and St. Chrysostom's Chapel sang a hymn. This was followed by the Doxology, accompanied by the bugles of the artillery. A reception was then held, the president being surrounded by the members of his Cabinet and the governors of twenty-nine states. Altogether, it was a far more elaborate ceremony than that accorded the first president, even though his current successor was hardly of Washington's stature.

The service at St. Paul's the next day was much simpler, being so far as possible a replica of the service following Washington's inauguration in 1789. The president and vice president (Adlai Stevenson, grandfather of his more famous namesake) were received by the bishop, the rector, and wardens and vestrymen of Trinity Parish, and were seated in Washington's pew. The governor of New York sat in the governor's pew, the mayor and members of the president's Cabinet were given appropriate places, as were ex-presidents Hayes and Cleveland. The entire floor of the chapel was reserved for invited guests, including governors, generals, justices, and members of both Houses of Congress.

Decorations of the chapel were, according to a contemporary account, "singularly beautiful." They included a pavilion with striped canvas, innumerable flags and tropical plants, masses of ferns, and on each column "an eagle in gilt copper, holding a shield and supporting coupled flags of 1789 and of the present time."

The service was begun by the rector, with Bishop Littlejohn of Long Island reading the first lesson and Bishop Quintard of Tennessee the second lesson. Concluding prayers were by Dr. Mulchahey; Bishop H. C. Potter delivered an address and gave the benediction. The Prayer Book used by the bishop was one formerly belonging to General Washington and used by him in Christ Church, Philadelphia.

A DECADE OF BUILDING

The last decade of the nineteenth century was an era of building in New York. The city's first steel "skyscraper" was built in 1889—the thirteen-story Tower Building, on Broadway just south of Exchange Place. When a hurricane struck, just before its completion, the architect, Bradford Gilbert, scaled the scaffolding and dropped a plumb line to prove to the skeptical that it would not blow out of line in a storm. When he came down, cheered by spectators, he and the owner, John L. Stearns, locked arms and marched up Broadway, "dumbfounding Trinity Church members just leaving the morning service, by singing in unison 'Praise God from whom all blessings flow,' " according to Ellis. The decade about to begin would mark the end of the proud boast that Trinity's steeple was the highest point in New York's skyline.

Far uptown, at Seventh Avenue and 57th Street, a mile north of St. Chrysostom's Chapel, Andrew Carnegie built the great music hall that was to bear his name; it was opened May 5, 1891 by Walter Damrosch, with Peter Ilich Tchaikovsky conducting one of his own works, the *Marche Solennelle.*

Still farther north, at Amsterdam Avenue and 110th Street, work was begun on the world's largest Gothic structure, the Cathedral of St. John the Divine. The need for a cathedral had been foreseen by Bishop Hobart as early as 1828; the idea was revived in 1872 by Bishop Horatio Potter, who urged his fellow churchmen to build the largest church in America. His successor, Bishop Henry C. Potter, appealed to all Christians, not only Episcopalians, for funds to build "this house of prayer for all people," and the response was immediate and generous.

Morgan Dix was an enthusiastic supporter of the new Cathedral. As early as 1885 he recorded in his diary:

> We had a call from Dr. Mallory, who brought me the astounding intelligence, 1st, that he had the promise of $5,000,000 for a cathedral in New York, on condition that a site could be procured; and 2ndly, that Col. Cruger had told him that the Vestry would be willing to give Trinity Cemetery [on upper Broadway, near 155th St.] for such a site. I encouraged him to proceed.

Dr. Dix, as a member of the committee of trustees appointed by Bishop Potter, had a prominent share in selecting the site at 110th Street from among several possibilities. The property was purchased for $850,000; later, in 1892, the Trinity vestry appropriated $100,000 as a gift from Trinity to the cathedral building fund.

Trinity Parish was also engaged in a large building project, the contruction of "the newest and grandest of Trinity's chapels of ease," on 92nd Street west of Columbus Avenue. The area between Central Park and Riverside Drive was then expected to become one of the choicest residential sections in the city; many of Trinity's parishioners and other "solid citizens" were already moving to that vicinity.

> Accordingly [says the parish history] the vestry felt justified in choosing this site for the new chapel's location. It did not take into consideration its past experiences. It forgot that St. John's Chapel had been the garden spot of its day. It was blind to the fact that Trinity Chapel, formerly in the heart of a favored section, was itself in the process of being left behind. It counted on permanence for the neighborhood in which the new chapel was to be built, and permanence is something which no student of New York's migrations can safely assume. It embarked on the enterprise of construction with an initial outlay of half a million dollars.

The architect of the new chapel, to be called St. Agnes', was William A. Potter, a brother of the Bishop of New York. The vestry was thinking in large terms; they called for him to design a chapel that would accommodate a congregation of 1,200 on the ground floor and 250 in the gallery, with a chapel accommodating 150 and capable of being opened to the rest of the church in case of great crowds. Adjoining the church was to be a large vicarage, parish house, and rooms for the junior clergy and the sexton. The cornerstone was laid by Bishop H. C. Potter on

May 19, 1890, with a sermon by the Rt. Rev. Hugh M. Thompson, Bishop of Mississippi.

Two years later, St. Agnes' Chapel was formally opened by Dr. Dix with a celebration of the Holy Communion and the introduction of the Rev. Dr. Edward A. Bradley, newly appointed to be in charge of the chapel. And on September 27, 1892 the chapel was consecrated by Bishop Potter.

The chapel, of Romanesque architecture, "combined with the simple dignity of nave and transepts a chancel rich and impressive. Marbles and mosaics gave it warmth and character. The eye went naturally to the sanctuary, raised high above the body of the church; no distracting features confused the picture." However, the great open tower above the crossing caused a problem in acoustics, which was long a source of concern to vicar and congregation alike.

In the tower was a truly magnificent set of four bells, designed to produce the "Westminster Peal." The largest bell weighed 6,750 pounds; the smallest, 1,150 pounds. The clappers were of lignum vitae (wood), "which produces sounds not so loud as when bells are struck by iron, but much softer and fuller."

St. Agnes' Chapel soon had a large and growing congregation and a Sunday school that became a model for the whole church. St. Agnes' also became noted for its music, under the direction of Dr. George Edward Stubbs. Within a year, beginning with green material, Dr. Stubbs developed a choir that gained fame for its rendition of the best compositions of English cathedral musicians.

Another chapel was added to the Trinity Parish system in 1892, under quite different circumstances. St. Luke's Church, at Hudson and Grove streets in Greenwich Village, had been an independent parish for seventy years, but changing circumstances and a disastrous fire a few years earlier had caused the St. Luke's vestry and congregation to determine to move to a new location at Convent Avenue and 141st Street. Trinity, which had originally donated the ground and given bond for a loan to build St. Luke's, thereupon decided to buy back the Hudson Street property and administer it as a part of the Trinity Parish.

St. Luke's Church had its beginning in 1820, when a small group of Episcopalians met at the home of Mrs. Catherine Ritter on West 4th Street to consider having a church of their own in the small community of Greenwich Village. The first service was held on October 27 of that year at Obadiah Parker's schoolhouse on Amos Street, now West 10th. Encouraged by Trinity Church (of which most of the members were communicants), the congregation was organized as a parish and its vestry elected the Rev. George Upfold (later Bishop of Indiana) as its first rector. Trinity Parish donated eight lots (later, in 1855, valued at $30,000) for a church and cemetery, and agreed to contribute $400.00 annually toward the rector's stipend. Similar aid, in varying amounts, was continued throughout the history of St. Luke's as a parish, though no control over its affairs was exercised by the mother church. The congregation worshiped in the Watch House of the States Prison on Christopher Street until its church was completed. It was consecrated by Bishop Hobart on Ascension Day, May 16, 1822.

As a parish, St. Luke's never had a very large communicant list, but developed much of the character of a village church. It was, however, fortunate in having a series of distinguished priests as rectors. Three of them later became bishops—George Upfold, Bishop of Indiana in 1847; Levi Silliman Ives, Bishop of North Carolina in 1831; William R. Whittingham, Bishop of Maryland in 1840. Another rector, the Rev. John Murray Forbes, became dean of the General Seminary. One of its assistant ministers, George Washington Doane, became Bishop of New Jersey. The parish was also the nurturing ground for some of the earlier religious orders, though most of these were short-lived. Among the distinguished laymen, the best-known was its first warden, Clement Clarke Moore, author of "'Twas the Night Before Christmas," and a professor at the General Seminary. His grave in Trinity Cemetery at Broadway and 155th Street is still the scene of an annual children's pilgrimage.

St. Luke's, now the third oldest church building on the island of Manhattan (St. Paul's Chapel and St. Mark's-in-the-Bowery being first and second oldest), was and is a simple but attractive rectangular brick building with a square central tower. In the early days, it was surrounded by stately elms and other trees and a graveyard, since removed. The vicarage was just south of the church and the parish house—once the home of Bret Harte, the novelist—to the north.

The interior originally contained a curved platform with a simple altar and a high pulpit above it. In 1875 this was enlarged, with the help of Trinity, to provide a recessed sanctuary and several large arches with a marble memorial altar. The latter was removed to the new church uptown in 1891.

A disastrous fire in January 1886 destroyed much of the sanctuary and damaged the church so badly that it had to be largely rebuilt. Again Trinity came to the rescue, but it was this mishap that probably led the vestry to decide to sell the property and move to the northern part of Manhattan, where a number of the parishioners had already built their homes. The Trinity Corporation thereupon agreed to purchase the Hudson Street property for $150,000 and to give an additional $20,000 toward the purchase of the site for the new church uptown.

At the time of the purchase, Trinity apparently intended to consolidate the work of St. Luke's with that of St. John's Chapel, only ten blocks farther downtown, and to build a new chapel to replace the two of them. This did not prove feasible, so St. Luke's, now a chapel of Trinity Parish, was administered by the clergy of St. John's Chapel. Many of the students at the General Seminary also assisted in the work at St. Luke's Chapel, where a large work speedily developed with the growth of the Greenwich Village community. It was not long, indeed, before St. Luke's Chapel had a larger following than St. John's, which was in a declining neighborhood. The Rev. Philip A. H. Brown was in charge of both chapels from 1892 until 1909, when St. John's was closed and the remaining communicants transferred to St. Luke's Chapel.

In 1896 Trinity Church was beautified by a truly handsome memorial, the bronze doors at the Broadway entrances to the church. They were given by William Waldorf Astor in memory of his father, John Jacob Astor, vestryman from 1865 and warden of the parish from 1884 to 1886, who died in February 1890.

The architect of the doors was Richard M. Hunt, one of the foremost men of the day in his profession. Under his direction, three sculptors designed and executed the doors in relief: Karl Bitter at the main portal, J. Massey Rhind at the north entrance, and Charles H. Niehaus at the south entrance.

Scenes from the Bible are shown on the main portals and the north door. They are depicted in a series of panels, with Old Testament scenes in the bottom panels of the main door and New Testament ones in the top panels. They include the expulsion of Adam and Eve from the Garden of Eden; the dream of Jacob, with angels ascending and descending; the Annunciation to the Blessed Virgin Mary; and the Empty Tomb after our Lord's resurrection. In the top panels are shown two scenes from the Apocalypse: the worship of the Church in glory and the Last Judgment. Above them are the twelve apostles seated on their thrones and our Lord standing, stretching forth his arms in welcome to the faithful. Other figures and designs surround the main panels.

On the north door, scenes depict the Passover in Egypt; the flight to a City of Refuge; deliverance of Paul and Silas from prison; healing of the lame man by St. Peter; and symbolical subjects.

The south door shows scenes from the history of Manhattan Island and of Trinity Parish: the arrival of Henry Hudson in 1609; the Rev. Henry Barclay, second rector, preaching to the Indians; the inauguration service for George Washington at St. Paul's Chapel; the consecration of four bishops at St. Paul's in 1832; the consecration of the present Trinity Church in 1846; and the dedication of the Astor memorial altar and reredos in 1877. A seated angel holds a scroll inscribed "King of Kings and Lord of Lords." Seals of the Society for the Propagation of the Gospel and of the corporation of Trinity Church complete the design.

One of the most conspicuous of the monuments in Trinity churchyard was also erected at about this time: the bronze statue of John Watts, last royal recorder of the City of New York and a loyal member of the parish both before and after the Revolution.

Since Trinity Parish now consisted of the mother church and eight chapels, scattered over a wide area, the vestry, in 1894, decided that each parish unit should be assigned a priest-in-charge with the title of vicar, and their assistants were thenceforth known as curates, rather than assistant ministers as in the past. Vicars were accordingly designated for the various chapels as follows: St. Paul's, Dr. William M. Geer (1894-1918); St. John's and St. Luke's, Philip A. H. Brown (1889-1909); Trinity Chapel, Dr. William H. Vibbert (1891-1910); St. Cornelius', Edward H. C. Goodwin (1870-1904); St. Chrysostom's, Thomas H. Sill (1869-1910); St. Augustine's, Dr. Arthur C. Kimber (1877-1909); and St. Agnes', Dr. Edward A. Bradley (1892-1898), followed by Dr. Charles T. Olmsted (1899-1902). Many of these newly designated vicars had actually been in charge of the respective chapels for some years previously, as indicated by the first date in parentheses. Trinity Church also had a designated vicar, the Rev. J. Nevett Steele (1890-1907). All, of course, were under the general direction and supervision of the rector, Dr. Morgan Dix.

TRINITY'S BICENTENNIAL

Trinity Church was 200 years old on May 6, 1897. In celebration of the bicentennial, a full week of special services and other observances were held in the mother church and the chapels, all of which were elaborately decorated for the occasion.

In Trinity Church, high on either side of the chancel arch, were mounted enlarged seals of the Society for Propagation of the Gospel (which had played such a large part in its early history) and of the Trinity Corporation, and massed flags. The latter seal is unique and always attracts attention for its symbolism. Based on Revelation 10:1-6, it depicts an angel with a rainbow around his head. He has a face like the sun; his right arm is raised and in his left hand he holds "a little book open." His feet are "as pillars of fire"; the right foot upon the sea and the left upon the earth. A child, representing the young colony of New York, kneels at his side and, in the background, is a square-rigged vessel in full sail, depicting the bringing of the Gospel to the New World. Beneath the angel's feet are palms and passion flowers and the inscription IVRO TEMPUS NON FORE AMPLIUS ("I swear that there shall be time no longer"). The inscription around the seal gives, in Latin, the name of the parish and the date of its foundation, 1697.

On a line with the two large shields, hanging on the clustered piers, ran a line of smaller shields depicting the arms of Canterbury and London; of Samuel Seabury, the first American bishop; of King William III, who issued Trinity's charter; of the Netherlands, to which New York had once belonged; of the New England colonies; of Washington; and of the United States.

Other shields, banners, figures, and colored lights decorated the walls. At the west doors stood the American flag and the British Union Jack. The organ gallery was draped with crescent garlands of bay, and the organ was flanked with two 12-foot banners commemorating St. Michael and All Angels and the Conversion of Constantine. The sills of the windows and, also, the chancel rail were solidly banked with flowers, chiefly azaleas, lilies, and tulips. The pavements of the church were strewn with bay and hemlock.

Special services were held throughout the week in Trinity Church and the chapels, with special music and sermons or addresses by noted preachers. But the principal service was a High Celebration in Trinity Church on Sunday, May 2, with the rector as celebrant and preacher. A contemporary account notes that "the rain which fell on the opening days of the bicentennial celebration intensified, by the outside gloom, the brilliancy of Trinity Church within." The organist-choirmaster, Dr. Messiter, and his assistant, Victor Baier, outdid themselves in the splendor of the music, climaxed by Sullivan's *Festival Te Deum,* in which the Trinity choir was augmented by that of St. John's Chapel.

The rector in his historical address noted that Trinity "has stood, and now stands, for the system which may be historically described as Anglo-Catholic Christianity." . . . The Oxford Movement, he said, was "the new-making, the uplifting of the Church," adding:

> We of this parish have gathered of its best fruit, while happily avoiding what marred its force and impaired its value. The closer study of the incarnation; the fuller appreciation of the sacramental system; the restoration of ritual dignity and the glory of the worship of Almighty God; the revival of religious orders of men and women; the return to the devout practice of confession; the expansion of ministries of mercy to all needy and suffering people; a somewhat clearer insight into the world beyond this visible scene; such are some of the fruits which came through the sowing at Oxford seventy years ago, and by which we have been helped, refreshed, strengthened in this place.

In prophetic vein, Dr. Dix went on record:

> Be it then remembered that this has been, and that it is so today, and that this testimony was borne here in this pulpit by the man who held the office of rector in 1897. What may come hereafter, no one can foretell. We trust that the pure Gospel of Jesus Christ may be preached here till the end of the world, if these walls shall stand so long, and that no corruptions, dim-

inutions, emasculations of that venerable and glorious revelation may ever find toleration here; but the future is in the sight of God and not in our view. Baleful influences may spread through our communion; false construction may be put on the terms of the Creed; an impure liberalism, a veiled rationalism, may corrupt men here and there and reach at last the highest seats in the Church; but we shall be in our quiet graves before that day arrives; and be it remembered, that for the first two centuries of her existence the parish was loyal and true and, as such, represented and distinctly stood for Supernatural Religion, Catholic Order, Church Authority, the Sacramental System, the Infallibility of the Word of God, and the All-Sufficiency of the Redeeming Blood of Christ shed for our Salvation on the bitter Cross.

Dr. Dix's statement was forthright and bold and his prophecy a discerning one. Three-quarters of a century later, as the venerable parish approaches its tercentennial, it contains ample food for meditation and reflection.

A Celebration of the Eucharist

11

Problems and Progress

1901-1913

As the nineteenth century drew to a close, Trinity Church and its eight chapels pursued their quiet rounds of services, relatively untouched by the Spanish-American War and the tumultuous politics of the nation and the city. New York, indeed, became a larger metropolis for, on January 1, 1898, Brooklyn became a part of Greater New York, as a part of Westchester county had three years before. The city now extended 36 miles north and south, with a population of 3,393,000—nearly double that of Chicago, its nearest rival. And it was in the midst of a tremendous building boom, but wages were low and 37 percent of the population was foreign-born, with many of them unemployed or poverty-stricken.

MINISTRY TO THE POOR

It was among the poor of lower Manhattan, living in crowded and unsanitary conditions, that Trinity had much of its social and missionary work. The mission house on Fulton Street had been doubled in size, through the generosity of William Waldorf Astor, and now had its own chapel seating 175 people. This sanctuary, known as St. Christopher's Chapel, served for many years as the spiritual center of the downtown mission work.

With the enlargement of the mission house, more ample quarters were provided for the Trinity Dispensary, which now held a Class I state license and was rated excellent in equipment and administration. A skilled private physician, Dr. Bennett S. Beach, donated his services so that patients could have, at trifling cost, services that would have cost them substantial fees in the doctor's uptown office. Cases needing hospitalization were referred to Trinity Hospital (up to its closing in 1907), or to St. Luke's Hospital, where several beds were endowed by Trinity.

Closely allied to the dispensary was the Downtown Relief Bureau. Here, assistance in cash or kind was given to individuals and families with marginal income when unemployment or illness caused undue hardship. The administrator of this bureau was Gilbert G. Hebberd, a trained social worker who was skilled in separating the genuinely needy from the beggars and panhandlers. He devised a plan whereby business concerns and individuals who made generous annual contributions to the work received tickets that could be distributed to the needy, in return for which they could receive a hot meal or other assistance.

Mr. Hebberd was prepared to supply groceries, coal, or even rent money to the poor and needy, but only after he had made a personal investigation of their needs. In a single year, Mr. Hebberd made 3,000 visits of investigation. During that period the bureau was able to help 1,836 persons in 411 families, and 895 individuals. In addition, 1,228 applications were referred to other agencies, hospitals, city welfare, or immigration service for help beyond the scope of the bureau.

The Sisters of St. Mary continued their social and missionary work at the mission house and made innumerable calls on the families of the poor. Their saintly foundress, Mother Harriet, died in 1886; Dr. Dix wrote shortly thereafter a monograph in which he told of her devoted and self-sacrificing life. But the Sisters continued their work at the mission house and also took children to Great River, Long Island, for relief from the slums and for happy summer holidays at Trinity Seaside Home. This property had been given to the parish by Mrs. William Kissam Vanderbilt, who lived nearby and who continued her generosity and personal interest in the maintenance of the project.

In 1900 Dr. Dix and his daughter Catharine spent a summer in England. The particular occasion of the trip was the acceptance by the rector of the degree of Doctor of Divinity at Oxford University—a signal honor that had been conferred on three previous rectors of Trinity, Drs. Barclay, Auchmuty, and Inglis. Dix, however, was the first American rector to be so honored. While in England, Dr. Dix participated in a bicentennial service of the Society for the Propagation of the Gospel, Trinity's benefactor in the early part of the eighteenth century. He also attended an intimate dinner at Lambeth Palace as guest of the Archbishop of Canterbury, Randall Davidson, when, he wrote in his diary:

> I made an awful blunder. A servant offered sherry, which I accepted. Suddenly, on looking up, I saw that not a single person but myself took wine! I subsequently learned that the Archbishop is a total abstainer, and I did not know it, but all

the rest did, and none ventured to take wine. Not disconcerted, however, I partook of my sherry with relish, thankful that I was not as other men.

Four years later, in the autumn of 1904, Dr. Dix had occasion to return the hospitality of Archbishop Davidson. At the invitation of J. Pierpont Morgan, the archbishop was visiting this country, primarily to attend the opening of the General Convention in Boston. (Mr. Morgan did not do things in a small way; as a deputy to General Convention, he customarily made the trip in his private car, sometimes with a special train, and rented a palatial villa to entertain the bishops and other deputies.) Dr. Dix took the opportunity to invite the archbishop to preach at Trinity, and that he did, on October 2, 1904. He was the first Archbishop of Canterbury to cross the Atlantic and, of course, the first to visit and preach at Trinity Church. Whether or not Dr. Dix offered him a glass of wine on that occasion is not recorded.

Before the visit of the Archbishop of Canterbury, however, another service at Trinity emphasized the British heritage of the parish. Queen Victoria died on January 22, 1901, and the United States as well as Britain went into mourning. Memorial services were held throughout the country on the day of her funeral, February 2, including one in Washington attended by President McKinley. Next in importance was the memorial service at Trinity Church, attended by the British consul-general, other officials of Her Majesty's government, and British residents of New York. Seats were reserved for some fifty foreign consuls, officers of the American army and navy, and English and Canadian societies. There were no decorations, except the British flag draped in mourning over the pulpit, and no sermon or address. The rector and vicar of

Trinity conducted a simple service of Creed, prayers, and lessons, and the benediction was given by the Archbishop of Ontario.

Only a few months later, in September, President William McKinley was shot while attending a fair in Buffalo and died a few days later. A dignified and solemn memorial service was held at Trinity, which was draped in mourning; the church was filled to capacity and crowds stood outside in the churchyard and on the sidewalks of Broadway.

Two other memorial services during that year are worthy of note. One, on October 27, 1901, commemorated the millenary (1,000th anniversary) of King Alfred the Great, coinciding with similar services held in England. The other, on December 5, commemorated one of Trinity's own sons, Robert Fulton, inventor of the steamboat. On this occasion a handsome monument and tablet were erected on the south side of the churchyard, the gift of the American Society of Mechanical Engineers.

Once again in 1901 the self-styled "heirs of Anneke Jans" cropped up and filed suit against Trinity, alleging that lands included in the gift of the Queen's Farm (now valuable city property) belonged by right to them. The suit was summarily dismissed by the court, which ruled that the controversy had been settled in favor of Trinity Parish as long ago as June 1847. In this instance the court also took action against the attorney for the plaintiffs, who had already been indicted in Pennsylvania for obtaining money under false pretenses from various persons supposed to be heirs of Anneke Jans. Further investigation proved that the alleged attorney was not a lawyer at all, but a layman practicing a fraud upon the court. The case was dismissed and the fraudulent "attorney" convicted and awarded a jail sentence. But delusions die hard, and in each generation the false Anneke Jans and Bogardus claims arise, only to be dismissed by the courts at the expense of the misled claimants.

In the spring of 1902 Dr. Dix went to Cambridge to attend the graduation of his son from Harvard and was surprised when President Eliot also awarded the honorary degree of Doctor of Divinity to Dr. Dix himself.

DR. WILLIAM T. MANNING

In the same year the vestry called to St. Agnes' Chapel a young priest, the Rev. Dr. William T. Manning, who entered on his duties March 22, 1903. Not only did the new vicar bring new life to the chapel, but the aging rector began to lean upon him heavily for much of the work of the parish. On December 12, 1904, upon nomination by Dr. Dix, Dr. Manning was unanimously elected by the vestry to be the parish preacher and assistant to the rector. Although Dr. Dix continued to be as active as his health permitted, more and more of the direction of the parish was entrusted to Dr. Manning and the two men worked in closest harmony and sympathy for the remainder of the rectorship of Dr. Dix.

The Rev. Dr. William Thomas Manning was a bright rising star in the firmament of Trinity Parish. Born in Northampton, England, May 12, 1866, he had migrated with his family to the United States at the age of sixteen, settling on a frontier farm in Nebraska. After about four years of what the father, John Manning, found to be an arduous and unrewarding effort to wrest a living from the Nebraska soil, he moved, with his wife, two sons and a daughter, to southern California, where the elder Manning, after a few lean years, settled on a small farm. The family were members of St. Paul's Church, San Diego, whose rector, the Rev. Henry Bond Restarick (later Bishop of Honolulu), found them an enthusiastic church family. William became a member of the choir, was soon made a lay reader, and placed in charge of the small mission church in Coronado.

It was the Rev. Mr. Restarick who opened the way for William Manning to enter the priesthood. He attended the University of the South, at Sewanee, Tennessee, where he became an ardent disciple of Dr. William Porcher DuBose, a distinguished theologian nurtured in the tradition of the Oxford Movement. Ordained deacon and priest, Manning served several parishes in California and then returned to Sewanee as professor of dogmatic theology. But Manning felt that his call was to the parochial ministry rather than to teaching and soon accepted a call to Trinity Church in Cincinnati, where he married Florence Van Antwerp. In 1896 Dr. Manning became the rector of St. John's Church, Lansdowne, Pennsylvania and, two years later, went to Nashville, Tennessee as rector of Christ Church, one of the oldest and strongest churches in the Diocese of Tennessee.

In Tennessee Dr. Manning was active in many diocesan affairs and was an examining chaplain. In 1901 he headed the deputation of the Diocese of Tennessee at the General Convention in San Francisco, where he attracted the favorable attention of Dr. William R. Huntington, head of the New York delegation in the absence of Dr. Dix. It was probably Dr. Huntington who recommended Manning to Dr. Dix. In any event, when there was a vacancy in the vicarship of St. Agnes' Chapel, Dr. Dix invited Manning to New York and offered him the post, which he accepted, despite many pleas that he remain in Nashville.

There is some indication that, from the outset, Dr. Dix, then seventy-five years old, saw in Dr. Manning a possible assistant who might, in time, succeed him as rector. The matter was brought to a head, however, in 1904, when Dr. Manning was elected Bishop of Harrisburg, Pennsylvania and seemed inclined to accept the call. Dr. Dix thereupon called a meeting of the vestry of Trinity Parish and proposed the election of Manning as assistant to the rector. The vestry agreed and, after two days of consideration, Dr. Manning accepted the post. Thereafter, although he remained vicar of St. Agnes', Dr. Manning worked closely with the aging rector in the administration of the parish, often presiding at vestry meetings when the rector was too ill to attend, and preaching on important parochial occasions.

One such occasion was the consecration of a new church for St. Cornelius' Chapel in October, 1906. This was a colorful military ceremony, with Bishop Greer officiating and the wardens and vestrymen of the parish, together with ranking military officers, attending. The sermon, written by Dr. Dix, was read by Dr. Manning, who also assisted the bishop in the service. The chapel itself was a small but beautiful one erected by Trinity Parish and later enriched with military flags and trophies by the vicar, the Rev. Edmund Banks Smith.

During this time, also, Dr. Manning was active in the negotiations leading to the addition of a ninth chapel to the Trinity Parish system. This was the Chapel of the Intercession, which, like St. Luke's, had a long previous history as a parish. The original church, a simple wooden structure at 154th Street and Amsterdam Avenue, had been consecrated in 1847. A new stone church, in Gothic style, had been built on the west side of Broadway between 158th and 159th streets in 1872. But this proved too costly for the small congregation and the church came near to being sold for debts.

As the city grew northward, however, the congregation of the Intercession grew, also, until it had virtually outgrown its facilities. Dr. Milo H. Gates, a priest of unusual vigor and initiative, became rector in 1904 and soon the parish numbered 600 communicants, with a Sunday school of 500 children. The church and parish house were badly overcrowded, but the parish still had a debt of $40,000 and was in no position to consider building new facilities. In 1906, therefore, Dr. Gates met with Dr. Manning and Hermann Cammann, the Trinity comptroller, and proposed that Trinity take over the Intercession as a chapel and, later, build a new church for the congregation on a part of the land set apart as the Trinity Cemetery. After prolonged negotiations and the settling of vexing legal problems, this was done, and in 1907 the parish was dissolved and became the Chapel of the Intercession, with Dr. Gates as its vicar.

Dr. Dix did not live long after the new chapel was added to the Trinity system. After preaching at Trinity Church with great vigor on Easter Day, April 19, 1908, the rector was taken ill, but there was no indication that his death was near. Dr. Manning left for Atlantic City for a brief rest after his own services the following Sunday. Three days later, he received an urgent telegram indicating that the rector was very low and sinking rapidly. He returned at once, but Dr. Dix had died before his arrival.

Morgan Dix was eighty-one years old and had been rector of Trinity Parish for forty-six years when he died on April 29, 1908. His leadership spanned the long period from the Civil War to the presidency of Theodore Roosevelt, marked by tremendous growth in the nation, the city, and the parish. He was widely regarded as the foremost priest of the Episcopal Church and as one of the most distinguished citizens of New York.

In accordance with his expressed wish, the body of Dr. Dix was removed to Trinity Church and placed in the entry, with the doors open to the altar. Watched over until the hour of the funeral by the clergy of the parish and the Sisters from the mission house, it was visited by throngs who filed by to pay their respects to his memory.

The burial was on Saturday, May 2, conducted by Dr. Manning, in a church packed with the late rector's friends and admirers, in the presence of visiting bishops and other clergy and representatives of the city and community. The service was simple and dignified, consisting of the Prayer Book order for Burial of the Dead and the Holy Communion. At the time of the funeral, the bells of all the chapels were tolled for thirty minutes and all pulpits in the parish and the rector's stall in Trinity Church were draped in mourning for six weeks.

The vestry lost no time in filling the rectorship left vacant by the death of Dr. Dix. At a special meeting on May 4, 1908, Dr. Manning was elected on the first ballot, and the next day he was formally inducted as the tenth rector.

Trinity Parish, with its mother church and nine chapels, now numbered some 8,500 communicants, with twenty-seven priests apart from the rector. In communicant strength and numbers of clergymen, it constituted one-tenth of the Diocese of New York and was larger than many of the dioceses of the Episcopal Church.

But changing conditions in New York City and in the parish itself made it necessary for the new rector and his vestry to take a hard look at the situation and to make some drastic changes in policy. Of the vicars in charge of congregations, four were still in the prime of life: Dr. Gates, forty-two, vicar of the new Chapel of the Intercession; the Rev. Caleb R. Stetson, thirty-eight, recently appointed vicar of Trinity Church; the Rev. William M. Geer, sixty, but still vigorous, vicar of St. Paul's Chapel; and the Rev. Edmund Banks Smith, forty-eight, vicar of St. Cornelius' Chapel. The other vicars, in some of the more difficult posts, had grown old in the service of the parish: Dr. Arthur C. Kimber, sixty-four, vicar of St. Augustine's Chapel; the Rev. Philip A. H. Brown, sixty-six, vicar of St. John's and St. Luke's Chapels, on leave of absence because of ill health; Dr. William H. Vibbert, sixty-nine, vicar of Trinity Chapel; and the Rev. Thomas H. Sill, seventy-four, vicar of St. Chrysostom's Chapel. The vicarship of St. Agnes' Chapel was, of course, vacated by the election of Dr. Manning as rector.

Within two years, however, three of the older vicars, Dr. Kimber, Mr. Brown, and Dr. Sill, had died, and the fourth, Dr. Vibbert, was retired at his own request.

To fill the vacancy at St. Agnes' Chapel, the rector appointed Dr. William W. Bellinger, formerly rector of Grace Church, Utica, New York. The Rev. W. G. W. Anthony, who had been a temporary summer assistant at St. Augustine's Chapel, became its vicar. The Rev. John Mockridge, formerly of St. Paul's Church, Louisville, Kentucky, was appointed to Trinity Chapel, and the Rev. Carl N. Moller, former rector of Christ Church, LaCrosse, Wisconsin, became vicar of St. Chrysostom's, although that appointment was not made until 1911. To St. Luke's Chapel, with oversight over St. John's Chapel, came the Rev. Edward H. Schlueter, one of the outstanding younger priests of the diocese. With newly appointed assistants to the mother church and most of the chapels, Dr. Manning thus early developed a strong leadership team for the parish.

DEATH OF A CHAPEL

But there were other grave problems to be dealt with, one of the first and greatest being the problem of St. John's Chapel. It had long been contemplated that the work of this chapel, only ten blocks from St. Luke's and in a declining neighborhood, should be combined with the latter congregation, and plans to demolish St. John's had been made as far back as 1894, but never put into execution. St. John's was one of the oldest and most beautiful of the Trinity chapels and its congregation, though small, had a fierce loyalty to it. One of the last acts of Dr. Dix had been the appointment of a vestry committee to review the matter and, in October 1908 this committee recommended that St. John's be closed and its congregation transferred to St. Luke's.

Accordingly, Dr. Manning announced the vestry's decision that St. John's Chapel would be closed on February 1, 1909 and that the congregation would be welcomed at St. Luke's Chapel. The announcement immediately aroused a great controversy in the parish, which was taken up and exploited by the newspapers and even some of the church press. Trinity Parish was accused of heartlessness and disregard for the feelings of its members and for work among the poor. Antiquarians deplored the impending destruction of what they considered the finest building in the city. Many of the remaining members of the congregation of St. John's joined in resisting the decision. Appeals were made to the courts and even to the state legislature to halt the action, but without success.

Within the parish itself, the annual election of vestrymen became a highly controversial one, with the congregation of St. John's and their supporters in some other chapels trying to substitute their own candidates for vestrymen whom they distrusted. Normally the annual election was a routine affair, with few qualified electors bothering to vote and only as many nominees as there were places to be filled. Now attempts were made in St. John's Chapel and elsewhere to enroll as many adult male contributors and communicants (the legal requirement for voting) as possible, and four candidates were nominated to oppose the four vestrymen thought primarily responsible for the decision.

Dr. Manning presided over the election with scrupulous fairness, each voter being handed two printed ballots with the respective slates of candidates. When the polls were closed, it was found that 653 votes had been cast out of a possible 1,421 and the "regular" candidates had secured 529 votes against 124 for the opposition ticket. On the following day the court handed down a decision vacating a temporary restraining order that had been obtained by the St. John's supporters. Thus the vestry won a double victory, later ratified by the appellate court to which the suit was appealed.

Dr. Manning moved swiftly to carry out the planned consolidation of the work of the two chapels at St. Luke's. However, he also arranged for a well-known evangelist, the Rev. William Wilkinson, to conduct street preaching in Wall Street and mission services in St. John's, so the actual closing of the latter chapel was deferred for the time being, though regular congregational services were terminated.

Actually, St. John's Chapel stood until 1918, when the widening of Varick Street and construction of a new subway caused the city to condemn the property and demolish the chapel. But the memorials and furnishings of the chapel, as well as the congregation, were transferred to St. Luke's Chapel in 1909 and, from that time, St. John's Chapel ceased to be a regular part of the Trinity chapel system.

TOWARD SOLVING SOME PROBLEMS

Partly as a by-product of the St. John's controversy, Trinity Parish also came under fire for its alleged exploitation of slum and tenement property held by the corporation. The vestry, indeed, had unwisely (and unsuccessfully) opposed a city ordinance requiring that a supply of fresh water should be piped to every floor of tenement dwellings, holding that it should not apply to the smaller buildings of two or three stories which constituted most of its holdings. Other charges against Trinity were proved to be largely without foundation. Testimony given by Col. William Jay, clerk of the vestry, before a legislative investigating committee, showed that many of the houses against which complaints had been filed did not belong to the parish at all, while others were on grounds owned by Trinity, but erected and maintained by lessees over whom the corporation had no control.

Dr. Manning was determined, nevertheless, that, even though Trinity might have no legal liability for its tenement property, it should remove all grounds for the charges against it. Thus in a sermon on May 16, 1909, he made clear his own position:

> I hold that in this matter we ought to set not only a high standard, but the very highest. Far better, if necessary, that all our charities should be given up and schools closed than that we should maintain any of them by revenue derived from properties in an insanitary or questionable condition.

Aware that no private investigation under the auspices of the Trinity vestry would prove acceptable, Dr. Manning urged the vestry to call in well-qualified and impartial outside consultants to make a thorough study of the situation. This was done under the auspices of the Charity Organization Society, with the aid of well-qualified public and private investigators.

In its initial report in 1909, the investigators submitted detailed studies on 334 houses owned directly by Trinity, but was unable to secure the cooperation of lessees of property on which 200 houses owned by them were situated. It was not until some years later that these leased properties could be included in the study.

Results of the study showed that the Trinity tenements had better sanitary conditions and less overcrowding than most such properties, but made specific recommendations for improvements in many of the buildings. As a result, Trinity, at considerable expense (involving substantial borrowing), moved swiftly to remedy conditions. By 1910, 225 tenements had been taken down as not worth reconditioning or to make room for commercial developments. A large bond issue was approved to make possible extensive renovation or rebuilding of commercial and residential properties, and a qualified inspector and director of social welfare was added to the Trinity staff to give constant supervision to its residential properties. Steps were also taken to recover houses located on leased properties, either by purchase or refusal to renew leases as they expired, and to renovate or demolish them. Thereafter, Trinity's tenements came to be recognized as models of their kind and the pattern of management became an example to be followed by others and a guide for future legislation on multiple dwellings in urban areas.

Dr. Manning also determined to remove the veil of secrecy from the financial affairs of Trinity Parish and thus dispel the rumors that it was making a vast fortune from its real-estate operations. On January 1, 1909, and annually thereafter, the corporation published a full, audited account of Trinity's financial affairs. The first report made headlines in all the papers and became a subject for wide comment in financial circles.

While the report showed that the parish was, indeed, by far the wealthiest church corporation in America, the public was surprised to find that it was less wealthy than inflated rumors had indicated and that its income was actually insufficient to meet the heavy demands of the religious, educational, and charitable work of the parish. It also made clear that no vestryman received any profit or benefit, direct or indirect, from his service to the parish, except in the case of those administering the estate or serving as legal counsel.

Meanwhile, of course, the religious activities of the parish continued their normal course. Trinity Church joined in the celebration in the autumn of 1909 of the tercentennial of Henry Hudson's discovery of the river bearing his name and the related centennial of the beginning of steam navigation with the launching of Robert Fulton's *Clermont*. Trinity had a special association with Fulton, whose sponsor was Chancellor Robert R. Livingston, warden of the parish just after the Revolution. When Fulton died in 1815, he was presumably buried beside his patron in Trinity churchyard, which also contains his monument erected in 1901.

A Hudson-Fulton service packed Trinity Church on September 26, 1909, with Bishops Darlington of Harrisburg and Walker of Western New York participating. Dr. Manning preached a remarkable sermon on the material progress of the past three hundred years, with references to Admiral Peary's recent discovery of the North Pole and the display of heavier-than-air machines put on by Wilbur Wright and Glenn Curtiss at Governors Island. As a part of the celebration, these remarkable flying machines demonstrated their ability, when the wind was right, by flying around the Statue of Liberty and even, on one occasion, as far up the Hudson as 125th Street.

While Lenten services had long been a feature of Trinity Church, Dr. Manning expanded the program to include daily noon preachers of widely differing viewpoints (though all Episcopalians), attracting large congregations from the Wall Street financial district and visitors to the city.

Other special services included one celebrating the jubilee of St. Stephen's College, a memorial service on the death of King Edward VII in May, 1910, and an observance of the 200th anniversary of the founding of Trinity School, originally the Charity School of the parish, in 1909.

The General Convention of the Church met in Cincinnati in October 1910. Its special guest was the Rt. Rev. John Wordsworth, Bishop of Salisbury. Dr. Manning and other church leaders met the bishop on his arrival from England, and the rector entertained him at a formal dinner party. The bishop later preached at Trinity, while his chaplain, the Rev. J. Spence Johnston, preached at St. Agnes' Chapel.

Dr. Manning was a deputy to the convention in Cincinnati and played a prominent part in it. The subject of Christian unity was very much to the fore and Dr. Manning, while insisting on the loyalty of the Episcopal Church to the Catholic tradition, was greatly interested in it. He therefore introduced a resolution calling for appointment of a commission of seven bishops, seven presbyters, and seven laymen to explore the possibility of a World Conference on Faith and Order. The resolution was adopted and J. Pierpont Morgan, also a deputy from New York, immediately offered $100,000 to meet the expenses of the preparatory work.

Bishop Anderson, of Chicago, became chairman of the joint commission, Robert H. Gardiner, of Maine, the secretary, and Dr. Manning head of the important subcommittee on the plan and scope of the proposed conference. In that capacity, Dr. Manning, with members of his committee, during the next three years, made visits to influential church leaders, including James Cardinal Gibbons, of Baltimore, to enlist their interest and support. In the summer of 1912, he sailed, with three bishops, to the British Isles and secured the endorsement of the Archbishops of Canterbury and York and the primates of the Anglican Churches in Scotland and Ireland. Others made similar calls on Protestant leaders in this country and abroad and gradually the project began to take shape.

While the first World Conference on Faith and Order did not actually take place until 1927 (because of the intervention of World War I), this became one of the roots of the ecumenical movement that was eventually to result in the formation of the World Council of Churches, of which most of the historic churches of the world are now members.

In 1911 Trinity Church was the scene of one of the colorful commemorative services that are a part of its tradition, this time to celebrate the centenary of the joint consecrations of Bishops Hobart and Griswold. Emphasis was on thanksgiving for these two great leaders who had done so much to bring new life and vigor to the church in the critical post-Revolutionary days and thanksgiving for the founding and work of Trinity Parish over a period of more than two centuries. Special remembrance was made of those, who as rectors and wardens, had guided the destiny of the parish through good years and lean ones, with a historical address by the Rt. Rev. Frederick J. Kinsman, Bishop of Delaware.

Work was also begun in 1911 on the building of a new Chapel of the Intercession at Broadway and 155th Street.

This was a large and imposing church in Gothic style, designed by the firm of Cram, Goodhue, and Ferguson. Its cost was estimated at half a million dollars, including a spacious parish house and vicarage; as usual, the final cost far exceeded the estimate. But the result was a large and beautiful group of buildings, admirably suited for the growing congregation of the chapel. The first service took place in the almost completed chapel on January 4, 1914, but the formal consecration of the completed buildings did not take place until May 25, 1915. By that time, the communicant strength of the Chapel of the Intercession had grown to 2,290, with a Sunday school of 668 pupils and 85 officers and teachers.

The General Convention of 1913 was held in New York City, but on this occasion Trinity Parish was not the host. Services were held in the unfinished Cathedral of St. John the Divine on Morningside Heights and the sessions in the adjoining new Synod Hall, built for the occasion by J. P. Morgan, with the House of Bishops meeting in the old Synod Hall. Dr. Manning again headed the New York deputation and was nominated for president of the House of Deputies, but lost to the Rev. Alexander Mann (later Bishop of Pittsburgh) by a vote of 258 to 242.

One of the issues at the 1913 General Convention was the proposal to change the name of the Church from "Protestant Episcopal" to something that would give greater recognition to its Catholic heritage, or at least not seem to weight it on the Protestant side. The proposal had also been made at the 1910 convention and had become a party issue on which there was strong difference of opinion. Dr. Manning was in favor of changing the name and had preached and spoken in favor of such a change, possibly to "American Catholic Church." When he preached on the subject at Trinity Church, some of the members of the vestry had protested, only to be told by the rector in no uncertain terms that it was not the function of the vestry to attempt to control the theological policy of the parish. But when it appeared that the General Convention might pass the proposed change by a slim majority against the bitter opposition of southern and some eastern dioceses, Dr. Manning moved to table the resolution and to refer to the Committee on Amendments to the Constitution a change requiring approval of such matters on the first reading to be made by a majority of two-thirds. The committee reported favorably upon the resolution, but it was not transmitted to the House of Bishops until too late for action, so both the proposed change of name and the amendment of the Constitution failed to be enacted.

The issue of the change of name was to become a hardy perennial, subject to vigorous and often bitter debate at every General Convention for half a century. It was not until 1964 that a satisfactory solution was found by the adoption and ratification of a preamble to the Constitution describing the church as "The Protestant Episcopal Church in the United States of America, otherwise known as The Episcopal Church (which name is hereby recognized as also designating the Church)." Unfortunately, Dr. Manning did not live to see the accomplishment of that happy compromise.

ALL SAINTS' CHAPEL

Shortly after the General Convention, Dr. Manning had the pleasure of officiating, with Bishop Greer, at the consecration of a lovely addition to Trinity Church as a memorial to his distinguished predecessor, Morgan Dix. This was All Saints' Chapel, erected at the northwest side of Trinity Church as a place of prayer and meditation and for weekday services and lectures. In later years, it was also used for the perpetual reservation of the Blessed Sacrament.

The plan for this chapel actually went back to June 13, 1910, when the vestry approved the project, and work on it had begun in December 1911. However, the work was delayed by strikes in the marble quarries and it was not until November 30, 1913 that the finished chapel was consecrated.

Designed by Thomas Nash in the style of fourteenth-century English Gothic to blend harmoniously with the main church, the chapel may be entered either from the church or from a main doorway on the Broadway side. The doorway is deeply recessed and surmounted by a canopied niche with traceried windows on either side, flanked by buttresses and octagonal turrets terminating in a gable with foliated cross. The interior is 65 feet long and 21 feet wide, with a normal seating capacity of 85 persons. There are three bays, with a shallow chancel two steps above the nave. The altar is backed with a reredos ornamented by a carved figure of our Lord in glory, flanked by St. Michael and St. Gabriel. On the inside wall are three recesses; one filled by the organ and screen, one opening to the cenotaph of Bishop Onderdonk, and one leading into the main church. The windows and ornaments of the chapel were given by parishioners and others as memorials, the windows on the north wall being in memory of Dr. Dix. It was not until two years later that the memorial effigy, representing the recumbent figure of Dr. Dix with his hands joined in prayer, designed by Isidor Konti, was added.

In a preliminary ceremony, on June 20, 1913, the body

of Dr. Dix was transferred with simple dignity from its temporary resting place in Trinity Cemetery to a crypt under the altar of the new chapel. The ceremony of consecration took place on Advent Sunday, following Morning Prayer in the main church. The procession, led by the sexton, William C. Broughton, and including the choir and clergy of the mother church, together with the vicars of the parish and Dr. Vibbert, vicar emeritus of Trinity Chapel, preceded Dr. Manning and the Rt. Rev. David H. Greer, Bishop of New York. Proceeding out to the churchyard, the procession entered the main door of the chapel where the bishop was received by the wardens and vestrymen. The bishop read the prayer of consecration and celebrated the Holy Communion, assisted by Dr. Vibbert, Dr. Geer, and Dr. Manning, and made a brief address. Later, at the 11 o'clock Eucharist, the rector referred to the new chapel and paid tribute to the revered memory of Dr. Dix.

12

World War I and Subsequent Changes

1914-1928

The year 1914, which was to witness the outbreak of World War I, began peacefully enough, especially in Trinity Parish. On Sunday, January 4, the first service was held in the new Chapel of the Intercession before a large congregation, despite inclement weather. The rector celebrated the Holy Communion, assisted by Dr. Gates, the vicar, and the Rev. A. S. Winslow, curate of the chapel, with the vestry occupying the front pews in the nave. The service marked a new "first" in Trinity Parish—the presence of women choristers as well as men and boys. However, the women did not participate in the procession, but sat vested in the "nuns' gallery" on the epistle side of the chancel above the organ console.

The new year was also marked by a change at Trinity Chapel on West 25th Street. Now in a business neighborhood and largely surrounded by foreign-born Americans who showed little interest in the Episcopal Church, the chapel seemed to have outlived its usefulness. However, the congregation was shocked when, on January 25, the rector announced that their vicar, Dr. Mockridge, was being transferred to the mother church as its vicar and that the Rev. J. Wilson Sutton would serve as priest-in-charge until the chapel could be closed and the property sold. Fortunately, the announcement did not receive the publicity that had attended the announcement of the impending demise of St. John's Chapel and, actually, the chapel was not closed at that time. Instead, under the leadership of Dr. Sutton (later designated vicar), and perhaps stimulated by the shock of the announcement, the chapel took a new lease on life and survived for nearly thirty years.

Dr. Mockridge also exercised vigorous leadership at Trinity Church, which had been without a vicar since Dr. Stetson had left in 1911 to become rector of St. Mark's Church, Washington, D.C.

Although Dr. Mockridge remained as vicar of Trinity Church only two years, he produced lasting results in the life of the mother church. Believing that the time had come for greater lay participation, he organized a men's committee with younger leadership than the old Trinity Church Association and organized them into subcommittees on religious work, social welfare, entertainment, and finance.

Concerned about the congestion, poverty, and disease in the vicinity of the mother church, Dr. Mockridge took the laymen, one by one, on tours of the depressed areas. Appalled at what they saw, the men decided to make a thorough survey of the "Washington Street District" and employed a trained social service secretary, J. Barton Myers, Jr., to supervise the study. The resulting report spurred the city and social agencies to adopt remedial measures. The men's committee also undertook to strengthen the existing work of Trinity Mission House and to organize sports and other activities among the men and boys of the neighborhood.

There was widespread unemployment and suffering in the city during the winter of 1914 and the Bowery was teeming with homeless men. Frank Tannenbaum, an organizer for the radical International Workers of the World, sought to dramatize the plight of the unemployed by invading churches and demanding food and shelter. Many churches barred the motley groups, sometimes with the help of the police, but Dr. Geer, vicar of St. Paul's Chapel, took a different approach. Knowing that the men had a real grievance, he invited Tannenbaum to bring his men to the chapel parish house on March 3 for an orderly protest meeting and conference. They came, 200 strong, following a rally at Rutgers Square, in which fiery speeches were made against the city and the church for their neglect and indifference.

Dr. Geer welcomed the men, served them a meal of sandwiches, bananas, and coffee, and then invited those without shelter to sleep in the chapel. The gesture aroused both praise and invective in the daily press, but served to dramatize the situation and led to a strengthening of unemployment and poor-relief agencies, both public and private.

TRINITY IN WORLD WAR I

With the outbreak of war in Europe in the summer of 1914, the parish found itself in the midst of the controversy between the isolationists, who wanted no part in the war, and those who felt that the United States should give every possible assistance, short of war, to the Allies. Dr. Manning early made it clear that he sympathized with the latter. In a sermon at a day of prayer proclaimed by President Wilson on October 4, the rector preached on the lessons of the war and declared that "God is speaking to us through this war." Recognizing that all, including Americans, shared responsibility for the breakdown of international order, he said:

> Through these fearful events God is showing us once again the need of true religion in the world. Men are asking in this crisis if Christianity has failed. . . . Christianity has not failed, but we have failed to be Christians. . . . This war shows us that the religion of Jesus Christ is the one hope of the world. Christianity is the one thing that has not failed.

With the sinking of the *Lusitania* in May 1915 the war came closer to America. At a missionary rally in the cathedral a month later, Dr. Manning deplored the neutralist attitude of many Americans and declared that, at times, war was not only right, but sometimes a clear Christian duty. It was a theme he was to stress many times in the months ahead, when German outrages brought this country steadily closer to military involvement. Increasingly he stressed the need for preparedness and struck out against pacifism and isolationism.

In a sermon at St. Paul's Chapel on October 30, 1916, commemorating the 150th anniversary of the chapel, Dr. Manning spoke out even more plainly on American policies in the war. At a time when President Wilson was seeking re-election with the slogan "He kept us out of war," the rector preached on the text, "What shall it profit a man if he shall gain the whole world and lose his own soul?" Applying the text to the nation, he asked: "Can we say that it has been our one concern to stand, at all cost, for the fundamental rights of mankind, or are we as people disposed to ask only that our own peace shall not be disturbed?"

We need a great awakening of the spirit of true Americanism, and a great reconsecration to our national ideal. There are influences at work today which are operating definitely to weaken the spirit of patriotism. . . . The attempt to identify the Christian religion with ultra-pacifism is a misapprehension of the truth and an injury to religion.

Dr. Manning went on to declare that "there is nothing that would be of such great practical benefit to us as Universal Military Training for the men of our land. . . . The danger of a democracy is not that it may be carried into militarism, but that it may be found unprepared to defend itself against militaristic aggression."

Dr. Manning's plea for universal military training aroused wide and immediate controversy, both in the church and in the public press. Almost every paper in New York featured it as an attack on American policy and a rebuke to President Wilson, but Dr. Manning stuck to his guns (no pun intended!) and hammered at the subject again and again in subsequent addresses and sermons. That many supported his views was indicated by a great ovation that greeted him in December, when he presided over a meeting in Carnegie Hall to protest Germany's actions in occupied Belgium, where the people were said to be starving while Belgian youths were deported to work in German war industries.

President Wilson was inaugurated for his second term on March 4, 1917. One of his first acts was to reveal the so-called Zimmermann papers, in which the German chancellor had instructed his Ambassador to Mexico to suggest that, if that country would declare war on the United States, it could count on German help to recover the southwestern states lost to the Americans in the 1848 war. On top of this, the German threat of unrestricted submarine war provided further provocation. On Good Friday, April 6, 1917, the Congress declared that a state of war existed between the United States and the German government. The die was cast and American neutrality was at an end.

In his Easter sermon at Trinity Church, Dr. Manning said:

> The Easter message today has a new depth of meaning for us as our country now rises to answer the clear call of God, to give itself to a great service, to perform, at whatever cost, a solemn and inexorable duty. . . . Christianity is the religion of love. But love can express itself just as truly through the right use of physical force as through mental or spiritual force. . . . The soldier in the trenches may be as Christ-like in his sacrifice as the doctor, the nurse, or the priest. . . .
>
> Because we believe in the message of Easter, because we believe that the whole world is to shine with the glory of the Risen Christ, we are willing and glad to take our part and share in this conflict.

Now that the country was fully engaged in the war, Trinity Parish girded itself to redoubled efforts in relief activities. Dr. Manning immediately called a meeting of the clergy in charge of the nine churches in the parish to make plans for wartime activities. He advised them to avoid the creation of needless new agencies and to continue to work with such well-established organizations as the Red Cross and Belgian Relief, with which most of the parish units were already cooperating. Workshops were manned practically every day and evening in each of the parish houses and in Trinity Mission House, with relays of volunteer workers. A committee of Trinity women opened a room where servicemen could rest, write letters, and have light refreshments. St. Paul's Chapel provided similar services.

A chaplains' committee of women undertook to supply

military chaplains with altar appointments, vestments, books, and other needs. They also provided a full set of altar appointments for the chapel at Camp Dix, in New Jersey, in memory of Dr. Dix, for whose father the camp was named. St. Luke's Chapel altar guild supplied altar linens to chaplains and St. Paul's Chapel provided French lessons for soldiers and nurses expecting to be sent overseas.

Dr. Manning was in frequent demand as a speaker for various patriotic groups and was appointed by Mayor Mitchell to official committees to welcome Allied representatives visiting this country. But, never one to advocate for others what he was not prepared to do himself, the rector volunteered to serve as civilian chaplain at Camp Upton, on Long Island. Here he held services each Sunday and major festival, both at the camp itself and in the base hospital attached to it. Much of his time was devoted to individual counseling with the officers and men, and he also served as an unofficial public relations representative to interpret the military to civilians through press interviews and feature articles.

When, in March 1918, the 77th Division was ready to go overseas, Dr. Manning was invited to accompany them as chaplain of the 302nd Engineers, to whom he had been ministering at Camp Upton. He was eager to accept the assignment and twice applied to the vestry for a leave of absence for the purpose, but the vestry was loath to have its rector absent for an indefinite period. After trying informally to dissuade him, they adopted a resolution invoking the requirement of Trinity's Charter that the rector be accessible at all times, declaring that they were, therefore, unable to accede to his request.

To Dr. Manning's regret, the engineers and the division

sailed for France without him. However, he remained at Camp Upton as chaplain to new units in training there and was also made an honorary chaplain to care for the families of the men who went overseas with the division. His work at Camp Upton continued until the end of October 1918, when a War Department ruling terminated the assignment of civilian chaplains to military installations. But by that time the war was nearly over and, on November 11, the armistice with Germany was signed.

Shortly after the close of the war, Dr. Manning was honored for his services by the award by the French government of the cross of a Chevalier of the Legion of Honor.

Despite his military activities, the rector did not neglect parish duties, though many to which he would normally have given his personal attention had to be delegated to the various vicars. Nor was he forgotten by the general church. Indeed, on June 5, 1917 he was notified that he had been elected Bishop of Western New York, but he promptly declined the election, believing that Trinity Parish had the first call on his services at this critical time.

Many of the members of Trinity Parish were, of course, in the military service. Two of the vestrymen saw active service: William Barclay Parsons, who went overseas with the 11th Engineers as a major and, later, was promoted through ranks to major-general; and John A. Dix, son of the late rector, who was a first lieutenant with the 310th Field Artillery. Two members of Trinity's men's committee, who later became vestrymen, were also in service: Dr. John B. Walker, who, as a major, was in charge of a hospital in France; and Col. George W. Burleigh, who served in the coast artillery for home defense.

A large service flag for the whole parish was hung on

two sycamore trees in the Trinity churchyard. When it was dedicated on Thanksgiving Day in 1917, it contained 450 stars for servicemen of the parish; by the end of the war, the number had increased to 910, including thirty-three gold stars for men of the parish who had been killed in action or died of wounds.

Despite Trinity's great resources, its expenses had long exceeded its income, and in May 1917 the vestry borrowed four million dollars from the Mutual Life Insurance Company to consolidate floating indebtedness and secure funds for improvement of the income-producing real estate.

The rectory on West 25th Street also had become too expensive to repair and maintain, and the widening of the street planned by the city would have required further expenses for alterations, as well as reducing the size of the property. It was, therefore, sold and Dr. and Mrs. Manning moved to a rented house on Washington Square.

Two distinguished visiting preachers came to Trinity in 1918: the Most Rev. Cosmo Gordon Lang, Archbishop of York, and the Rt. Rev. Charles Gore, Bishop of Oxford. Both of these English prelates were also taken by Dr. Manning to pay visits to Camp Upton.

The Archbishop of York drew tremendous crowds on a Sunday morning at the Cathedral of St. John the Divine and at an afternoon service at Trinity Church, where he also preached at the noonday services during the week. The archbishop then made a tour of the major cities in the east and middle west, returning to preach the three-hour service on Good Friday at Trinity.

With the continuing of wartime demands and increasing inflation, economy became the watchword of the parish. In April 1918 the vestry voted to terminate the parish day-school system at the end of the current term, leaving only the school at St. Agnes' Chapel, which continued under local auspices. With the shortage of fuel, churches were left unheated during the week and, sometimes, even on Sundays, but the loyal communicants, bundled in overcoats, continued faithful in their attendance.

At St. Paul's Chapel, the Rev. Dr. Geer, the last of the vicars whose service in the parish dated back to the days of Dr. Dix, announced his retirement and was given the title of vicar emeritus. He was succeeded as vicar by Dr. Joseph P. McComas, who was also responsible, under Dr. Manning, for the work at Trinity Church and the mission house.

NEW PLANNING AND ACTION (1919-1921)

With the end of the war, Dr. Manning turned his attention to the many problems of the parish that required new planning and action.

The first of these problems was posed by the decision of the Mother Superior of the Community of St. Mary to withdraw the Sisters from Trinity Mission House. This was apparently partly because of disagreements with the rector about certain of the Sisters' extra-liturgical devotions and partly because of the desire of the community to pursue its work in other than parochial fields. However, one Sister remained until June 1919 in order to give time for other arrangements to be made. Sister Lucy, who was greatly beloved by the people among whom she worked, was also permitted to continue her care of Trinity Seaside Home at Great River in the summers of 1919 and 1920.

The rector immediately set about finding a replacement for the Sisters at the mission house and, by the fall of

1919, two members of the Sisterhood of St. Margaret arrived to continue the work. The new Sisters, Miriam Margaret and Clare, and their successors, soon won a place of honor and affection and were to continue their quiet but effective work in the Trinity Mission House until its closing in 1956 and, thereafter, in Trinity Church and the missions in the lower east side of Manhattan.

In the closing days of 1918 the rector announced that the system of pew rentals in Trinity Parish would be discontinued and that, thereafter, all pews would be free. The proposal was long overdue, but as some pewholders at Trinity, St. Paul's, and St. Agnes' had contracts running well into 1919, it took some time for the new policy to become fully effective. Moreover, the vestry, mindful of the loss of income from the rental of pews, made a strong appeal to parishioners to make annual contributions in lieu of rentals—an appeal that met with only moderate success at that time.

The subject of spiritual healing under the auspices of the church was beginning to receive attention, especially in England, but, also, to a limited degree in this country. Dr. Manning became greatly interested in the movement, partly as a recovery of a neglected part of the ancient heritage of the church and partly as an offset to such modern movements as Christian Science. Learning that a noted Anglican layman, James Moore Hickson, who had done remarkable work in this field, was shortly to visit this country, the rector invited him to conduct a healing mission and instruction at Trinity Chapel, where Dr. Sutton was also doing some training in the deeper meanings of the spiritual life.

Mr. Hickson came initially for two weeks in the spring of 1919, but so wide did his appeal prove to be that the mission was extended for a month and resumed a year later. The mission began each day at 10 o'clock with prayers, in which people joined, and continued throughout the day. Each person was prayed for individually and those who desired it received the laying on of hands at the altar rail. Mr. Hickson was careful to point out that his work was in no way a substitute for medical care, but was supplementary to it. He also warned those who came not to expect instantaneous relief or miraculous cures, but to be patient and constant in prayer. There were, indeed, no miraculous cures, but sometimes immediate relief of a striking kind was marked.

Subsequently, at the General Convention in Detroit, where Mr. Hickson held a meeting, Dr. Manning succeeded in having a resolution adopted to form a commission on the ministry of healing. A notable result of the work of this commission was the restoration to the Prayer Book in its 1928 revision of a service for Holy Unction and the laying on of hands for the healing ministry.

With relief from war activities and postwar adjustments, Dr. Manning was able to resume his activities in behalf of Christian unity. He felt that the sad spectacle of supposedly Christian nations locked in deadly warfare lent particular urgency to the cause of better understanding between churches in Europe and America, with something like a "League of Churches" as the spiritual counterpart of the League of Nations, then ardently advocated by President Wilson, though ultimately rejected by the United States Senate.

On the national scene Dr. Manning also had high hopes for a proposal known as the "Concordat," whereby Congregational and other Protestant ministers were to be ordained as priests by bishops of the Episcopal Church without renouncing their ministry in their own religious bodies. A study by a committee of the House of Bishops, headed by Bishop Hall of Vermont, had made an adverse report on this proposal, pointing out many practical difficulties. Undaunted by this report, Dr. Manning joined with other leaders in the Episcopal Church in issuing a document entitled "Proposals for an Approach Toward Unity," which became a basis for constitutional and canonical proposals at the General Convention of 1919.

Dr. Manning presented the proposals at a mass meeting in Arcadia Hall, Detroit, on the eve of the convention and became one of the leading advocates in the House of Deputies. Here he found himself in the strange position of being opposed by deputies who, like himself, were considered Anglo-Catholics. The House of Bishops passed the proposed constitutional enabling amendment and, in the House of Deputies, it came to the Committee on Amendments to the Constitution, of which Dr. Manning was chairman. Here it was amended, to require certain safeguards, and Dr. Manning then presented it on the floor of the House where, after vigorous debate, it was adopted. To become effective, however, it had to be put over to the next General Convention in 1922 for ratification and the passage of enabling canonical legislation.

To anticipate the story, the constitutional amendment was ratified in 1922 and a canon "Of Ordination in Special Cases" adopted, but it was hedged about with so many restrictions that it was to have little practical effect. By that time, the "Concordat" with the Congregationalists was virtually a dead letter, as their leaders had lost interest in it.

Meanwhile Dr. Manning became involved in a controversy over the reservation of the Blessed Sacrament, primarily for administration to the sick, which had surprising repercussions in Trinity Parish. Dr. Manning opposed reservation and wrote strong letters to the church press against the practice. In reply the Rev. William B. Kinkaid, then rector of the Church of the Advent, San Francisco, who had served for four years on Trinity's staff, wrote that "but a short time ago, to my knowledge, three out of the nine churches and chapels [of Trinity Parish] had the practice of perpetual reservation."

The rector immediately questioned each of his vicars to determine the facts in the matter. He found that there was, indeed, perpetual reservation of the sacrament in three places: the Sisters' oratory at Trinity Mission House; the side chapel in St. Luke's Chapel; and St. Paul's Chapel, where the sacrament was reserved in an aumbry in the sacristy, but without a light burning before it.

Dr. Manning admitted that he did not have full jurisdiction over the Sisters' chapel, which was, in any event, not in one of Trinity's chapels. When Fr. Schlueter, vicar of St. Luke's, protested that the reserved sacrament was necessary for emergency ministrations to the sick, he was allowed to continue the practice except on Sundays and Thursdays—a curious compromise which made the vicar unhappy, but to which he reluctantly agreed. The reserved sacrament at St. Paul's was in a place where it could not be easily used as a focus for worship. Dr. Manning wrote to *The Living Church* that, both in Dr. Dix's rectorship and his own, reservation was at times permitted for administration of the sacrament to the sick and dying, "but 'Perpetual Reservation' for worship has never been permitted in any of our nine churches. The above statement as to the practice of Trinity Parish has been submitted to the Vicars and is assented to by all of them as correct."

Thus, by distinguishing between reservation for the

sick and reservation "for worship," Dr. Manning managed to save face over the flat contradiction of a former curate. And he did have a good point, for what he was really objecting to was the growing custom in some Episcopal churches of using the reserved sacrament as the center for services of Adoration and Benediction, which he regarded as Roman Catholic excesses. It is, perhaps, significant that within a decade he permitted perpetual reservation to be instituted in a chapel of the Cathedral of St. John the Divine.

Once again, on November 19, 1919, Trinity Church was host to a member of the British royal family. This was Edward, Prince of Wales, who was later to reign briefly as King Edward VIII, and then to abdicate the throne and become known as the Duke of Windsor. Prince Edward was seated in the same pew that had been occupied by his grandfather, Edward VII, when he, as Prince of Wales, had visited New York in 1860. In a short address, Dr. Manning recalled the historic connections of Trinity Parish with the British royal family, beginning with the granting of Trinity's charter by William III in 1697, and welcomed the prince as representative of the country with which the United States had been associated in the recent war.

A year later, on September 16, 1920, the Wall Street area was rocked by the explosion of a bomb left in a horse-drawn wagon in front of the offices of J. P. Morgan and Company, just a block from Trinity, at Wall and Broad streets. Thirty-five people were killed and some 130 injured, fifty-three of them seriously enough to be hospitalized.

The explosion occurred at noon, just as services were beginning in Trinity Church and St. Paul's Chapel. In a short time, five of the parish clergy—Dr. McComas, Frs. Veazie and Strombom of Trinity Church, the Rev. George B. Cox of St. Paul's Chapel, and the Rev. Edmund Banks Smith of St. Cornelius' Chapel—rushed into the streets and then to the Broad Street and Volunteer hospitals to minister to the injured and the dying. When the news reached the rector, who was vacationing at his summer home in Maine, he returned immediately to make further hospital visits and to comfort the sufferers and their families. The perpetrators of the outrage were never identified, but Dr. Manning, in his sermon at Trinity the next Sunday, made a strong plea for brotherly love to heal the hatred and lack of unity of which the crime was symptomatic.

MANNING ELECTED BISHOP OF NEW YORK

Bishop Greer of New York, now sixty-five years old and in ill health, was unable to preside at the diocesan convention in May 1919 and his suffragan, the Rt. Rev. Charles S. Burch, took the chair. Bishop Greer had sent a message to the convention requesting the election of a second suffragan bishop to assist him, but the convention, feeling that help could be given more rapidly by securing outside bishops to take confirmation and ordination services, delayed action on the bishop's request. However, within a week of the convention, Bishop Greer died and the diocese was left without an episcopal head.

A special convention was called for September 17, 1919 to elect a new Bishop of New York. The leading candidates were thought to be Dr. Ernest M. Stires of St. Thomas' Church and Dr. Manning of Trinity, though Bishop Burch and Dr. Charles L. Slattery of Grace Church were also nominated. However, Bishop Burch took the lead on the first ballot and was elected on the third ballot, with Dr. Stires second and Dr. Manning third.

Dr. Burch served only a little more than a year as Bishop of New York, for he died on December 20, 1920, leaving the diocese with neither diocesan nor assistant bishop. A special convention was therefore called for January 26, 1921 to elect a new bishop.

In preconvention caucuses and discussions, interest centered on Drs. Stires, Slattery, and Manning, each of whom had vociferous supporters and equally vocal opponents. The daily papers gave much attention to reports and speculations on the outcome of the forthcoming election. But what was really a matter of internal concern to the Episcopal Church became a public issue when, on the day of the convention, Hearst's *Evening Journal* made a bitter personal attack on Dr. Manning with an editorial under the heading: "Is an English Bishop necessary? Why? Is there no fit American?" Copies of the newspaper with its scurrilous attack were on sale at the door of the Synod House and were naturally bought by most of the delegates, who soon showed their displeasure at what they regarded as the unwarranted interference of a newspaper in the business of the Episcopal Church.

Again Drs. Stires, Slattery, and Manning were nominated, as was the Rt. Rev. Nathaniel S. Thomas, Bishop of Wyoming. Bishop Thomas was little known in the diocese, and so received few votes on the three ballots. On the first ballot Dr. Manning had a slight lead in both clerical and lay votes, with Dr. Slattery second and Dr. Stires a close third. The second ballot was much the same, but on the third ballot the name of Dr. Stires was withdrawn and Dr. Manning received enough votes in each order to be declared elected.

Probably the much-resented attack on Dr. Manning by

the Hearst newspaper was as much a factor in his election as were his ability and popularity. During the nominating speeches, Dr. Manning's supporters had made it clear that the rector had come to this country at the age of sixteen and had become an American citizen at the age of twenty-one and that his loyalty to this country was beyond doubt. With three well-qualified candidates, this doubtless was a strong element in the transfer of votes to Dr. Manning when Dr. Stires' name was withdrawn. Dr. Stires immediately moved to make the election unanimous and this was done as Dr. Manning, now bishop-elect, was led to the platform amid general applause.

DR. STETSON ELECTED RECTOR

With the election of Dr. Manning as Bishop of New York, it became necessary for the vestry of Trinity Parish to look for a new rector. A committee on nominations was chosen on February 14, consisting of Warden Richard Delafield and Vestrymen William B. Parsons, Nicholas F. Palmer, S. Edward Nash, and George F. Crane.

Except in the case of Trinity's first two rectors, the vestry had always filled vacancies in the rectorship by an active or former clergyman of the parish. On this occasion there were two vicars, Drs. William W. Bellinger of St. Agnes' and Milo H. Gates of the Chapel of the Intercession, who were, perhaps, equally qualified to succeed Dr. Manning. Faced with a difficult choice, the committee also looked outside the parish for a nominee, and on April 11 they unanimously recommended the Rev. Dr. Samuel Smith Drury, headmaster of St. Paul's School, Concord, New Hampshire. However, the names of Drs. Bellinger and Gates were also reported and a special meeting of the vestry was called for April 18 to consider the nominations.

At that meeting, presided over by Dr. Manning with eighteen of the twenty-two wardens and vestrymen present, Dr. Drury was elected with 11 votes against 4 for Dr. Bellinger and 3 for Dr. Gates. It was decided to ask the rector-elect to take office on or about September 15, and Dr. Manning thereupon submitted his own resignation to take effect the same date.

The rector-elect was a distinguished priest and noted educator with a dozen or more years of teaching experience and three years of missionary service in the Philippine Islands. He asked time to consider the call to Trinity but, after careful consideration, decided that his duty really lay with the school as his primary interest was in Christian education. On May 3, therefore, Dr. Drury wrote the vestry declining the election. It was, so far as the records indicate, the first time in Trinity's more than two centuries that any priest had turned down election to its rectorship.

Dr. Manning was consecrated Bishop of New York at the Cathedral of St. John the Divine on May 11, 1921. A few days before, a delegation of Trinity parishioners presented him with an episcopal cross and ring and a set of episcopal vestments, as well as many individual gifts. Bishop Manning was particularly happy that his old friend and bishop in his Nashville days, Bishop Gailor of Tennessee, was the preacher at his consecration and that Drs. Bellinger and Gates served as his attending presbyters.

The vestry was again faced with the choice of a new rector and Bishop Manning graciously agreed to continue as rector until his successor was chosen. Thus, once more, as had been the case in the early nineteenth century, the offices of Bishop of New York and rector of Trinity Parish were, for a time, combined.

The second election took place on October 21, 1921,

with Bishop Manning again presiding and seventeen wardens and vestrymen present. Drs. Bellinger and Gates were again nominated, but the committee's recommendation favored the choice of the Rev. Caleb Rochford Stetson, former vicar of Trinity Church (1907-1911) and, for the past ten years, rector of St. Mark's Church, Washington, D.C. In the balloting, Dr. Stetson received 10 votes, Dr. Bellinger 4, and Dr. Gates 3. The election was thereupon made unanimous and a notification committee was appointed.

Dr. Stetson accepted the election, and the date of his induction was set for St. Thomas' Day, December 21, with Bishop Manning's resignation to take effect at the same time. The return of a priest who was familiar with the traditions of the parish and remembered with affection by the members of Trinity Church met with general approbation by vestrymen and parishioners alike, and had the hearty approval of his predecessor, Bishop Manning, who had worked closely with him in the years when he had been Trinity's vicar.

CHANGES IN CHURCH AND CHAPELS (1922-1928)

The religious ceremony of institution of Caleb R. Stetson as eleventh rector of Trinity Parish was held in Trinity Church on January 25, 1922. It was conducted by Bishop Manning, who noted that it was the first time in the long history of the parish that a former rector had officiated at his successor's institution.

Dr. Stetson was quite a different type of person from his predecessor, though with the same loyalty to the Catholic tradition of the Episcopal Church and the same conservative point of view. A New Englander, born in Braintree, Mass. (coincidentally also the birthplace of William Vesey, Trinity's first rector), he was a graduate of Harvard and had studied medicine for a year at Johns Hopkins University before deciding to enter the ministry. His theological training, begun at the Virginia Theological Seminary, was completed at the General Theological Seminary and he was ordained deacon in 1898 and priest the following year by the Rt. Rev. Henry Yates Satterlee, Bishop of Washington. His early ministry was in the Diocese of Washington, where he built up a mission from 250 families to about 670 families, and built a basement church, parish hall, and vicarage.

Called to Trinity Church in 1907, Dr. Stetson spent four years as vicar of the mother church, where he gained a familiarity with the parish that stood him in good stead ten years later, when he returned as rector. During his time as vicar, he had lived with the other unmarried clergy of the parish in the clergy house at 61 Church Street, at the west end of St. Paul's Churchyard. However, during his period as rector of St. Mark's, Washington, from 1911 to 1921, he had been married to a cousin, Helen Stetson Richards. Accordingly, a new rectory was purchased for him at 56 Park Avenue—a five-story house with no elevator, typical of the townhouses of the day.

Most of the vicars of Trinity's chapels were the same ones who were serving when Stetson had been vicar of Trinity Church—Dr. Bellinger at St. Agnes', Dr. Gates at the Intercession, Fr. Schlueter at St. Luke's, and Dr. Banks Smith at St. Cornelius'. Fr. Moller had been appointed vicar of St. Chrysostom's just as Dr. Stetson was leaving in 1911 and Dr. Sutton, now vicar of Trinity Chapel, had been on the staff of the mother church when Stetson was vicar. Two vicars new to Dr. Stetson were Dr.

McComas at St. Paul's Chapel and the Rev. Lloyd D. Rhodes at St. Augustine's. Junior clergy numbered twelve, with three curates each at Trinity Church and St. Agnes' and two at the Chapel of the Intercession.

Trinity Church had no vicar, but had been under the direction of Dr. McComas. This combination of the work of Trinity Church and St. Paul's Chapel did not appeal to the new rector, so he called to Trinity as senior curate, and later priest-in-charge, an able former curate, the Rev. William B. Kinkaid.

The vestrymen were also mostly well-known to Dr. Stetson, including the two wardens, Richard Delafield and Stuyvesant Fish. The latter had succeeded Hermann Cammann, who had resigned in 1921 as warden, but continued as a senior vestryman. George F. Crane was the comptroller. One vestryman, Nicholas F. Palmer, died in January 1922. To succeed him, Stephen F. Bayne was elected. Mr. Bayne was a school-board official and superintendent of the Sunday school at the Chapel of the Intercession; he was later to serve as a warden of the parish and his son, the Rt. Rev. Stephen F. Bayne, Jr., has become one of the most distinguished bishops of the church.

Dr. Stetson also had another important post to fill, that of organist of Trinity Church. Dr. Victor Baier, who had spent his entire musical career at Trinity, had died in August 1921. His place during the interim was filled by the assistant organist, Moritz E. Schwartz, who was approaching retirement age. Dr. Stetson had a keen appreciation of church music and appointed as organist an exceptionally capable musician, Channing Lefebvre, formerly assistant organist at the Cathedral of St. John the Divine.

With his staff thus completed, Dr. Stetson turned his attention to the administration of the large and sprawling parish, which now numbered 9,640 communicants in nine congregations, with 2,700 pupils and teachers in the nine Sunday schools. In addition, the Trinity Mission House, under the direction of the Sisters of St. Margaret, had a large religious and social-service program which touched some 300 families on the lower West Side. The children of the mission house congregation now attended a weekly Children's Eucharist in Trinity Church, at which the children themselves sang the service and, later, received instructions by the clergy and the Sisters. Subsequently, with the adoption of the released-time program in the public schools, these instructions were given on weekdays, leaving Sunday as a day specifically for worship.

Unlike Dr. Manning, Dr. Stetson left the direction of financial affairs almost entirely to the vestry and the comptroller. The debt accumulated before and during the late war had been largely liquidated and the parish appeared to be in a good financial state.

The city and nation also reveled in a kind of prosperity, though much of it was soon to prove illusory. Gambling in the stock market, largely on margin, became a way of life, even for clerks and small businessmen. Prohibition was largely a farce, leading to thousands of speakeasies, many of them within a stone's throw of the church and chapels. Bootlegging led to hijacking and gang warfare and widespread corruption, while morals became increasingly lax among young and old alike.

Dr. Stetson was no reformer, but he was greatly concerned about the growing laxity, especially in the areas of divorce and remarriage, against the evils of which he spoke out boldly. He was also particularly concerned about the young people and did all he could to provide them with a wholesome environment and sound instruction in religion and morals.

Radio was now becoming popular, the first commercial

broadcasting station having been opened in 1920. Two years later, Station WEAF in New York invited Trinity to broadcast some of its services, but the offer was at first refused. However, on Christmas Eve 1922 the carol singing was broadcast from Trinity Church and, a week later, on New Year's Eve, the chimes of Trinity Church were heard on the air—as far away, it was said, as Cuba.

Dr. Stetson supported the requests of the vicars of St. Luke's and St. Chrysostom's chapels for trained social workers and made similar provisions for Trinity Mission House. An offering of $10,000 at the Ascension Day service in 1922 was used for the repair and refurnishing of the Seaside Home at Great River, where children from depressed areas were taken for happy summer holidays.

But some of the chapels appeared to have outlived their usefulness and new arrangements had to be made. At St. Augustine's Chapel, the change in the neighborhood from German and Italian to Jewish had caused the church's distinctive ministry to dwindle. The small religious work was continued by Fr. Rhodes, but the parish house was turned over to the social-service commission of the diocese and became a largely secular work under the name of "Houston Community House."

At St. Chrysostom's Chapel, at Seventh Avenue and 39th Street, the situation was even more acute. The neighborhood had long ceased to be a residential one and the chapel was increasingly hemmed in by stores, warehouses, and office buildings. After a thorough survey, it was decided to close the chapel and encourage the few remaining communicants to transfer to the nearby parish of St. Clement's Church. Arrangements were made to care for the rather considerable number of Negro communicants under diocesan auspices or in other chapels of the parish. The final service was held at St. Chrysostom's on

February 10, 1924, with Bishop Manning and Dr. Stetson officiating. The building was then sold and demolished to make way for another commercial structure.

At Trinity Chapel a new organ, costing about $20,000, was built to replace the one dating from 1855. It was blessed by the rector on November 11, 1923, with a service and recital by the chapel organist, W. Hunter Beckwith.

At the instigation of Mr. Lefebvre, Trinity Church also acquired new musical facilities in 1924. In 1846, when the present Trinity Church was built, there was but one organ in a loft at the rear of the church. This was augmented in 1864 by a chancel organ, but the double arrangement required two organists, whose constant problem was to play in complete accord. This sometimes resulted in absurdities, as on one occasion when the two organists disagreed on the tune to be played and each persisted with his own selection until the hymn was finished. Now two organs were built (though some of the stops of the original organ were retained) and coupled electronically so that both could be played from a single console in the chancel. Built by the Skinner Organ Company, the double instrument cost $42,000.

New arrangements were also made at St. Cornelius' Chapel on Governors Island when the Rev. Edmund Banks Smith retired as chaplain in 1924. The War Department now had a more adequate chaplaincy service than it had before World War I and desired to appoint its own chaplains to all army posts. The arrangement with Trinity Parish was therefore modified by mutual agreement so that the army would appoint a chaplain who was a priest of the Episcopal Church, and Trinity would maintain the chapel and provide the music. Under this policy, Chaplain Thomas E. Swan became the military chaplain and was also made honorary vicar of St. Cornelius' Chapel. The arrangement worked well and was to be continued with successive military chaplains until the post was closed and the command turned over to the Coast Guard in 1966.

During 1924 the vestry spent considerable sums in enlarging and improving the chancel and choir at St. Luke's Chapel and in making repairs and improvements at St. Agnes' Chapel and its parish house. Trinity also virtually rebuilt St. Clement's Church, to which most of the congregation of St. Chrysostom's had been transferred.

The most extensive changes, however, were made at St. Paul's Chapel. The classic simplicity of that colonial building had been marred during the nineteenth century by unwise "improvements" not in harmony with its notable architecture. Dr. Stetson and Thomas Nash, the parish architect, made plans to restore the chapel to bring it more into accord with its original appearance and, at the same time, to effect necessary repairs. The latter, however, proved to be more extensive than originally contemplated and problems of widening the street and digging foundations for a new subway further complicated the situation.

The major problem connected with the subway construction concerned the parish buildings on the chapel property. These included the offices of the rector, comptroller, and real estate employees; the quarters for unmarried clergy; and the parish house used by guilds and other church organizations. At first it was hoped that these could be shored up while the city excavated under them, but this proved not to be feasible and in 1927 the buildings were vacated and the property on which they stood was sold to the city, which demolished the structures.

The refurbishing of St. Paul's Chapel was further hampered by the death, in January 1926, of the architect, Thomas Nash. Essential repairs to the fabric were completed, but the restoration that had been contemplated had to be deferred to a later date.

In 1927 Trinity Parish was able to render a unique ecumenical service to the growing Russian Orthodox community in New York. Many Russians were living in the area; some had migrated to this country in the early years of the twentieth century and others had left their homeland after the Bolshevik Revolution of 1917. In 1905 their spiritual leader, Archbishop Tikhon, had moved his see from San Francisco to New York, where the beautiful Cathedral of St. Nicholas on East 97th Street was built, largely at the expense of the czarist government. Tikhon returned to Russia in 1907, where he was promoted to positions of increasing power, finally becoming the first Patriarch of All Russia, just after the relatively mild Kerensky revolution. When the Bolsheviks came into power, however, they took steps to suppress the Orthodox Church in Russia. Patriarch Tikhon was placed under house arrest, and thereafter the Russian Church was largely controlled by bishops appointed by the communist authorities, or willing to be subservient to them.

In the United States the leadership of the Russian Orthodox Church fell to Archbishop Platon, who returned to Russia at the outbreak of war and became Metropolitan (Archbishop) of Odessa. In 1919 Metropolitan Platon visited America, but was unable to return to Odessa as the communists were then in control. He therefore remained in the United States, in charge of Russian Church affairs in this country.

However, the communist government also wanted to control the Russian Orthodox Church in the United States and, under their influence, the Russian synod chose a priest, John Kedrovsky, who was an American citizen, and consecrated him as Archbishop for the Church in America. Archbishop Kedrovsky soon returned to New York and sought to take over the Cathedral of St. Nicholas on the ground that it was the property of the Russian government. In this he was opposed by Metropolitan Platon, with the support of most of the 250 Russian parishes in this country. A legal battle ensued, with two distinguished lawyers of the Episcopal Church, George Zabriskie and George Gordon Battle, representing the Metropolitan. However, after more than three years of litigation, the United States courts ruled in favor of Archbishop Kedrovsky and awarded the cathedral to him and his supporters.

Metropolitan Platon thereupon appealed to Bishop Manning for a place of worship for his followers. Bishop Manning and Dr. William C. Emhardt, of the department of the National Council dealing with foreign churches, turned to Trinity Parish for help in solving the problem, and Dr. Stetson in 1926 took up the matter with the Trinity vestry. After considering various possibilities, the vestry decided to divide the large St. Augustine's Chapel with a soundproof wall and to allocate the larger part of it to the Russians, together with parts of the parish house not used for community activities. This was done, with the smaller part of the chapel being retained for services of the Episcopal Church.

The Russian community united to make their part of the chapel a beautiful and typical Orthodox church, which was dedicated on May 22, 1927 as the Cathedral of the Holy Virgin Protection. The remodeling had cost the vestry $30,000 and an additional $2,500 a year was allocated for the Metropolitan's living quarters.

Thus in a time of crisis for their Russian neighbors, Trinity Parish extended its role of Mother of Churches to provide them with a center of worship. The happy association of the two churches in sharing the same building was to continue for sixteen years, by which time the Russians were able to buy and remodel a church on East 2nd Street for their exclusive use.

Meanwhile the services and Americanization activities of St. Augustine's Chapel continued under the priest-in-charge, Fr. Rhodes, until his resignation in 1928 and, thereafter, for ten years under the Rev. George LaPla Smith, with the assistance of a new parish worker, Evelyn Anderson. By 1929 Fr. Smith could report a Sunday school of ninety-five pupils, a number of active guilds, and an increasingly cordial relationship with the large and growing Russian congregation.

At the mother church, Dr. Stetson and Fr. Kinkaid quietly modified Dr. Manning's stand against perpetual reservation of the Blessed Sacrament. A beautiful sanctuary lamp, a memorial to a former vestryman, Ambrose S. Murray, Jr., was installed in All Saints' Chapel, which was increasingly used for private prayer and meditation, and the sacrament was reserved there and used for the sick and dying. The same practice gradually spread to all the chapels except St. Agnes' and Trinity Chapel, even including the military St. Cornelius' Chapel on Governors Island.

13

The Great Depression and World War II

1929-1945

The year 1929 started quietly, with little to indicate that, before it was over, there would be a market crash that would mark an economic and social watershed in American life. Harding "normalcy" and Coolidge prosperity had been succeeded by Hoover optimism of "a chicken in every pot" and two cars in most garages. New York City alone had more automobiles than all of Europe and land values in the city had increased in ten years by 75 percent, with Park Avenue rentals of $40,000 not uncommon. The Wall Street financial district was teeming with activity and money was borrowed freely for speculative purposes. It seemed that national prosperity was ever-increasing and eternal, and fortunes were being made—mostly on paper—by all who cared to put their money into stocks purchased on margin, often on the basis of someone's "hot tip."

The year was ushered in with gala celebrations at Broadway and Wall Street, where 2,000 thronged in and about Trinity Church for watchnight service and the striking of the bells at midnight. Other thousands gathered at Times Square in the center of the "Great White Way." Both Trinity Church and St. Paul's Chapel began the practice of having a priest sitting at a table at the door of the church during the noon hour for consultations on matters both trivial and profound—a practice that was to be continued and prove of great help to many in the depression years to come. Dr. Stetson joined the increasing numbers of leaders who contended that prohibition was a failure and should be repealed, or at least modified to permit light wines and beer.

Trinity Church was a place of tranquility in the midst of the frantic activities of Wall Street. "Finance has no place in our sermons," said Dr. Stetson in a widely published syndicated interview:

> Those who step out of the turmoil of Wall Street into the church are not looking for tips on the market. . . . The financial district may be the terrible, heartless place that some say it is, but one thing is sure—the busiest place in the world is not too busy to go to church.

THE DEPRESSION YEARS

Then came the crash. On "Black Thursday," October 24, 1929, prices of stocks began falling and brokers began calling for more money on margin accounts. By noon panic had set in; everybody wanted to sell and nobody wanted to buy. Endeavors of leading bankers and brokers to stem the tide proved fruitless. In the next few days, prices continued to decline; by November 13 it was reported that thirty billion dollars of supposed values had vanished. Nine million savings accounts were wiped out, 85,000 businesses became bankrupt, and 5,000 banks failed. The Great Depression, which was to last for several years, had begun.

Unemployment began to assume serious proportions in 1930 and became increasingly grave in 1931 and 1932. Like a blight it spread from one part of the city to another until hardly anyone remained unaffected. Even those who retained jobs found their paychecks cut again and again, and hunger began to stalk the poor. Gaunt men stood on street corners and outside churches trying vainly to sell apples or pencils or begging for a pittance to keep their families fed and clothed, however inadequately. Soup kitchens drew long lines of shivering and hungry men and women. Children stayed out of schools for lack of shoes and warm clothing.

In the absence of an adequate public-welfare system, churches were called upon for ever-increasing relief activities. In Trinity Parish, chapels like St. Augustine's on the east side, St. Luke's in Greenwich Village, and St. Paul's in the business district were the first to feel the pinch. The rector's opinion was that a parish should begin by helping its own people and this was done through increased social-service activities. But it soon became apparent that this was not enough and the church was challenged to make relief of the distressed thousands a major undertaking.

The churches of the city set Sunday, April 27, 1930 as the first of many "Unemployment Sundays," with appropriate sermons and appeals for generous contributions for relief. Assistance was rendered at first directly by individual churches, some of which opened soup kitchens and distributed food and clothing, but this soon proved inadequate and more centralized efforts were required.

In the Episcopal Church the main burden fell on the diocesan City Mission Society, which administered a cen-

The Trinity Choir

ter at Lafayette and Bleecker streets, near cheap lodgings such as the Mills Hotel. The Rev. Leslie E. Sutherland, superintendent of the society, preached at the Chapel of the Intercession and other churches, appealing for assistance. Toward the end of October, Bishop Manning issued an appeal for $250,000 to help the City Mission Society to carry its load. Trinity Parish responded with a gift of $10,000 immediately and a like amount early in the following year.

The city also sponsored an Emergency Relief Committee, known as the Prosser Committee from its head, Stewart Prosser. In November the Trinity vestry voted a generous grant as the first of many contributions to the work of this committee. It also reimbursed Fr. Schlueter half of the $2,000 he had given from his personal funds for relief of the poor in Greenwich Village and authorized him to rent a house near the vicarage to accommodate those of his people who had lost their homes and needed temporary shelter.

In the mother church and all of the chapels, unemployment relief in various forms became the main activity. All did what they could to the limit of their abilities and resources, in a multitude of ways that defy enumeration or classification. At St. Augustine's Chapel, meals were provided for children each day. At the Chapel of the Intercession, on the edge of Harlem, special attention was given to the needs of the Negro community, which had grown in ten years from 1.5 percent to 10.3 percent of the population in the area served by the chapel. Other chapels, as well as the mother church, gave assistance to the poor and the unemployed in a variety of ways.

The vestry was also generous in its contributions from capital funds and income on its real-estate holdings, but the corporation was also suffering from the depression. By

November 1931 its annual income was $400,000 below normal. By the following year, twenty-one of the important Trinity business properties were in financial difficulties, with the spectre of foreclosure of the mortgages arising, with resulting loss of the income-producing land. To avoid such a contingency, the corporation waived some of its ground rents, and even paid the overdue real-estate taxes of some of its tenants.

Meanwhile the parish continued its normal round of services and ministrations to the spiritual needs of its people. Special services were held on various occasions, notably a memorial service at Trinity for Marshal Foch and a commemoration of the one-hundredth anniversary of Bishop Hobart's death. Trinity Chapel had a series of special services celebrating its seventy-fifth anniversary.

At the Chapel of the Intercession, Dr. Milo H. Gates celebrated his twenty-fifth anniversary as rector and vicar, and shortly thereafter announced his resignation to become Dean of the Cathedral of St. John the Divine. To fill his place, the rector, with approval of the vestry, brought from Providence, Rhode Island, where he was rector of St. Stephen's Church, the Rev. Dr. Frederic S. Fleming, who began his work as vicar on April 13, 1930. It is interesting to note that when he was called, Dr. Stetson wrote in his diary: "I wonder if he might follow me as Rector in a few years' time?"

The time was to prove even shorter than the rector had anticipated. In the fall of 1931 Dr. Stetson went to Denver as a deputy to the General Convention, where he sponsored the report of the Commission on Church Architecture and participated in a heated debate on a proposed new canon on marriage. When a deadlock developed on the question of remarriage after divorce, he proposed a compromise amendment which, while not recognizing such remarriage in the church, would provide for restoration to communicant status of members remarried outside the church. The amended canon, while not entirely satisfactory to either side, was adopted and was to function reasonably well as the church's marriage law for ensuing decades.

On his return, Dr. Stetson was faced again with serious problems in the parish. Chief among these was the deteriorating financial situation, but others concerned discord in the vestry over the corporation's business affairs and problems in the mother church, where Fr. Kinkaid was replaced as priest-in-charge by the Rev. Thomas A. Sparks, to take effect in September. In addition, Dr. Stetson began the year 1932 with a severe cold and his health grew steadily worse. He officiated at a service at St. Paul's Chapel commemorating the 200th anniversary of George Washington's birth and preached at the festival Ascension Day Eucharist at Trinity Church in May. But, in June, shortly before he and Mrs. Stetson planned to leave for a vacation in Europe, he was stricken with "indigestion" and went into St. Luke's Hospital for a rest and checkup. There, on June 15, while reading the morning paper with his breakfast, he suddenly collapsed with a heart attack and died almost immediately.

Dr. Stetson's unexpected death was a shock to his people, who had come to love the quiet and reserved, but friendly, priest who had been their rector for ten and a half difficult and trying years. The clergy of the parish and the Sisters of St. Margaret kept perpetual vigil over his casket at All Saints' Chapel until the funeral service and requiem, celebrated by Fr. Kinkaid, assisted by Drs. Bellinger and Fleming. Bishop Manning read the committal and accompanied the body to Trinity Cemetery and, for the second time in little more than a decade, Trinity Parish was without a rector.

DR. FLEMING BECOMES RECTOR

The vestry did not act hastily in the selection of a successor to Dr. Stetson as rector of Trinity Parish. Fortunately, in view of the fact that Dr. Stetson had planned to spend the summer in Europe, the vicar of St. Paul's Chapel, Dr. Joseph P. McComas, had recently been appointed as assistant to the rector. In that capacity he administered the parish during the vacancy, and in September Fr. Sparks, whose appointment as priest-in-charge of Trinity Church was one of Dr. Stetson's last acts, began his work at the mother church. Fr. Kinkaid, who had been nominated by the Presiding Bishop as priest-in-charge of the American Church in Munich, was taken ill and died at St. Luke's Hospital before he was able to assume his new post.

During the interim another unique service was held at St. Paul's Chapel to commemorate the consecration a century before of four bishops, now depicted also on one of the bronze doors of Trinity Church. Bishop Manning celebrated the memorial Eucharist, with the Rev. H. Percy Silver, rector of the Church of the Incarnation, preaching the sermon.

On November 14, 1932 the vestry elected the Rev. Dr. Frederic S. Fleming as the twelfth rector of Trinity Parish. Although Dr. Fleming had served only two years in the parish, as vicar of the Intercession, he had served with distinction in the dioceses of Chicago and Rhode Island and had twice declined election to the episcopate —as Bishop Coadjutor of Northern Indiana and as Bishop of Olympia, in the state of Washington, both in 1924. A native of Maine, he was forty-six years of age. His induction took place on December 12 and his institution as rector on January 25, 1933, with Bishop Manning officiating.

Dr. Fleming quickly found himself heir to all the problems that had faced his predecessor and which had probably hastened his death. Chief among these was the financial problem, which was rapidly becoming acute.

The policies pursued by Mr. Cammann and Mr. Crane, as successive comptrollers responsible for Trinity's real estate and other investments, had by 1932 successfully replaced most of the corporation's obsolete housing properties with modern business buildings, rented on long leases, and had enabled the parish to build up a liquid reserve of over $2,000,000. But Mr. Crane and his chief assistant, W. F. L. Aigeltinger, were both well over seventy years of age and the vestry realized that their replacement would be difficult, especially as most of the details of business administration of the parish were known only to them. Crisis was precipitated when both of these able administrators resigned or retired early in 1933, and in fact both of them died before the end of that year.

Lawson Purdy was appointed acting comptroller on April 1 and Alden D. Stanton became his chief assistant. Both were men of wide experience and ability. They proposed, however, that Trinity's business affairs should no longer be handled directly by the vestry, but should be entrusted to a subsidiary corporation operated by professional real-estate men; and this proposal was adopted by the vestry.

This is not the place to review the financial history of the parish during the depression years. Like all business organizations, the corporation suffered disastrous losses, complicated in Trinity's case by its double role as a religious organization and as a real-estate operating company.

Suffice it to say that the $2,000,000 reserve was soon dissipated in the payment of debts and that the situation steadily became worse as the depression deepened. To protect its estate and prevent foreclosures on leased property, Trinity often had to assume the debts of the lessees and to take title to some of the leased buildings and operate them at a deficit.

By 1936 Trinity reached its maximum indebtedness of more than $23,300,000 and a later study indicated that the corporation was perilously close to bankruptcy for ten anxious years.

Nevertheless, Trinity was able to maintain its mother church and chapels and to carry on its religious and charitable activities during this critical period. The rector never ceased to emphasize that the work of the parish was to minister to the souls of the people entrusted to its care and in this he was fully supported by the clergy and the members of the vestry.

Nor did Trinity forget its role of Mother of Churches, though it was forced to curtail the size and scope of its gifts outside the parish. Nevertheless, it continued to assist weaker parishes and to contribute generously to the General Theological Seminary, the Beekman-Downtown Hospital, Hobart and Trinity colleges, and other church, charitable, and educational institutions. Contributions to the diocese and the City Mission Society, primarily for unemployment relief, totaled nearly $125,000 during these critical years.

For several months after he became rector, Dr. Fleming continued to live at the vicarage of the Chapel of the Intercession and also gave personal attention to the direction of that chapel. He and Mrs. Fleming had no desire to move into the rectory at 56 Park Avenue with its flights of stairs leading to the living quarters on the third, fourth, and fifth floors. The vestry, therefore, put the old house up for sale and rented an apartment on East 90th Street, to which the Flemings moved in May 1933. This served until 1936, when another apartment was rented at 1 Lexington Avenue. Finally the vestry bought a cooperative apartment at 133 East 64th Street, which served as the rectory for the rest of Dr. Fleming's incumbency and that of his successor.

As vicar to succeed him at the Intercession, Dr. Fleming called the Rev. Wallace John Gardner, rector of St. Paul's Church, Flatbush, Brooklyn. Dr. Gardner served in that capacity until 1936, when he was elected Bishop Coadjutor of New Jersey. He was succeeded by the Rev. Dr. S. Tagart Steele, who served as vicar from 1937 to 1943.

One of Dr. Fleming's concerns was to draw together the members of the mother church and the chapels, in order to develop more of a sense that they were one parish and concerned with each other's life and worship. This he did through united services of the whole parish in Holy Week and Advent, as a common preparation for their Easter and Christmas communions. Later Trinity Sunday became the occasion for the annual service for the whole parish.

Since the demolition of the parish house at St. Paul's in 1927, the offices of the rector and Trinity's clergy had been in rented quarters in the Wall Street area. In 1934, however, the parish acquired a modern twenty-five-story building at 74 Trinity Place, directly behind the church, by buying up the bonds from its bankrupt owners. Most of the building was occupied by offices, but the vestry decided to use as much of it as necessary for parish purposes. Hobart Upjohn, the parish architect, supervised adaptation of the upper floors for its new purpose. A rector's office and study were designed for half of the twenty-fifth floor, with a reception room and secretary's office. The other half was made into a unique vestry room, built after the manner of the chapter houses in English cathedrals. The room is vaulted and divided into three bays, with leaded windows high above the vestry stalls which line three walls, with a platform and seats for the rector and clerk on the fourth wall. Coats of arms and names of original pewholders decorate the vestry stalls, including such famous names as Governor Fletcher, the Earl of Bellomont, William Huddleston (the first parish schoolmaster), James Emott, and his famous client, Captain William Kidd.

Other offices for parish use were located on the twenty-fourth floor, and the basement was redesigned as a parish hall. This became widely used for noontime recreation and was furnished with comfortable chairs, magazines, and other books. There were also practice rooms for the Down Town Glee Club and Golden Hill Chorus and meeting places for guilds and organizations. Later, facilities were installed for small Communion breakfasts.

In 1935 it was found that cracks were developing in the tower of Trinity Church. The foundation of the tower was gradually sinking and extensive repairs were necessary to make it secure.

With the constantly changing population of New York, the work of several of the chapels underwent changes. Trinity Chapel, under its vicar, Dr. Sutton, found an added ministry among the Swedish community. The Rev. Donald H. Morse succeeded Fr. Sparks at Trinity Church and developed a special ministry to the sick, as well as taking great interest in downtown musical groups. Trinity Mission House, under the Sisters of St. Margaret, developed a ministry to people of Slavic origin, many of whom became communicants of the church. The worship at St. Christopher's Chapel, in the mission house, was greatly stimulated by the Rev. Robert Cornell, whose special concern was the mission house ministry. On his death in 1938 the mission house congregation raised funds for a statue of the Blessed Virgin and Child, dedicated in his memory. He was succeeded by the Rev. Charles Asa Clough, who later became Bishop of Springfield, Ill.

Although Dr. Fleming loved to preach, he had little sympathy with those who used the pulpit as a sounding board for social, economic, or political views. In 1936 he received wide attention in the public press for his suggestion, probably with tongue in cheek, that there be "a moratorium on preaching for the period of one or two years." He was soundly denounced by some of his Protestant brethren, but defended by others.

Trinity Church itself had many visiting preachers, often English bishops and priests touring this country in behalf of some worthy cause or other. So frequent were their appearances at one period that a vestryman was heard to mutter, "I wish the rector would have visiting preachers who could speak the English language so an American can understand them."

At Whitsunday 1937 Dr. G. Edward Stubbs completed forty-five years as organist and choirmaster at St. Agnes' Chapel. Under his guidance, the choir of men and boys at St. Agnes' had become recognized as one of the best in the country and his textbook on choir training became the standard on the subject. Following a gala anniversary celebration, the vestry granted Dr. Stubbs a leave of absence, but on December 26 he died at the age of eighty. He was succeeded as organist of St. Agnes' by Kenneth White.

A fourth religious order came to Trinity Parish in 1939

when three Sisters of the Order of St. Anne were assigned to work as teachers and parish visitors at St. Luke's Chapel. They were to remain at St. Luke's for ten years, after which they were replaced by Sisters of St. John Baptist.

For two years Dr. Fleming had attempted to administer Trinity Church, St. Paul's Chapel, and Trinity Mission House as a single entity, with the rector in direct control and the other clergy rotating among the three posts. This had been tried by other rectors and never proved very satisfactory. It was complicated in this case by the rector's recurring spells of illness, which often left the churches for three or four months without his supervision. He therefore appointed Fr. Morse as priest-in-charge of Trinity Church, the Rev. James Green as priest-in-charge of St. Paul's Chapel, and Fr. Clough in charge of the mission house. The Rev. Thomas J. Williams succeeded the Rev. G. LaPla Smith as priest-in-charge of St. Augustine's Chapel, after Fr. Smith retired because of failing health, and served until 1945.

In Advent 1939 Dr. Fleming invited three laymen to give a series of Advent talks on successive weeks in Trinity Church. They were Spencer Miller, Jr., a labor-management specialist; Professor William Lyon Phelps, of Yale University; and Professor Hoxie N. Fairchild, of Columbia University. So successful was this first experiment in having lay speakers at the noonday services that it was repeated from time to time in later years, often with members of the vestry serving in this capacity.

By 1939 the worst effects of the Great Depression had been dissipated and the country was entering into a new era of business activity. Trinity Parish, too, was slowly emerging from the mountain of debt accumulated during the depression years, though its financial situation was still precarious. Lawson Purdy had resigned as comptroller and was succeeded by Alden D. Stanton—the first time that the office had been held by one who was not also a warden or vestryman. Under his direction the corporation resumed the management of its own real estate, under the name of Trinity Operating Company, and steps were also taken to diversify their investments to include corporate securities.

But war clouds were again gathering on the horizon; indeed, much of the new prosperity in America was based on war-related industries. In Europe the rising stars of Benito Mussolini and Adolf Hitler were causing apprehension. The civil war in Spain and the invasion of Ethiopia by the Italians presaged greater threats.

The worst fears were realized when, in August 1939, Nazi Germany and communist Russia invaded Poland. World War II had begun. Although at first the United States seemed far removed from the conflict, events were moving inexorably toward the involvement of this country. The next five years were to be increasingly critical ones and, once again, the soul of America was to be tried in the crucible of war.

MORE CHANGES

The years 1940 to 1945 were also critical ones for Trinity Parish, marking an agonizing reappraisal of its work, leading to the closing of two of its chapels and some radical readjustments in others, as well as in the mother church.

There was also a major turnover in the membership of the vestry, which in the past had rarely required more than one or two replacements in a year. Three vestrymen died in 1940: Colonel William Burleigh, who had served since 1931 and had been clerk for several years; W. Sanders Davies, elected in 1936; and Frederick H. Moore, whose service on the vestry dated from 1920. In 1941 Dr. John Erskine of Columbia University, who had been a vestryman since 1916 and warden since 1939, resigned; in 1942, Judge T. C. T. Crain, John B. Walker, C. Aubrey Nicklas, and Archibald M. Shrady died and Harry Forsyth resigned.

Many of these vestrymen, all of whom had rendered faithful service, had represented the mother church or one of the chapels. Now, it seemed impossible to fill all the vacancies from members of the parish and Dr. Fleming turned to leading churchmen of other parishes to fill some of the places. As Trinity was the mother parish of Manhattan, it was felt that any churchman who lived or worked in New York City was eligible for election to the Trinity vestry; thus, from this time forward, some served in double capacities as vestrymen of Trinity Parish and also as wardens or vestrymen of other parishes in the city or the suburbs.

As the vestry was reconstituted, John A. Dix continued as one of the wardens and Stephen F. Bayne was elected in 1941 as the other warden. New men on the vestry included Albert Stickney, elected vestryman in 1939 and clerk in 1940; Lindsay Rogers, also elected in 1939; Frederick E. Hasler, Joseph W. Barker, Allan Davies, J. Taylor Foster, Willis H. Booth, Colonel William M. Chadbourne, Pierpont V. Davis, Captain John A. Gade (U.S.N.), William N. Westerlund, Charles W. Gerstenberg, Richard H. Mansfield, William B. Given, Jr., and W. Gibson Carey. Wendell L. Willkie, unsuccessful presidential candidate against Franklin D. Roosevelt, was also elected in 1942, but resigned the next year. Thus by 1943 fifteen of the twenty vestrymen were new or had served less than four years. Of the five continuing ones, Judge Philip J. McCook received leave of absence for war service (as did Joseph W. Barker), leaving only four veteran vestrymen: Admiral Reginald R. Belknap, Harry Woodburn Chase, Carl W. Ackerman, and the senior vestryman, Woolsey A. Shepard, to complete the roster. When Mr. Dix resigned as warden in 1945, he was succeeded in that post by Admiral Belknap.

As early as 1936 Dr. Fleming had appointed a vestry committee on parochial policy to study the whole question of the policy and scope of the parish and the effectiveness of the chapels. While the membership of the committee varied from year to year, among those who served during the most critical years were the two wardens, Mr. Dix and Dr. Bayne, Dr. Erskine (until his resignation), Admiral Belknap, Dr. Barker, Dean Ackerman (of the Columbia School of Journalism), and Dr. Chase (Chancellor of New York University). Under the guidance of this important committee, the vestry had to make some hard decisions about the work of Trinity Parish in relationship to the community, to other churches, and to the Diocese of New York. Three of the chapels—Trinity Chapel, St. Agnes', and St. Augustine's—were to bear the brunt of these difficult decisions.

Trinity Chapel, on 25th Street, west of Broadway, had long been considered a problem chapel. It was no longer in a residential district and as far back as 1917 Dr. Sutton had been sent there with the expectation that he would gradually terminate its work. Instead, for some years, Dr. Sutton had succeeded in infusing new life into the old chapel and had actually increased its membership and instilled new spirit into its people. But it was a losing battle, and by the early 1940s it was apparent that there was little or no future for the chapel as a part of Trinity Parish. Moreover, there were a number of Episcopal churches nearby that could easily absorb its remaining communicants.

On the other hand, there were two Eastern Orthodox congregations that were interested in purchasing the substantial property. One was the Russian Orthodox Cathedral, now worshiping in a part of St. Augustine's Chapel; the other was a Serbian Orthodox congregation which was also seeking a site for a new cathedral. In 1942 the vestry decided to accept the offer of the Serbian Orthodox. Dr. Fleming offered to transfer Dr. Sutton to the staff of the mother church and to provide quarters for him to continue the work of his guilds and other organizations of his congregation. However, Dr. Sutton declined the offer and, instead, accepted a position as associate rector and later rector, of St. Stephen's Church, at 69th Street near Broadway.

The sale was made, and on June 11, 1944 the former Trinity Chapel was consecrated as the Cathedral of St. Sava of the Serbian Orthodox Church. Bishop Manning and Dr. Fleming, with bishops of the Greek and Russian Orthodox churches, attended the service, at which the Serbian Bishop Dionysius officiated.

The fate of St. Agnes' Chapel, on West 92nd Street near Columbus Avenue, was a more unhappy one, reminiscent of that of St. John's Chapel a generation before. This had been the largest and, at one time, the most prosperous congregation in the Trinity system. Even in 1942 it listed 2,060 communicants, but the figure was misleading as most of the people on its rolls lived at a distance and actually attended other churches. But Dr. Bellinger, who for more than thirty years had instructed them, married many of them, baptized their children, and ministered to them in sickness and in health, could not bring himself to transfer them or to remove their names from the chapel list. Although the vicar was more than eighty years old, he was still active and resisted any suggestion that he might retire.

The property on which St. Agnes' stood was wanted by nearby Trinity School, itself an offspring of Trinity Parish, though with its own board of directors, of which Dr. Bellinger was one. Another member was Dr. Erskine, warden of Trinity and a member of St. Agnes' Chapel. At first Dr. Bellinger agreed to the transfer of the parish hall to Trinity School, but when it appeared that the trustees wanted the entire property he opposed the plan, despite the fact that Dr. Erskine favored it. Bishop Manning also gave his approval to the plan, perhaps reluctantly, since St. Agnes' had been his chapel before his election as rector of Trinity. At last, in November 1942, terms were agreed upon and the transfer of the property to Trinity School was consummated the next year.

Dr. Bellinger was deeply grieved. He could not bring himself to announce the decision to his congregation, although the fact was reported in the newspapers. Sick at heart, the vicar tried to continue his usual rounds, but in the middle of Lent he failed in body, too, and was taken to St. Luke's Hospital where he died on April 6, 1943.

It was not until June 1943 that the rector and vestry sent a formal announcement to the congregation of St. Agnes', advising them that the chapel was about to be closed and inviting them to transfer to Trinity Church or one of the remaining chapels. Some did so, or asked to be transferred to other parishes, but most of them made no response or expressed bitterness at the impending destruction of their beautiful church following the death of their beloved vicar. The chapel was closed on July 1, 1943.

The final blow came when wreckers began the heartless destruction of the chapel. Its altar, stained-glass windows, and various memorials had been placed in storage for future distribution to other churches, but apparently no one remembered the cornerstone. It was thrown into the rubble by the wreckers and there it was found by one of the former parishioners, who retrieved the contents placed in it at the time construction was started half a century before. It was the almost ghoulish ending to a sad and tragic story.

The third "problem chapel," St. Augustine's, met with a somewhat happier fate than Trinity Chapel and St. Agnes'. Demolition of tenements to widen the streets of the lower east side and the replacement of others by new federal and municipal housing had by 1943 greatly reduced the population in that area and those who remained were mostly Jewish. The Russian congregation, which occupied the major part of the divided church, removed to another building on East 2nd Street with many expressions of gratitude for the years that they had shared with the congregation of St. Augustine's as beneficiaries of the generosity of Trinity Parish. Obviously the time had come to give serious thought to the future of the work at St. Augustine's and the parochial policy committee devoted many hours to such consideration.

Fortunately, there was another Episcopal church near by—All Saints', at Henry and Scammel streets, a few blocks to the south and east of St. Augustine's. This church, though nominally an independent parish, had long been receiving substantial aid from Trinity Parish, as well as from the diocese. All Saints' had a history dating back to the early nineteenth century, its cornerstone having been laid by Bishop Hobart in 1827. The building itself was a large and historic one—the only remaining church in New York with the remnants of a gallery originally built for slaves, but probably never so used, as slavery was abolished in New York in the very year it was built. Its most recent rector had been the Rev. H. McL. Farnsworth, who resigned in 1944.

The way was therefore cleared for a combination of the work of All Saints' and St. Augustine's, centering at All Saints' Church, under the direction of Trinity Parish. Accordingly, St. Augustine's church and parish house were sold and the two churches were combined as All Saints'-St. Augustine's. On January 15, 1945 the Rev. Herman A. Berngen was named priest-in-charge of the combined work.

Fr. Berngen, thirty-five years old at the time of his appointment, was experienced in both parochial and social work and soon brought new life to the combined churches. He established cordial relations with the Henry Street Settlement, just across from the vicarage, and even with the Orthodox Jewish synagogue across from the church. The Sisters of St. Margaret, from the Trinity mission house, helped him in making a survey of the area, taught in released-time classes, and worked especially with women and children.

Fr. Berngen soon found that his most rewarding work was with the Negroes and Puerto Ricans who were beginning to move into the neighborhood, together with some Chinese and white families, many of whom had been associated with the old St. Augustine's. With services in the chapel twice a day, music, and a welcome open door, he soon attracted many, particularly among the children and young people. He did not try to compete with the settlement house and other social agencies, but welcomed all who would come with the warmth, color, and drama of Catholic worship, combined with the simplicity and zeal of Evangelical piety.

By 1949 the amalgamation of the two churches was complete and the parish organization of All Saints' Church was dissolved. The building was purchased by Trinity Parish, and thereafter it was designated simply as St. Augustine's Chapel. Fr. Berngen continued as vicar until 1952, when he resigned to become vicar of a mission in the state of Washington. His death occurred on June 13, 1959.

At the Chapel of the Intercession, Broadway and 155th Street, Dr. Steele continued as vicar until August 1, 1943, when he accepted a call to become rector of St. Luke's Church, Germantown, in Philadelphia. In his place, Dr. Fleming called the Rev. Joseph S. Minnis, rector of Christ Church, Joliet, Ill. Like the other chapels, the Intercession was undergoing many changes in an area that was rapidly becoming mostly Negro and Puerto Rican. Black membership in the chapel grew gradually, especially among children and young people. The total communicant strength remained relatively steady, at about 2,000, but, by 1951, some 40 percent of the Sunday school was Black and many Negroes attended the early services.

St. Luke's Chapel, in Greenwich Village, retained many of the characteristics of a village church, despite the increasing commercialization of the area. Fr. Schlueter was a great pastor and knew his people as few clergymen in New York do. It is said that at one time he turned up at a military camp half an hour before reveille, got one of the recruits out of bed, and told him that he had a pass for him for the day, and he should return to his church to be baptized. When the young man protested that he had some doubts about the Christian religion, Fr. Schlueter replied: "I know all about that, but God wants you to be baptized and He will clear up your difficulties if you let Him." Whether the story is true or not, it illustrates the direct approach and personal concern of Fr. Schlueter, who was greatly beloved not only by the members of St. Luke's but by the shopkeepers and residents of the neighborhood.

Fr. Schlueter also attracted the interest of men and women who had community leadership ability. Among his lay workers were: Mrs. Vladimir G. Simkhovitch, founder and head of Greenwich House; Harriet P. Bronson, a director of the New York Altar Guild; Dr. Abby Porter Leland, a leading physician; and Elizabeth McCracken, writer and journalist.

Fr. Schlueter also maintained and personally directed a summer camp for the boys and girls of the chapel congregation at his summer home in West Cornwall, Connecticut. When he retired in 1945, at the age of sixty-eight, he sold the property to the vestry, which continued the boys' camp as Camp Schlueter and later developed there a conference center for parish and other groups.

As successor to Fr. Schlueter, the Rev. Dr. Leicester C. Lewis served for four years, unfortunately marked by ill health. Dr. Lewis was noted as a scholar and preacher and did much to develop a first-rate faculty at St. Luke's School, which was rapidly becoming one of the leading day schools in the city. He died on March 18, 1949, while reading the galley proofs of the latest volume in the official parish history.

Dr. Lewis was succeeded by the Rev. Paul Weed, Jr., who had been a curate at St. Luke's from 1936 to 1942 and then rector of the Church of St. James the Less, Philadelphia. He had also assisted Fr. Schlueter during the summers at the West Cornwall camp, and so was well known by the congregation, who welcomed his return as their vicar.

St. Paul's Chapel continued on an even keel, despite several changes of vicars during this period. In 1939 this venerable chapel had observed the 150th anniversary of President Washington's inauguration, and through the years it continued its observance of patriotic occasions. The British Harvest Festival, which had been inaugurated by Dr. McComas at St. Paul's, was transferred to Trinity Church in 1938, but continued as an annual festival for those of British descent with the clergy and many of the people of the chapel participating.

Fr. Green served as priest-in-charge of St. Paul's for only a year, 1940-1941, and then went to the Cathedral of St. John the Divine as headmaster of the choir school. His successor, the Rev. Robert J. Gibson, served as vicar until 1947, when he was succeeded by the Rev. Charles W. Newman until 1949, and then by the Rev. Robert C. Hunsicker.

A feature of St. Paul's Chapel was the noonday Mass on weekdays, widely attended by workers in the financial district. St. Paul's was also the place from which frequent musical services were broadcast, generally with Andrew Tietjen, assistant organist of Trinity Church, at the organ.

Dr. Lefebvre resigned as organist at Trinity Church in 1941 to go to St. Paul's School, Concord, N. H. and, later, to the Philippines as organist at the new cathedral in Quezon City. He was succeeded by George Mead, Mus. D., who, as son of the sexton at St. Paul's, had grown up in Trinity Parish and had been assistant organist for some years before going to another post in Brooklyn. Dr. Mead continued and enhanced the high musical standards set by his predecessor and was ably assisted by Mr. Tietjen, who became assistant organist at about the same time.

TRINITY IN WORLD WAR II

The Japanese attack on Pearl Harbor on December 7, 1941 again plunged the nation into war. In accordance with President Roosevelt's proclamation designating January 1 as a national day of prayer, special services were held at Trinity and its chapels on New Year's Day in 1943 and each year thereafter through 1945. Special intercessions were added at other services and the noonday services at Trinity and St. Paul's attracted business people who frequently filled the churches, especially in Lent and Advent. Again, many of the young people of the parish volunteered or were drafted for military service and special intercession was made for them at the Sunday services. The Trinity Mission House alone had a roster of eighty men and four women in the armed forces and three of them were killed in action.

Judge Philip McCook, one of the senior vestrymen, resigned from the New York Supreme Court to accept a commission as colonel in the Judge Advocate Branch, despite the fact that he was seventy years old. It was his third war; he had been a private in the Spanish-American War and a major in World War I. Another vestryman, Dr. Joseph W. Barker, went to Washington as special assistant to the secretary of the navy, and others of the vestry were engaged in some form of war work, though mostly in New York.

With the threat of submarine warfare and possible air

attacks, New York had a dimout every night and food and fuel were rationed. In order to save the churches' treasures in case of attack, the parish transferred valuable church plate, artistic treasures, and historical documents to vaults in various places.

On April 12, 1945 news came of the death of President Roosevelt and memorial services were held throughout the parish, as in other churches everywhere. Then came the news of the armistice in Europe (prematurely, as it turned out) and the bells of Trinity rang out while tons of ticker tape filled Wall Street. Services of thanksgiving were held hourly for two days in Trinity and St. Paul's and both churches were filled many times over.

Then, on August 6, 1945, came the incredible news of the dropping of the atomic bomb on Hiroshima. Canon Bernard Iddings Bell, who was preaching that noon at Trinity, scrapped his prepared text to denounce the act, and added:

> It is doubtful if Christian missions in the Orient, at least under American and British auspices, can matter ever again. The Orient has long perceived that Anglo-Saxon diplomacy is based not on Christian principles, but on a canny imperialist expediency; now it has been shown that American methods of war are cosmically and cold-bloodedly barbarous beyond previous experience or possibility.

But many, remembering the barbarity of the Nazi and Japanese troops, did not agree with Canon Bell and welcomed the Bomb as averting the necessity of an invasion of Japan, with possibly even greater casualties on both sides. Less than two weeks later came the news of the surrender of Japan, and again the churches were filled with men and women giving thanks that the war was, indeed, at an end. Fr. Morse, preaching at Trinity, announced that there would be forty days of observance in church and chapel, "offering to God in penitent thanksgiving for the winning of another chance to promote and preserve His peace and order in the world by really obeying Him."

Now began a series of homecoming parades up Broadway, past Trinity Church and St. Paul's, with more showers of ticker tape. The first of these was to welcome General Jonathan Wainwright, released after three years of imprisonment by the Japanese. Passing the clergy assembled on the steps of Trinity, he saluted them and later recalled in an interview that his grandfather, for whom he was named, had been a minister of Trinity Church for three different periods between 1819 and 1854, two of them while he was also Provisional Bishop of New York.

World War II was, indeed, over. With the establishment of the United Nations, peace may have seemed just around the corner. But, a generation and two wars later, true peace has not yet come to this country or to the world. And the problem of the Bomb and its even more horrendous successors is still with us.

14

Renewal of Mission and Stewardship

1946-1966

The one-hundredth anniversary of the dedication of the present Trinity Church, the third on the same site, came in 1946 and the 250th anniversary of the parish in 1947. The rector and vestry decided to make the entire year, from May 1946 to May 1947, a time of celebration of this double anniversary.

As early as 1941 preparation for the year-long celebration began. A vestry committee, consisting of John A. Dix, Dr. Charles W. Gerstenberg, and Captain John A. Gade, began to gather material for a well-balanced program. The Rev. Dr. E. Clowes Chorley was commissioned to write a brief history of the rectors and the chapels, with a chapter on "The Music of Old Trinity" by Canon Edward N. West and one on "Trinity School and Trinity Parish" by Lawrence T. Cole. This was published by the Church Historical Society under the title, *Quarter of a Millennium.* In addition, new guide books were compiled for the church and some of the chapels. A magazine, *Trinity Par-*

St. Paul's Chapel and Churchyard Today

ish Herald, was begun in 1946 and continued until the spring of 1951.

As the time drew nearer, the Rev. Charles W. Newman was added to the parish staff as secretary of the anniversary celebrations, with responsibility for planning and overseeing the various special services.

THE CELEBRATION OF TRINITY'S QUARTER MILLENNIUM

The festival year began with the Ascension Day Eucharist on May 30, 1946. The music was Beethoven's *Mass in C,* with orchestral accompaniment, and the preacher was the Rev. Hughell E. W. Fosbroke, D.D., dean of the General Theological Seminary. On September 15, the twenty-fifth annual British Harvest Festival was held with the massing of banners and flags and the preacher was the Most Rev. Geoffrey Francis Fisher, Archbishop of Canterbury.

Other special services during the year honored the Eastern Orthodox churches, the Religious Orders of the Episcopal Church (held at St. Luke's Chapel), and Trinity's contributions to the music of the church.

In 1947 the month of January was devoted to Trinity's part in the growth of Christian and secular education. Special emphasis was placed on Columbia University, founded with Trinity's help as King's College; on Hobart College, begun by Bishop Hobart and named after him; and on Trinity School, which had its origin in Trinity's earliest years as the Charity School of the parish. The principal service, in which representatives of these and other educational institutions participated, was held at the Chapel of the Intercession.

In February Trinity Parish was featured on a nation-wide radio broadcast, with the rector as speaker and music by the Trinity choir. March was devoted to the relationship of Trinity with churches in New York founded or aided by the parish and with the Dutch Reformed, Methodist, Presbyterian, and Lutheran churches with which it had been associated in the early years.

The festival year reached its climax on Ascension Day in 1947. Trinity Church, newly reconditioned throughout, was decorated with twenty-nine banners hung throughout the nave representing churches and institutions associated with the history of the parish, as well as with a profusion of flowers and ferns. The musical setting of the Eucharist was Cesar Franck's *Messe Solonelle* with a forty-piece orchestra and choir conducted by Dr. Mead, with Mr. Tietjen at the organ. The Mass was sung by the rector, Dr. Fleming, with two vicars, Drs. Lewis and Minnis, as deacon and subdeacon. Five bishops, as well as the clergy of the parish, were in the procession. The sermon was preached by the Rt. Rev. J. W. C. Wand, Bishop of London, who spoke of his predecessor, Bishop Compton, designated as rector of Trinity in its royal charter promulgated in 1697. As the crowds wishing to attend could not be accommodated, the entire musical service was repeated the following Sunday.

As a souvenir of the festival year, 250 medals were struck to mark the anniversaries, most of them being distributed to guests at a gala dinner given Bishop Wand on May 22, 1947.

Many gifts were given to the parish on the occasion of these anniversaries, including a magnificent lectern Bible sent by King George VI, a silver chalice and paten given by the dean and chapter of Canterbury Cathedral, and gold ones from the dean and chapter of St. Paul's Cathedral, London. The parish, in turn, made gifts to King

George VI and to British churches, as well as generous benefactions to the Diocese of New York, the Episcopal City Mission Society, and other organizations and churches, including the Jewish Civic Center Synagogue and the Roman Catholic Church of Our Lady of Victory.

On April 1, 1948 Canon Bernard C. Newman became vicar of Trinity Church. A graduate of Harvard and General Theological Seminary, he had served his entire previous ministry in the Diocese of Pittsburgh, which he had represented three times in the General Convention. He was a brother of the Rev. Charles Newman who, after completion of the 250th anniversary celebrations, became vicar of St. Paul's Chapel. (To distinguish between the two brothers, the vicar of St. Paul's was commonly called Fr. Newman and the vicar of Trinity, Canon Newman.)

At Trinity Church, Canon Newman was able to share his work with two competent curates, the Rev. Dr. Charles T. Bridgeman and the Rev. Robert C. Hunsicker. Later, when Fr. Hunsicker became vicar of St. Paul's following the resignation of Fr. Newman, the Rev. Benjamin R. Priest was appointed and began work at Trinity in April 1950.

Canon Newman and his assistants began an organized program of visiting the families of the church and reorganized and strengthened the guilds and other activities. In addition Dr. Bridgeman (also known as canon from his previous work at the Anglican Cathedral in Jerusalem) took major responsibility for Trinity Mission House, and Fr. Priest, who had special training in psychological counseling, devoted much of his time to spiritual direction and the hearing of confessions.

The Rev. Donald H. Morse continued to be a tower of strength, especially through his preaching at weekday services, but in 1950 Fr. Morse was given a year's leave of absence because of ill health. However, his health continued to deteriorate and he never returned to the parish, but lived quietly in his boyhood home at Bradford, Mass. until his death of a heart attack on February 15, 1955.

During these years, the rector's health was a matter of increasing concern, both to the vestry and to himself. In the year 1948 Dr. Fleming virtually lost his voice and continued to have great difficulty with his throat. In November 1948 he entered the hospital, where his left vocal cord was removed. Thereafter, he could speak only in a hoarse whisper. After a second operation in December, he began, with a good teacher, a long and arduous process of learning to control his breath and his voice, but for a long time he was unable to preach or to celebrate publicly. It was not until Christmas 1949 that he could enter in his diary: "My first mass to be celebrated at altar anywhere since May 19, 1948."

Not until October 1950 was Dr. Fleming able to preach, and then only with the aid of a special microphone set up in the pulpit of Trinity Church. But the rector was failing in his general health, also, and it became increasingly difficult for him to attend to parish business.

On June 19, 1951 Dr. Fleming wrote to the vestry, tendering his resignation to take effect October 1, "with earnest request that it be accepted." Dr. Bayne, as senior warden, summoned a special meeting of the vestry two days later and the rector's resignation was accepted in accordance with his expressed desire. Arrangements were made for his retirement allowances and for such hospitalization as might be necessary. The rector was then brought into the meeting and gave his blessing to the vestrymen. Shortly thereafter Dr. Fleming entered a rest home in Connecticut and he was never able to return to the parish. He died five years later, on June 19, 1956, and was buried in the Trinity cemetery near the Chapel of the Intercession, where he had once been the vicar.

The Rev. Dr. Joseph S. Minnis, vicar of the Intercession, was named assistant to the rector, and as such became the acting rector while the vestry pursued the task of seeking a new rector of Trinity Parish.

Because of the importance of Trinity Parish, recommendations and suggestions poured in from all directions and the vestry soon had a list of a hundred or more "possibles." Some clergymen, indeed, wrote to recommend themselves, including one who cited as one of his qualifications that his wife was a direct descendant of King Alfred the Great. Somehow this failed to impress the hardheaded businessmen who made up the Trinity vestry.

Quietly and unobtrusively, usually in connection with a business trip, individual vestrymen would drop into churches whose rectors were on the "possible" list and report their impressions to the nominating committee. Gradually the list of "possibles" was whittled down until only two names remained under serious consideration. One of these was the Rev. Dr. John V. Butler, who had been a curate at the Chapel of the Intercession from 1931 to 1933 and was currently the rector of Trinity Church, Princeton, N. J.; but Dr. Butler had been the Princeton rector for only three years and made it clear to his supporters on the vestry that he was not prepared to leave that post at the time, even for the rectorship of Trinity Parish. The other was the Rev. Dr. John Heuss, head of the Department of Christian Education of the National Council.

Dr. Heuss had been called from the rectorship of St. Matthew's Church, Evanston, Ill., to bring new leadership to the educational work of the national church. The General Conventions of 1946 and 1949 had given generous support to his work, which included publication of the

Church's Teaching Series and far-reaching plans for a new curriculum for church (Sunday) schools, but he made it clear at the outset of his employment by the National Council that he would serve for only five or six years, and would then return to the parochial ministry.

On December 10, 1951 John Heuss was elected unanimously as thirteenth rector of Trinity Parish and the vestry was happy to announce his acceptance a few days later.

NEW MISSION AND STEWARDSHIP (*1952-1966*)

The ancient ceremony of Induction was held for the new rector on January 14, 1952. However, the service of Institution did not take place until June 3, as Dr. Heuss still had many commitments to fill before his work for the National Council was completed. During the intervening months, however, he met with the vestry, the vicars, and parish organizations and made some preliminary visits to the chapels.

The parish was a smaller but better organized one than that to which his predecessor had come. In addition to the mother church, there were now but five chapels: St. Paul's, St. Luke's, the Intercession, St. Augustine's, and St. Cornelius'. The total communicant strength was 3,932, though the list of more or less active parishioners numbered about 5,000. The debt accumulated during the depression, though considerably reduced, had not been entirely liquidated. The fabric of several churches and parish houses was in need of extensive repairs and refurbishing.

But, more important than these physical matters, Dr. Heuss felt, was the need of strengthening the spiritual life of the parish with a greater sense of commitment and responsibility on the part of its people. To his vicars and others in position of leadership, he stressed early in his rectorship what he called "a four-pronged attack" on these human problems. In varying words, he set forth the four objectives of his ministry in Trinity Parish:

1. Deepening the fellowship of each congregation, with a central core of devoted people who, in turn, would leaven their several congregations through regular worship, prayer, and work.
2. Building up an intercongregational fellowship and unity, with emphasis upon giving through a projected annual every-member canvass.
3. Development of a center at West Cornwall for conferences, "where deep life-shaking experiences and learning could take place."
4. Development of a College of Pastoral Work, to "bring groups of urban clergy here to share with us what we are doing to create a true Christian parish."

Three of these objectives were to be accomplished during the rectorship of John Heuss; the fourth, for various reasons, had to be deferred to the rectorship of his successor. In other areas, new types of ministry were also to be developed as the occasion and opportunity arose.

In one area, however, the parish was already in the process of developing a new ministry, which was shortly to result in a new chapel of Trinity Parish, known as St. Christopher's. Slum dwellings and old tenement houses on the lower east side were being torn down to make way for new low-cost housing, partially subsidized by the federal, state, and city governments. The largest of these was the vast new Alfred E. Smith housing project at the eastern end of Henry Street, near the Brooklyn Bridge. This and other similar developments brought hundreds of families, mostly Black and Puerto Rican, into the neighborhood in which there were few churches, either Catholic or Protestant. Although Trinity had a chapel at the opposite end of Henry Street, it was just too far away to serve the new community effectively. Thus it proved to be impractical for the new people to be ministered to by St. Augustine's Chapel.

It was the vicar of that chapel, Fr. Berngen, who first brought the matter to the attention of Dr. Fleming, in the latter days of his rectorship. Shortly before his resignation, Dr. Fleming called the parochial policy committee of the vestry into special session to consider how Trinity might extend its ministry to these people. Canon Newman, assisted by a team of students from the General Theological Seminary, made a survey of the area. Temporary quarters were rented, at first in the basement of a housing project on Cherry Street, and later in another location nearby. Sister Constance Margaret, S.S.M., gathered together some of the children for released-time education, and in the summer of 1952 Canon Bridgeman conducted a summer vacation school. Dr. Fleming's resignation caused no interruption in the work, which met with a greater initial response than had been anticipated.

When Fr. Berngen left St. Augustine's Chapel in 1952, Dr. Heuss brought to the parish an experienced urban mission priest, the Rev. C. Kilmer Myers, to be vicar of that chapel while the Rev. Edward Chandler, who also had experience in that type of work, served as priest-in-charge of St. Christopher's, assisted by the Rev. William A. Wendt.

As might be expected, Dr. Heuss began immediately to work toward the achievement of the first two points of his "four-pronged attack." At the mother church and the chapels, devotional organizations such as the Brotherhood of St. Andrew and the women's guilds were strengthened and a systematic program of parish visitation was begun. The Sunday schools were emphasized and new teachers recruited. At Trinity Church, the Rev. William W. Reed, formerly Archdeacon of Western Michigan, was appointed and put in charge of the church school, now transferred from the mission house. The Rev. Victor Hoag, a well-known educator, performed the same function for the Chapel of the Intercession.

At 74 Trinity Place, clergy and staff quarters were remodeled and enlarged to occupy the twenty-first to twenty-fifth floors. A dining room, with provisions for a private chapel and meeting rooms, was built on the second floor. A director of communications, Ellsworth Wallace, was appointed, with special responsibility for planning the first every-member canvass. A picture guide, *Our Life in Old Trinity Parish,* was prepared and, later, a new periodical, *Trinity Parish Newsletter,* was begun, with Mr. Wallace as editor.

In 1954, after intensive preparation, the first every-member canvass was undertaken, opening with a "Loyalty Sunday" in each congregation. Over 2,000 pledges were received—a notable result in a parish whose members had largely been content to leave financial matters to be administered by the vestry from business income. Money received through the pledges was not used for the maintenance of the churches, but was entirely designated for missionary work inside and outside the parish.

The Conference Center at West Cornwall, housed in the remodeled farmhouse and other buildings, began to be used for retreats, quiet days, and parish life conferences, both for the people of Trinity Parish and for others. Mr. and Mrs. Dexter M. Stephens were in charge of it. At the same time, the camping facilities for boys were improved, with a new swimming pool and other recreational and educational facilities and, in time, a second camp for girls was developed at Sharon, Conn.

The day school at St. Luke's Chapel was greatly stimulated in 1955 by the building of a modern school, preserving the atmosphere of a nineteenth-century dwelling on the street side but open to a garden quadrangle and playground on the inside. This was a part of the remodeling of the historic St. Luke's block, which modernized the buildings while preserving the quaint exteriors that had been one of the attractions of Greenwich Village.

In 1954 the Rev. Dr. Joseph S. Minnis, who had been vicar of the Chapel of the Intercession since 1943, was elected Bishop Coadjutor of Colorado. He was succeeded by the Rev. Robert R. Spears, Jr., who had been rector of St. Peter's Church, Auburn, N. Y. Fr. Spears served until 1960. This largest of Trinity's chapels was a beehive of activities. With a full schedule of Sunday and weekday services, the Intercession attracted a wide cross-section of the multiracial upper Broadway community. Under the direction of its organist, Clinton Reed, the chapel had four choirs and an oratorio society. Its Sunday school had the highest enrollment in fifteen years and was one of the largest and best in the diocese. Parish house activities included basketball and dances in the big gymnasium and annual Christmas fairs and gala spring fiestas. But the center of its activities was the altar where every day was begun with a 7 o'clock Eucharist, followed on Thursdays by a breakfast for those who had to hurry off to work or to school. The normal staff complement for the Chapel of the Intercession was four priests and nine lay workers and every family on its list of some 2,000 communicants was called on at least once a year.

Fr. Spears resigned as vicar in 1960 to become rector of Trinity Church, Princeton, N. J. Later he became Bishop of Rochester, N. Y. His place at the Intercession was taken by the Rev. C. Kilmer Myers, transferred from the Lower East Side Mission. However, Fr. Myers served as vicar of the Intercession only three years, when he resigned to become director of an urban training mission in Chicago, later becoming Suffragan Bishop of Michigan and then Bishop of California. The Rev. Dr. Leslie J. A. Lang became vicar on September 1, 1963.

In 1965 the Chapel of the Intercession celebrated the fiftieth anniversary of the consecration of its present building. Observances during the year included: a festival of the arts, which included a Jazz Mass; a musical service featuring Haydn's *Lord Nelson Mass*; an anniversary dinner at the Concourse Plaza Hotel; a "hootenanny" presented by the young adults; and numerous other festivities for adults and children.

The religious observance of the anniversary was a solemn procession and festal Eucharist on Whitsunday, at which Dr. Heuss preached. On Trinity Sunday the Eucharist for the whole parish, normally held at Trinity Church, was held at the Intercession, with sermon by the Rt. Rev. Stephen F. Bayne, Jr., who had been raised as a member of the chapel congregation and whose father had been superintendent of its Sunday school and, later, a vestryman and warden of Trinity Parish.

St. Cornelius' Chapel continued its ministry to the army troops at Fort Jay, Governors Island, with army chaplains who also served as honorary vicars of the chapel. These included Chaplains Eric I. Eastman (1951-1953), Harry G. Campbell (1953-1955), John E. Kinney (1955-1958), John C. Francis (1958-1961), Alister C. Anderson (1961-1963), and Russell O. Kirsch (1963-1964).

But in 1965 the century-long association between the Episcopal Church and the army at Governors Island was brought to a close. On the last day of that year, the army finally closed its post on the island, which was to be taken over by the U.S. Coast Guard the following June.

In a ceremony at St. Cornelius', a plaque was unveiled commemorating the army's stay on the island and was accepted for Trinity Parish by Canon Newman. The honorary vicar, Chaplain Raymond P. Hoffman, gave an address relating the history of the chapel. The day was closed with the firing of a salute and the ceremonial lowering of the flag while the national anthem was played. Chaplain Hoffman remained at St. Cornelius' until the end of June, while the army completed the work of dismantling its post.

St. Paul's Chapel, with the Rev. Robert C. Hunsicker as vicar, was not content with its role as historical monument, but took its full share in community and social enterprises. The staff made daily visits to the Beekman-Downtown Hospital and was represented on the Community Planning Board. In addition, the clergy participated in a joint ministry to work with the authorities and transients at Ellis Island. While it was still an immigration center, they also had a far-reaching personal counseling and pastoral ministry.

The two chapels on the lower east side were now under a common vicar: Fr. Myers until 1960, and then the Rev. William W. Reed. Under the vicar's general oversight, St. Augustine's and St. Christopher's each had a priest-in-charge and several curates, as well as a devoted and growing staff of lay workers. Among the clergy who served these two chapels at various times during this period were: Frs. Edd L. Payne, William G. Love, Robert Lloyd Williams, Gerald Fairweather, Samuel L. Snodgrass, Jr., Peter A. Marks, Louis A. Meyer, Donald C. Hagan, William D. Dwyer, Gilbert S. Avery, Merrill O. Young, Maurice A. M. Garrison, Walter N. Thompson, Stephen J. Chinlund, Rafael deSota, and James L. Miller.

Services in both chapels were in English or Spanish and, often, bilingual. Extensive youth programs were held and an effective effort was made to turn gang activities into constructive social channels. Summer programs were held with boys and girls of all ages and many were given outings at the Seaside Home on Long Island or the camps at West Cornwall and Sharon, Conn.

The Trinity Mission House was closed in 1956 and the Sisters transferred to the lower east side work, with a new convent on Oliver Street. The congregation was transferred to Trinity Church, where they formed the nucleus of the 9 o'clock Sunday Mass, followed by breakfast and church school classes.

Extensive repairs required the closing of St. Augustine's for a time and there was fear that it might not be possible to reopen the historic church. This was done, however, after expensive remodeling and the vestry also acquired adjoining land on which a parish house was built.

The vestry was also changing, as death or resignation removed some of the older members and new ones took their places. Albert Stickney, vestryman since 1939 and clerk from 1940 to 1955, died in the latter year. He was replaced as clerk by Ellis H. Carson from 1955 to 1959, and then by Andrew Oliver.

Stephen F. Bayne, a lifelong member of the Chapel of the Intercession, vestryman since 1922 and warden since 1941, died in August 1956. The other warden, Admiral Reginald R. Belknap, died March 30, 1959. New wardens were Frederick E. Hasler and Dr. Joseph W. Barker.

New vestrymen elected during the period 1951 to 1962 were G. Keith Funston (president of the New York Stock Exchange), Lewis B. Cuyler, R. Keith Kane, Richard K. Paynter, Jr., Adrian M. Massie, Andrew Oliver, Herbert G. King, Theodore Baumeister, Kempton Dunn, George A. Murphy, and J. Eugene Banks.

A. Elliott Bates continued as comptroller until his retirement in 1960, when he was succeeded by Desmond L. Crawford. Under their careful management, Trinity's mortgage indebtedness was liquidated and the commercial properties, as well as the churches, were modernized and maintained in good repair. And, with the reconstruction of St. Luke's block, Trinity Parish no longer held any residential property except that used as vicarages or homes for the other clergymen of the parish.

In 1964 construction began on a massive addition to Trinity Church and the remodeling of a part of the church itself. The major part of the work was the building of a wing at the southwest corner of the church to house an exhibit hall, a choir room, vesting rooms, and small conference rooms. At the same time a new entrance was designed for the Trinity Place side of the church, with a cloister and flight of steps to the sidewalk. The result was not only a handsome addition to the church, but the provision of more adequate facilities for the clergy and choir. Also it made it possible for members of the congregation to cross directly from the church to 74 Trinity Place, where Communion breakfasts and dinners were held on Sundays when most eating facilities in the Wall Street district were closed.

The new structure was to be dedicated on Ascension Day 1965, with the wing as a thanksgiving and memorial to Trinity's tenth rector and the tenth Bishop of New York, the Rt. Rev. William T. Manning. However, strikes and other delays intervened, and by that date only the exterior had been substantially completed. On that day, however, just prior to the orchestral Eucharist, the cornerstone was formally laid by the Rt. Rev. Horace W. B. Donegan, Bishop of New York, assisted by Dr. Heuss and

Bishop Bayne. In his sermon Bishop Donegan reviewed the history of Trinity Church during the rectorship of Dr. Manning and paid high tribute to him.

Completion of the alterations and the furnishing of the new wing took another year. On Ascension Day 1966 Bishop Donegan again was the preacher. Just before the sermon he proceeded with the clergy and vestry into the new wing where the various rooms were blessed, as was the new cloister and the "cherub gate." But on that occasion there was, unhappily, no rector to participate and to see the completion of his dream, for John Heuss had entered into eternal life two months earlier.

DEATH OF DR. HEUSS

March 20, 1966 began for Dr. Heuss much as any other Sunday. He and Mrs. Heuss attended the 9 o'clock Mass at Trinity Church and had breakfast in the parish cafeteria. At the 11 o'clock Eucharist, the rector preached a Lenten sermon. Then he had lunch, again in the parish dining hall, and lingered to visit with the members of the choir and congregation. On the way home, he dropped off a vestryman and his wife at their apartment and continued with Mrs. Heuss to the rectory on East 64th Street. The afternoon and early evening were spent quietly, with the reading of the Sunday papers, perhaps some writing and telephone calls, a family supper, and an hour or two of television. The rector retired early, but did not complain of illness. Mrs. Heuss stayed up to watch the 11 o'clock news on TV. When she went to their room, she found her husband dead of a heart attack.

The congregation and Dr. Heuss' many friends were shocked at the sudden and unexpected death of the rector. Although he had twice had leaves of absence for health reasons, he had fully recovered and had seemed to be in good health.

Canon Bernard C. Newman had been appointed assistant to the rector a few months earlier and the vestry promptly designated him as acting rector. The burial office was held at Trinity Church a few days later, with Bishop Donegan officiating and Canon Newman celebrating the Mass of Requiem. In the sanctuary was the Most Rev. John J. Maguire, Coadjutor Archbishop of New York and personal representative of Cardinal Spellman—the first time a Roman Catholic prelate had participated in a Eucharistic service at Trinity. It was a symbol of the respect in which Dr. Heuss was held by all—Episcopalians, Protestants, Eastern Orthodox, Roman Catholics, and men of every faith or none.

Burial, by special dispensation, was in the Trinity churchyard, which had been closed to further interments except in existing vaults since 1831. Later, a memorial cross was erected over the vault provided by the parish for his burial.

One of Dr. Heuss' last acts had been to write an Easter message for the *Trinity Parish Newsletter*. The message, published after his death, became in a sense a farewell message from him. He wrote:

> Easter is not an argument. It is an announcement! It is not a syllogism. It is a shout that God is alive. He is very much alive and we in Trinity Parish know it. So, Happy Easter and thanks be to the living God!

15

Striking Out in New Directions

1966-1971

At the time of his death, Dr. Heuss had been planning to lead a small pilgrimage of vestrymen and members of Trinity Church to England, primarily to participate in the celebration of the 900th anniversary of Westminster Abbey. In his place, Canon and Mrs. Newman led the group, which included the two wardens and their wives (Mr. and Mrs. Hasler and Dr. and Mrs. Barker), two vestrymen and their wives (Col. and Mrs. Herbert J. King and Mr. and Mrs. Ellis H. Carson), and the comptroller, Desmond L. Crawford, and Mrs. Crawford.

A second purpose of the trip was to make an official visit to the Church of St. Mary-le-Bow in London. This parish, which was the prototype for Trinity Church (and so mentioned in the charter), had been enjoying increasingly close relationship with Trinity through visits of its rector, the Rev. Joseph McCulloch, and through aid given by Trinity to the London church to assist in rebuilding after World War II. Now, in an expression of friendship and thanksgiving, the two wardens of Trinity Parish were inducted as honorary wardens of St. Mary's, for the bombed-out church of St. Mildred's, Bread Street, which stands nearby.

At Westminster Abbey, in the course of a special service, Canon Newman unveiled a plaque "in grateful memory of King William III, who, in 1697, granted a Charter and a generous gift of land to Trinity Church, establishing it as the first Anglican church in the city of New York; and of Queen Anne, who in 1705 granted Trinity Church the Queen's Farm and Garden on Manhattan Island." The Bishop of London, the Rt. Rev. Robert W. Stopford, as well as the dean and chapter of the Abbey, participated in the ceremony.

Now the vestry was again faced with the choice of a new rector. While various names were suggested and considered, attention was soon focused once more on Dr. John V. Butler, who was then dean of the Cathedral of St. John the Divine. Not only had he once served as a curate at the Chapel of the Intercession, but he had been a close friend of Dr. Fleming and Dr. Heuss and had often preached at Trinity or one of the chapels at their invitation. He was, therefore, more familiar with the parish and with the plans of his predecessor than any priest except Canon Newman, who was within a year or two of retirement age. On August 1, 1966, at a special meeting of the vestry, Dean Butler was unanimously elected as fourteenth rector of Trinity Parish and his induction was set for three months later.

Meanwhile, St. Paul's Chapel was engaged in a year-long celebration of its 200th anniversary. In preparation, St. Paul's had at last completed the work of restoration to much of its appearance in the eighteenth century. The climax of the observance was a service of worship on

October 30, attended by the vestry and a large number of dignitaries representing religious, educational, and governmental organizations. The Hon. John V. Lindsay, mayor of New York, himself an Episcopalian, gave an address, largely historical, and the Rt. Rev. John E. Hines, Presiding Bishop, preached the sermon. An interesting feature was the participation by four bishops whose predecessors had been consecrated at the famous service in St. Paul's in 1832.

Two days later, on All Saints' Day, at Trinity Church, Dr. Butler was inducted and instituted as rector of Trinity Parish. For the first time in Trinity's long history, the two services were combined, with the ceremony of Induction at the door of the church being followed immediately by the office of Institution by the Bishop of New York. In his sermon Bishop Donegan noted that Dr. Butler "is not just the rector of an historic parish; he is rector of the parish to which, in all Christendom, the Lord has entrusted the most talents, and from which the Lord will require the most by way of accounting in stewardship." The bishop also suggested a rethinking of the whole chapel system of Trinity Parish: "Today we must ask ourselves if the long continuation of the chapel status is not in reality a serious criticism of the parent body." No doubt the same thoughts were in the new rector's mind, as subsequent events were to show.

TRINITY INSTITUTE

One of the first objectives to which Dr. Butler addressed himself was the "unfinished business" of Dr. Heuss' fourth aim—development of a college of pastoral work for the clergy of the whole church. Within three months of his institution, Dr. Butler was able to announce the founding of Trinity Institute, with the Rev. Dr. Robert E. Terwilliger as its first director. In the initial announcement, it was stated:

> Trinity Institute will be organized on the lines of similar centers in Europe, particularly in Holland, France, and Germany. It will be theologically oriented to provide a situation in which the clergy can be assisted in understanding and expressing the Christian Faith in contemporary terms. The minor purpose would be the development of expertise in dealing with present-day problems. It would provide opportunity for the clergy to become cognizant of the sociological, political, and psychological developments pertaining to their work.

Quarters for the new institute were found at Windham House, on West 108th Street, which had formerly been a residential training center for women church workers.

On September 30, 1967 Trinity Institute was inaugurated with a special convocation at Trinity Church, marked by an address by the Most Rev. Michael Ramsey, Archbishop of Canterbury, on "Jesus Christ in Faith and History." The assembly was a distinguished one, with guests from the Eastern Orthodox, Roman Catholic, and Protestant churches, the faculties of the General and Union Theological seminaries, as well as the rector, clergy, and vestry of Trinity Parish. It was a brilliant but simple ceremony consisting only of a bidding prayer, a statement by Dr. Terwilliger setting forth the aims of the institute, and the archbishop's address, concluding with a hymn and a blessing by the Bishop of New York.

The first conference at the institute, on November 29, attracted more than 120 priests to a conference on the significance and use of the new Liturgy of the Lord's Supper, approved for trial use by the 1967 General Convention. Addresses were given by the Very Rev. Samuel J. Wylie, Jr., dean of the General Seminary, by Canon Edward N. West of the cathedral, Dr. Benjamin Minifie of Grace Church, and Fr. Donald L. Garfield, of the Church of St. Mary the Virgin. It was the first of many such conferences and convocations.

During the next several years Trinity Institute attracted priests from all parts of the country and clergymen of other communions, also. A series of conferences for bishops was attended by almost every active bishop of the Episcopal Church. Distinguished theologians from this country and Europe read papers and led discussions on contemporary theological questions, and experienced priests and pastors dealt with such questions as urban renewal and ministry, liturgy, worship, and pastoral care.

The highlight of the first few years of the institute was a special seminar for bishops in the spring of 1970, led by Archbishop Ramsey and Leo-Jozef Cardinal Suenens, Primate of Belgium, on the "Future of the Christian Church." A session at Riverside Church, open to the public, attracted more than 2,000 people and was filmed for American and German television. The two prelates were also welcomed by Terence Cardinal Cooke, Roman Catholic Archbishop of New York, at St. Patrick's Cathedral.

LITURGICAL CHANGES

At Trinity Church, the rector turned his attention to modernization of the liturgy and fabric of the sanctuary. While dean of the Cathedral of St. John the Divine, Dr. Butler had worked closely with Canon West in developing a "customary" for the celebration of the Holy Eucharist, as an example to parishes. This involved, among other things, a free-standing altar so that the clergy could celebrate facing the people, as contemplated in the trial liturgy. He soon concluded that certain changes in the structure of the church were desirable in order to implement the contemplated changes in the liturgy and obtained the approval of the vestry to alter the chancel accordingly.

> It seemed to me on coming to Trinity [Dr. Butler wrote] that the pulpit [on the epistle side] was too high and hazardous, with little eye-to-eye contact with the congregation; that the high altar was too far removed, the chancel steps dangerous, and the choir stalls too cramped, not to mention the communion rail. So without changing the choir pavement we removed four choir stalls, leaving two on each side. We removed the communion rail also. All this fine woodwork is safely in storage. Of course this meant housing the choir normally in the gallery, but George Mead [the organist] preferred this acoustically. We built a wood platform at the level of the former communion rail flooring, extending it to the first bay of the nave. . . . We had an identical pulpit or ambo constructed and placed it on the epistle side, far to the front. We moved the old pulpit to the gospel side, way front and with only two shallow steps up.
>
> With the two pulpits, we now had provision, as at St. Mary-le-Bow, for dialogue sermons; also a proper place for reading of the epistle, or the prayer of intercession. We had an altar designed of wood, with two polychromed candlesticks.

With the new chancel arrangement, the Eucharist is normally celebrated with three sacred ministers facing the people, not only on Sundays but at daily noon Masses. The chancel is covered with red carpeting and communion rails are at the sides. Those wishing to receive the sacrament standing, do so at the center and those who prefer kneeling receive at the side rails. The choir is normally in the gallery at the rear of the church except while it participates in processions.

Canon Bernard C. Newman, who had served as vicar of Trinity Church for twenty years and as assistant to the rector since 1966, retired on April 1, 1968. At a "service of appreciation" on Passion Sunday, the rector and vicars concelebrated the Holy Eucharist and Bishop Bayne was the special preacher. Canon and Mrs. Newman were also tendered a farewell dinner by the rector and vestry, as well as a reception by the congregation.

To succeed Canon Newman as vicar of Trinity Church, the rector appointed the Very Rev. Donald R. Woodward, who had been dean of Grace and Holy Trinity Cathedral in Kansas City, Mo., since 1958. Fr. Woodward had been a curate at the Chapel of the Intercession from 1940 to 1943, so it was really a return to the parish for him.

The Rev. Benjamin R. Priest, who had exercised a notable ministry in Trinity Church since 1950, retired December 19, 1969.

Dr. George Mead, Jr., retired as organist and choirmaster of Trinity Church on June 9, 1968. A lifelong member of the parish, he served as a boy in the choir at St. Cornelius' Chapel, and at the age of eleven became an acolyte and choir member at the mother church. He attended the Trinity Day School and, later, Columbia University, where he became a member of Phi Beta Kappa and went on to take the degree of Master of Arts in Music. The university later awarded him the degree of Doctor of Music.

In 1925, when he was not yet thirty years old, he was employed at Trinity Church during the summer "to play the hymns for three months for three days a week when there is no organ recital." He served as assistant to Channing Lefebvre from 1926 to 1936 and then accepted a position as organist at the Central Congregational Church in Brooklyn. In 1946 he succeeded Dr. Lefebvre as organist and choirmaster of Trinity Church. He also served as director of the Down Town Glee Club and the choir of the Friendly Sons of St. Patrick.

At Trinity Dr. Mead composed and arranged works in various forms, including a notable work entitled "With Instruments of Music," written for the dedication of the new organ on Ascension Day 1961. Another work, "A Fantasy for Organ," won a prize from the American Guild of Organists. His recitals and concerts, both at Trinity and at Symphony Hall, won him wide acclaim in the musical world.

Dr. Mead was succeeded as organist and choirmaster at Trinity by Larry King, who continued Trinity's high musical standards and added to them significant contemporary experimental and electronic compositions.

When Dr. Butler had become rector in 1966 he was a widower, his wife, Mary McKee Butler, having died nearly a year previously. On June 14, 1969 Dr. Butler was married at St. Paul's Chapel to Ruth Dear Towner, widow of the late Reginald Finch Towner, Sr., of Montclair, N. J. The ceremony was performed by Bishop Donegan, assisted by Bishop Bayne. Dr. Butler thus became the fourth rector of Trinity to be married while holding that office, the others having been the first rector, William Vesey, the second, Henry Barclay, and the ninth, Morgan Dix.

NEW DIRECTIONS

One of Trinity's most noteworthy gifts as Mother of Churches was a grant of $45,000 made by the vestry in 1968 for purchase of a site for a church in the Philippine

Islands. Dr. Butler had twice visited the Philippines, both times in connection with visits to India on behalf of the Executive Council (formerly National Council) and the Commission on Ecumenical Relations.

The Episcopal Church and the Philippine Independent Catholic Church had ratified a concordat of full communion in 1964 and their ecumenical activities were undergirded by a joint council with the Presiding Bishop of the Episcopal Church and the Supreme Bishop of the Independent Church as co-chairmen. Clergy for both churches in the Philippines were trained at St. Andrew's Seminary in Quezon City and many of their missionary efforts were joint projects.

Both churches were represented by communicants in Davao City, on the island of Mindanao, but neither had an adequate church in that rapidly growing area. Plans were made for a new church to be headed by priests of both communions, but it was impossible to find land at a price that the churches or the joint council could afford.

Familiar with the situation, Dr. Butler presented the problem to the Trinity vestry, which generously voted the necessary funds.

The gift was used to buy property at a central location in the Philippines' third largest city and the two churches, with the aid of the joint council, built the Church of the Resurrection, which was consecrated on June 12, 1970. Two bishops of the Philippine Episcopal Church and two bishops of the Philippine Independent Church concelebrated the first Mass to inaugurate this truly ecumenical and Catholic ministry. Trinity, at about this time, made a further substantial gift toward the building of a parish house for the church in Davao.

The Rt. Rev. Stephen F. Bayne, Jr., was a son of Trinity Parish and had always had a great interest in it, though most of his active ministry had been exercised elsewhere.

After service as rector of St. John's Church, Northampton, Mass., as chaplain at Columbia University, and as a navy chaplain in World War II, he was elected and consecrated as Bishop of Olympia, Wash., where he exercised jurisdiction from 1947 to 1959. He then became the first executive officer of the Anglican Communion, with headquarters in London, until 1964. Returning to this country, he served the Executive Council of the church as first vice president and chairman of the staff program group until 1970, when he became a member of the faculty of the General Theological Seminary.

During all these years, Bishop Bayne was a frequent visitor and preacher at Trinity Church and its chapels, especially the Intercession, which had been his home church before his ordination. When in 1965 he began his ministry in the Executive Council, he was appointed as honorary minister of Trinity Parish, and in 1970 was elected assistant to the rector, succeeding Canon Newman in that position. Although his duties at the seminary (of which he later became dean) occupied most of his time, he participated in many festival services in the parish, as celebrant or preacher, and in the activities of Trinity Institute.

Assisting in the many changes in the parish were a talented group of younger priests who served as curates at the mother church or exercised special ministries in the Wall Street area. Among them were Frs. Davis Given, John W. Moody, Robert F. Herrick, and Birney W. Smith, Jr. Exercising special ministries were the Rev. Robert C. Worthey, who became director of the urban conference center and the parish boys' camp in 1968, the Rev. John M. Corn, director of special ministry in the courts beginning in 1969, the Rev. William B. Gray, director of communications and editor of the *Trinity Parish Newsletter*, and the Rev. John D. Swanson, director of "A Seminary of the Streets." Both of the latter began their specialized work in July 1970.

Also serving Trinity as a staff member was a perpetual deacon, the Rev. Samuel E. Benson, ordained to the diaconate in 1966 after retirement from business. Long a faithful and active layman, and often subdeacon at the mother church, he was now able to continue his devoted service in the ordained ministry, which had been his desire for many years.

Much of Trinity's ministry now became youth-oriented. The basement of 74 Trinity Place, which had served as a parish hall, was remodeled into a coffeehouse known as "74 Below," with a recording studio and entertainment facilities. Here, on weekday noons, young people gathered (and some older ones, too) to enjoy rock music and other entertainment while having a light lunch from the coffee bar. Movies, lessons, live entertainment, and talent contests characterized this informal gathering place, which became increasingly popular.

Other groups, including two chapters of Alcoholics Anonymous, held regular meetings and a methadone clinic was conducted under joint auspices of Trinity Parish and Beekman-Downtown Hospital.

On October 15, 1969 Wall Street was the scene of a mass demonstration calling for a moratorium in the Vietnam War, with thousands of men and women demanding "peace now," after ten years and more of conflict in southeast Asia. There were counter-demonstrations, too, but the violence that was feared failed for the most part to materialize.

Trinity Church, in the heart of the demonstration area, took an active and constructive part in the rising tide of protest. Beginning at the conclusion of the 8 o'clock Mass, the names of Americans who had died in the war were solemnly read from the pulpit. An increasingly large and constantly changing congregation soon filled the church. At hourly intervals, the reading of names was interrupted briefly for organ music or for reading of prayers by Fr. Moody or Fr. Herrick. A part of the day-long ceremony was filmed for national television.

At noon the regular mid-day Mass was a requiem in recognition of the day, with altar and celebrant vested in black. When the service was over, the reading of names was resumed. At the next "break," Fr. Woodward welcomed the congregation and stated the purpose of the observance: "to pray for peace, to witness for peace, to do everything in our power to make the principle of peace the foundation of our society in the future." After a hymn, Rabbi Julius Mark read an Old Testament lesson, after which Judy Collins and a Black folk singer, accompanied by a guitar, sang. Bill Moyers, former press secretary for former President Johnson, gave an address and the service was concluded with a "prayer of commitment" by the Rev. Christopher Mooney, S.J., president of Woodstock College.

At a similar protest demonstration in the Wall Street area in the spring of 1970, Trinity Church had a somewhat more grim role to play. Following the incursion into Cambodia by United States forces and the killing of four students in a protest demonstration at Kent State University, Wall Street again became a focus for protest and counter-protest. On May 6 white-coated students and faculty members from several medical and nursing schools attended an impromptu service at Trinity and afterwards offered to man a first-aid center in the exhibit hall in the Manning Wing if one were needed in this troubled week.

At noon on May 8, while a Mass for peace and commemoration of the slain students was in progress, casualties from the mob violence outside began to be brought in and soon the doctors, medical students, and nurses had to use the clergy vesting room and sacristy, as well as the exhibit hall, to care for the injured and those suffering from shock. In all, some sixty persons were treated, mostly for minor injuries.

But happier occasions were more common at Trinity Church and often overflowed into the churchyard, especially during noon hours when office workers were able to participate.

Festivals featuring rock musicians and folk singers and dancers were held, both in the church and in the churchyard, particularly in the summer time. Some church members, including a few of the vestrymen, thought these were undignified for the ancient parish; others welcomed them as a new kind of contemporary ministry to people "where they are." On occasions the churchyard was festooned with balloons to celebrate the joy of life. The luncheon crowds enjoyed the festivities and the peaceful dead did not object. Indeed, Mrs. John Heuss, widow of the thirteenth rector, specifically requested that her husband's grave be included in the balloon decorations. At no time were these more secular activities permitted to interfere with the regular round of Sunday and weekday services of prayer and sacramental worship.

The chapels also extended their activities to cover the needs of their respective communities, as well as to minister to their own members.

St. Augustine's and St. Christopher's held full activities to help counter the "long hot summers" which often brought the threat of violence and gang warfare to lower

Manhattan. They took many and varied forms—breakfasts, picnics, athletic events, and services of witness and concern.

At St. Augustine's, the Rev. Jeffrey T. Cuffee served as priest-in-charge from 1964 to 1968, when the Rev. John G. Murdock became vicar. The chapel celebrated its one-hundredth anniversary in 1969 with an outdoor procession and festival Eucharist.

St. Christopher's, whose vicar was the Rev. Carlos J. Caguiat, observed the fifteenth anniversary of its consecration on May 26, 1968 with a gala dinner at 74 Trinity Place. Three years later, in May 1971, St. Christopher's was closed as a chapel of Trinity Parish, with the expectation that the Diocese of New York would provide Spanish-language services in the area. Continued under Trinity's auspices, however, was the "Seminary of the Streets" under the direction of Fr. Swanson and his associates, with an office in the former chapel building.

At St. Luke's Chapel, the long and fruitful ministry of the Rev. Paul Weed came to a close with his retirement on October 1, 1971. Fr. Weed had begun his ministry at St. Luke's as a curate in 1936 and had been vicar since 1949. One of his last acts as vicar was to celebrate and preach at a Mass of Thanksgiving commemorating St. Luke's 150th anniversary and to be guest of honor at an outdoor art show and festival in the afternoon. The Rev. Ledlie I. Laughlin, Jr., former dean of Trinity Cathedral, Newark, was chosen as his successor.

St. Luke's also honored Mrs. Katherine Taylor in 1971 on her twenty-fifth anniversary at St. Luke's School, of which she had been the principal since 1956. The Rev. Wilbur C. Leach, curate at St. Luke's since 1950, also resigned at the end of the year.

At St. Cornelius' Chapel on Governors Island, now transferred to the U.S. Coast Guard, activities continued with a totally new constituency. Navy chaplains now replaced the former army ones and, since the Coast Guard could not undertake to supply chaplains of the Episcopal Church, they might be of any denomination. However, the first one, the Rev. Samuel R. Hardman, was a priest of the church and was made honorary vicar. When no priest was available, celebrants for the Sunday Eucharist were supplied by arrangement with the Armed Forces Division of the Executive Council, but usually there was at least one chaplain of the Episcopal Church on the post.

By 1971 there was almost a complete turnover in the vestry of the parish. J. Eugene Banks became a warden in 1968. New vestrymen since 1964 were Donald C. Cook, John L. Gibbons, Robert S. Davies, Warren H. Turner, Jr., Charles H. Lawrence, Curtis Roosevelt, William E. Hutton, Robert A. Robinson, Richard E. Stewart, E. Allen Dennison, Paul A. Norton, James S. Coles, Steward R. Bross, Jr., and Thomas H. Wright, Jr. (clerk of the vestry). Dr. Joseph W. Barker continued as senior warden (until 1972 when he was succeeded by George A. Murphy). Other senior vestrymen were Ellis H. Carson, G. Keith Funston, Lewis B. Cuyler, Herbert G. King, and Kempton Dunn. These were the men who were to serve with the rector in the development of the far-reaching plan for parish reorganization known as "One Peppercorne."

"ONE PEPPERCORNE"

Although tremendous progress had been made in the 1960s in making the ministry of Trinity Parish more relevant to the rapidly changing communities in which the mother church and chapels were set and to the diocese, the national church, and the ecumenical scene, the rector and vestry felt that a complete restudy of the function of the parish was in order. In May 1969 an ad hoc committee was appointed by the rector and vestry to review the whole question of the nature of the parish, the use of its human and financial resources, and the broad policies to be followed in the 1970s.

The rector, Dr. John V. Butler, was the chairman of the committee, with four vestrymen as other members: Lewis B. Cuyler, Kempton Dunn, Curtis Roosevelt, and Warren H. Turner, Jr. The Rev. George H. Woodard was retained as consultant and worked with a group of Chicago-based advisers in developing the study. Bishop Bayne, drawing upon the most varied experience of any American bishop, was also of inestimable assistance.

The resulting report was called "One Peppercorne," after the nominal rental asked by King William III in 1697 for the land given for the foundation of the church in New York. Adopted by the vestry on September 24, 1970, the report called upon Trinity "to make a transition over several years to being a parish that again provides the city and the whole Church with powerful leadership by demonstrating how any church can faithfully use all its resources to maximum effect." This would require expansion and reorientation

—in the preaching, liturgical and pastoral ministries
—in ways that effect fundamental changes in the human condition and experience—both spiritual and physical
—in the discernment of God's will in the issues of the day and in making faithful responses
—in ways that contribute to the freeing of men and women from dependency on others for decision-making and support so as to demonstrate a hopeful belief in God and in all His People, and

—toward showing the real possibility of a diverse people living in a metropolis with respect for each other and jointly pursuing common Christian purposes.

As goals for the 1970s, the report called upon Trinity Parish

I. To be the parochial presence and ministry in Lower Manhattan
- —Including Trinity Church and St. Paul's (having encouraged and assisted the present chapel congregations to achieve self-government)
- —as ecumenical as proves possible
- —closely allied with the Diocese of New York
- —conducting a multiplicity of effective ministries in the business, residential and transient populations of the neighborhood.

II. To act as an operating trust or foundation disbursing or otherwise utilizing to the fullest extent the resources of the Parish for the work of the Church
- —operating some programs directly
- —making primarily strategic seed grants of adequate size and design to have significant transitional effect upon the human condition
- —in close alliance with the Diocese of New York and the national Episcopal Church
- —in cooperation or coalition with other agencies as indicated ad hoc.

Highlights of the report were published in the *Trinity Parish Newsletter* for November-December 1970 and were distributed to the clergy and congregations in pamphlet form. Lay leadership groups were formed in the mother church and each of the chapels to study the implications of "One Peppercorne" and to devise ways of implementing it in their own congregations and communities. Conferences of the clergy, Sisters, and staff members met to consider implications for the parish leadership.

On the parish level the plan called for appointment of five deputies to the rector: for Special Ministries, for Downtown Ministries, for Parish Administration, for Grant Programs, and for Parish Resources. "Key to the new organization of the parish," it was announced, "will be greatly increased involvement of laity and staff in decision-making and development of ideas. . . . In keeping with the spirit of Peppercorne, the authoritarian, paternalistic style of the past will be replaced by a participatory style."

The first of the newly designated deputies was Warren H. Turner, Jr., who resigned from the vestry to become deputy for parish administration August 1, 1971. Durant Stroud, who had been acting comptroller, became his assistant since the new structure eliminated the office of comptroller, dating back in Trinity's history to the early nineteenth century. Desmond L. Crawford, formerly comptroller, was appointed financial adviser to the rector.

The financial aspects of "One Peppercorne" were immediate and dramatic. The budget for gifts and allowances, which had been at a level of about $120,000 a year, was raised to approximately $1,000,000 and, in addition, the giving of Trinity Parish to the work of the Diocese of New York rose from $250,000 to $500,000 in 1971. All of this was made possible by the decision not to add profits from real estate and investments to capital funds (except for a reserve for emergencies), but to use most of the current income of the parish for grants and special projects.

Appointment of the other deputies called for in the report and further implementation of "One Peppercorne" were deferred until the election of the fifteenth rector, for Dr. Butler had already signified his intention to retire. He had entered upon the rectorship at the age of sixty, but had never felt that he was called to a "holding operation." Like Pope John XXIII, he had opened windows so that the winds of change could enter in, but it would be up to his successor to carry out most of the changes that had been introduced or to modify them as circumstances might require.

Although the parish knew that the rector was approaching the time of retirement, most of the members were surprised when he announced at the end of 1970 that he wished his retirement to be effective on April 29, 1971, when he would become sixty-five years old. He agreed, however, to continue as rector until the election of his successor, provided that it take place before the end of the year. However, in May, he moved with Mrs. Butler to their retirement home in Montclair, N. J., commuting to New York four or five times a week to attend to the affairs of the parish, and in the summer he spent most of his time at their summer home in Chatham, Mass.

The vestry was thus left free to seek a new rector and this they did, under the guidance of a nominating committee which held frequent meetings during the year. For the first time the clergy of the parish were officially given a share in making recommendations, which were carefully considered by the committee, as were those received from other sources inside and outside the parish.

On October 4, 1971 the vestry elected the Very Rev. Robert Ray Parks, D.D., dean of St. John's Cathedral, Jacksonville, Fla., and a member of the Executive Council, as the fifteenth rector of the Parish of Trinity Church in the City of New York. For the past twelve years, Dean

Parks had led the church and the Jacksonville community in renewal, with extensive programs in health, housing, care of the aged, and education. It was these concerns, as well as his qualities of leadership in worship and spiritual matters, that led the vestry to elect him unanimously and to rejoice when he signified his acceptance of the election.

With his successor chosen, Dr. Butler announced that his resignation would be effective December 31, 1971 and that the rector-elect would take office as of January 1, 1972.

The Introduction of Fr. Murdock, St. Augustine's Chapel

16

275 Years Young

1972

The Rev. Robert Ray Parks, D.D., was instituted at noon on January 26, 1972 as the fifteenth rector of Trinity Parish. The church was filled with parishioners and friends of the new rector, including about one hundred who had come from Florida in a chartered plane for the happy occasion. Archbishop Ramsey, in New York for another seminar at Trinity Institute, was in the procession, as were clergymen of the Roman Catholic and Protestant churches and representatives of churches and institutions that Trinity had founded, endowed, or otherwise aided in its 275 years of ministry.

In his sermon Bishop Donegan referred to some of the highlights of that long and fruitful history: He noted Trinity's early concern with "the slaves brought to our country without knowledge of where they were going and manifestly against their will," adding:

> The abuse which Trinity received as a result of this ministry constitutes an indelible part of colonial history. Yet the first totally integrated school in this city was sponsored by Trinity Parish in the eighteenth century. . . .

Robert Ray Parks, the Fifteenth Rector

Twenty-four parishes were either built or endowed by Trinity within the present diocese of New York. Four parishes in Long Island and innumerable parishes in Western New York were either established or maintained by Trinity. The diocese of Albany alone has been given the current equivalent of more than a half million dollars, and the diocese of Western New York was inaugurated by a settlement of the modern equivalent of $350,000. . . . As I had reason to note some years ago, by 1909 it was estimated that Trinity Parish had built, established, endowed, or aided fourteen hundred and four institutions. It is an astonishing record of financial responsibility.

During the last sixty-three years, Trinity Parish has aided an additional 238 churches and institutions. The Mother of Churches has literally hundreds of children, not only in this country but in Britain, the Philippines, and other parts of the world.

Certainly Trinity had come a long way from the pioneer days in which Captain Kidd had lent his privateer runner and tackle "for the hoiseing up stones" to build the first outpost of Anglicanism on Manhattan Island, and when King William III had granted a royal charter to the church with the proviso that "the quitrent . . . be one pepper corne as desired." And, the work was still continuing, though fortunately it was no longer necessary for an armed vestryman to accompany a missionary priest setting forth to preach in the unfriendly wilderness of Connecticut, as Caleb Heathcote had done in 1706.

As Bishop Donegan gave his charge to the fifteenth rector, one may perhaps, with a little imagination, think of the unseen spirits of Dr. Parks' predecessors standing beside him to lend their strength and encouragement in carrying forward the task:

William Vesey (1697-1746), who planted a Christian mission in a pioneer colony and defended it against the whims of royal governors and the scorn of dissidents;

Henry Barclay (1746-1764), the Indian missionary who exercised his ministry to both free men and slaves and who participated in the founding of King's College;

Samuel Auchmuty (1764-1777), who, after years of faithful ministry, returned from exile to find his beloved church in ashes;

Charles Inglis (1777-1783), whose loyalty to king and country cost him his parish and his home;

Samuel Provoost (1784-1800), who rebuilt his church and steered it in new paths of freedom in a new nation;

Benjamin Moore (1800-1816), whose gentle firmness brought reconciliation to a divided church and community;

John Henry Hobart (1816-1830), who planted the church firmly throughout the state and nourished it with his watchword of "evangelical truth and apostolic order";

William Berrian (1830-1862), whose quiet ministry and sacramental teaching were a witness to unity in a nation rapidly plunging toward civil war;

Morgan Dix (1862-1908), who wisely guided the church, both locally and nationally, through four tumultuous decades;

William T. Manning (1908-1921), who added new dimensions of social conscience and ecclesiastical statesmanship;

Caleb R. Stetson (1921-1932), who maintained a haven of peace and faith amid secular crisis and financial collapse;

Frederic S. Fleming (1932-1951), who saw the church decline and then rise phoenixlike after years of depression and war;

John Heuss (1951-1966), who brought a new sense of mission and stewardship to a congregation grown complacent;

—and, still very much alive, Dr. Parks' immediate predecessor, John V. Butler (1966-1971), who led the ancient church into new forms of ministry to the contemporary world.

But, as Trinity celebrated its 275th anniversary and progresses toward its tercentennial, it is not concerned so much with the past as with the present and the future. Bishop Donegan stressed this note in his charge to the new rector:

> In ancient days it was noted that few people spoke English in this city. The problem now is not whether they speak English but whether they speak the same language. And, as I see it, Trinity's future must be a current adaptation of its past—to speak to people, the modern slaves, the young, the disaffected, the cynical, the alcoholic, the drug addict, the social drop-out, the freak, the Jesus people, and all the rest of the unhappy and disillusioned exactly where they live.
>
> My dear brother, you have been chosen not only by the corporation of this venerable parish to be its rector, but also you have been chosen unanimously by the vicars and the younger clergy who make this parish run. Your election and their approbation has only this to say about the past, that both groups believe you to be able to mould a great past into a yet greater future.
>
> Obviously, your ministry will be a highly specialized one. But be of good cheer, dear brother; God in His strange way regards each person ever born as the object of a specialized ministry. No man in the history of this parish has started his ministry with more love on his side. Brother, I bid you both enjoy it and do it.
>
> I ask the vestry, vicars and other clergy, the men and women of Trinity Parish, to remember your Rector constantly before God; he will need your trust, your loyal support, your love, and above all your prayers.
>
> God bless him. God bless you.

Notes on Sources

This is not, in the main, a work based on original research. It is a summary of the highlights of Trinity Parish in the City of New York, based upon the official parish history, with reference to standard histories of the Episcopal Church, New York City, and the nation, supplemented by diaries and other reference materials bearing on the subject. More recent chapters are based on parish yearbooks and periodical and other publications on file in the parish archives.

The work cited as "the official parish history" is in six published volumes and one not yet published, all compiled by order of the Corporation of Trinity Parish, as follows:

A History of the Parish of Trinity Church in the City of New York:

VOLS. I-IV. By Morgan Dix. 1898-1906.
VOL. V. By John A. Dix and Leicester C. Lewis. 1950.
VOL. VI. By Charles T. Bridgeman. 1962.
VOL. VII. By Charles T. Bridgeman and Clifford P. Morehouse.

Other official historical publications of the parish include:

Quarter of a Millennium. By E. Clowes Chorley. Church Historical Society, Philadelphia, 1947.

Gifts to Churches, Organizations and Persons Outside the Parish of Trinity Church. Privately printed, 1966.

The Trinity Church Association and Trinity Mission House, 1876-1956. By Charles T. Bridgeman. Privately printed, 1956.

First Recorded Minutes Regarding the Building of Trinity Church in the City of New York. Privately printed, 1964.

In relating the history of Trinity Parish to that of New York City, I have relied frequently upon *The Epic of New York City*, by Edward Robb Ellis (Coward McCann, Inc., New York, 1966). This is particularly true in the first chapter, giving the Colonial background, and in references to the draft riots and the Confederate plot during the Civil War, as well as in other places where this excellent book is cited. I am grateful to the publishers for permission to use the material in this way.

For the "visit of a stranger" in 1744, I am indebted to *Gentleman's Progress*, edited by Carl Bridenbaugh (University of North Carolina Press, Chapel Hill, N.C., 1948).

For the story of Captain Kidd (pp. 19-21), I have drawn upon *The Island* (the story of Gardiners Island, New York) by Robert Payne (Harcourt, Brace, New York, 1958).

For the period of the Revolution and the British occupation of New York City (pp. 57-70), I have been greatly helped by the thesis by Gwenith Heuss Severance on *Trinity Parish During the American Revolution,* submitted to Wesleyan University under the title, "A Loyalist Church During the American Revolution" in partial fulfillment of the requirements for the degree of Master of Arts in Liberal Studies. Manuscript, April, 1969.

The official parish history dismisses the story of "Gentleman Joe" (pp. 175-79) in three paragraphs. It is worth a whole book, and fortunately W. A. Swanberg has written one: *The Rector and the Rogue*. Charles Scribner's Sons, New York, 1968. I have taken my account mostly from that source, with permission of the publishers.

Books of Church History used as reference include:

A History of the American Episcopal Church. By William Wilson Manross. Morehouse-Gorham Co., New York, 3rd edition, 1959.

The Story of the General Theological Seminary. By Powel Mills Dawley. Oxford University Press, New York, 1969.

Men and Movements in the American Episcopal Church. By E. Clowes Chorley. Charles Scribner's Sons, New York, 1946.

Frequently consulted on the history of the United States:

The Oxford History of the American People. By Samuel Eliot Morison. Oxford University Press, New York, 1965.

On the history of New York City:

Incredible New York. By Lloyd Morris. Random House, New York, 1951.

The Age of the Moguls. By Stewart H. Holbrook. Doubleday & Co., Garden City, N.Y., 1953.

Biographies and diaries:

Some American Churchmen (chapter on John Henry Hobart). By Frederick C. Morehouse. The Young Churchman Co., Milwaukee, 1892.

The Diary of Philip Hone. Edited by Allan Nevins. Dodd, Mead & Co., New York, 1936.

The Diary of George Templeton Strong. Edited by Allan Nevins and Milton Halsey Thomas. The Macmillan Co., New York, 1952.

The Diary of Morgan Dix. Unedited microfilm, in Archives of Trinity Parish.

Prudently with Power (biography of Bishop Manning). By W. D. F. Hughes. Holy Cross Publications, West Park, N.Y., no date.

Mrs. Seton, Foundress of the American Sisters of Charity. By Joseph I. Dirvin, C.M. Farrar, Straus & Cudahy, New York, 1962.

Diaries of Caleb R. Stetson and Frederic S. Fleming; memoranda of John V. Butler. Manuscripts in Trinity Archives.

Index

(Names of Rectors of Trinity Parish are marked with an asterisk.)